Mediumistic Romance

If I Didn't Love You So Much

Valter Turini

By the Spirit of
Monsignor Eusébio Sintra

Translated into English by
Isabel Lucero Puchuri Sulca
Lima, Peru, December 2023

Original Title in Portuguese:

"Se eu não te amasse tanto assim"

© VALTER TURINI, 2009

Translated from the Spanish version by J. Thomas Saldias, MSc., 2023

Revised by:
Beatriz Rueda Stella, Campinas, SP, Brazil.

World Spiritist Institute
Houston, Texas, USA
E-mail: contact@worldspiritistinstitute.org

If I Didn't Love You So Much…

Can a sincere and true love transcend death? Monsignor Sintra presents us with a moving period novel about the inauspicious fate of the couple, Sylvie and François–Armand. Set in 19th century France, the plot also covers aspects of the work of Allan Kardec, the Codifier of Spiritism, plus the founding of the Paris Spiritist Society, as well as an attractive plot involving intriguing cases of obsessions.

Valter Turini

If I Didn't Love You So Much… How could the indelible flame of love, strongly enveloping two creatures, simply be consumed by the death of one of them…? Through the pages of this novel, Monsignor Eusébio Sintra demonstrates, in a highly efficient and captivating way, the unfolding of a plot that presents, as a backdrop, the intense relationship between two souls strongly yoked by passion: Sylvie and François–Armand, but whose relationship is suddenly interrupted by an unexpected event…

The spiritual author, through the mediumship of Prof. Valter Turini, skillfully weaves a thought–provoking plot to show us that the power of love transcend death itself, and presents the countless communications from beyond that were received at Paris Spiritist Society as incontrovertible proof of this, under the command of the ineffable Allan Kardec, the illustrious codifier of Spiritism, to testify, for the first time in human history, and in a form rigorously based on scientific and philosophical principles, that spirits can and, if they so wish, do communicate with us, the incarnate, through the doors of mediumship.

About the author

Valter Turini, the medium, was born in Rinópolis, São Paulo (SP), on February 9, 1952. He taught Portuguese in the São Paulo state school system and in private schools until he retired in 2003.

He made his debut as a psychographer with the work *O Sorriso de Pedra* (The Smile of Stone), although he had already been involved in Spiritist work as a medium and speaker since 1973, when as a boy of 21, he began studying and practicing Spiritism at Cairbar Schutel school, alongside Benedito Borges, a renowned medium and one of the pioneers of Spiritism in the city of Dracena, SP.

> "Though I speak with the tongues of men and of angels, if I have not love, I am as sounding brass, or as a clanging cymbal."
>
> (I Corinthians 13:1)
>
> *Si un jour la vie t'arrache à moi Si tu meurs que tu sois loin de moi Peu m'importe si tu m'aimes Car moi—je mourrais aussi Nous aurons pour nous l'éternité Dans le bleu de toute l'immensité...* [1]
>
> L'hymne à l'amour
>
> Piaf/Loug

---

[1] If one day life takes you away from me If you die and are far from me I don't care if you love me, For I'll die too We'll have eternity to ourselves Within the blue of all immensity... Ode to Love

Piaf/Lougy

Contents

If I Didn't Love You So Much… 3
About the author 5
Words from the Spiritual Author 9
Chapter 1 12
    Clash of Ideals 12
Chapter 2 36
    Hearts in love 36
Chapter 3 60
    A Trip to the Countryside 60
Chapter 4 84
    Turning Tables 84
Chapter 5 107
    Sorrow and Resentment 107
Chapter 6 129
    In Champagne 129
Chapter 7 152
    A Tragedy Strikes 152
Chapter 8 174
    Goodbye to Sylvie 174
Chapter 9 197
    Faced with Extreme Pain 197
Chapter 10 221
    In Charenton 221
Chapter 11 244
    In the Darkness of Madness 244

Chapter 12...267
   Spirituality Reveals Itself...............................267
Chapter 13...288
   Spiritism..288
Chapter 14...308
   Monsieur Allan Kardec....................................308
Chapter 15...329
   The Société..329
Chapter 16...348
   A Case of Healing...348
Chapter 17...367
   A Chance Encounter 367
Chapter 18...387
   A Friendship is Born 387
Chapter 19...407
   A fatal accident...407
Chapter 20...429
   Reality and Dreams..429
Epilogue...449

Words from the Spiritual Author

In the annals of human history, the 19th century was perhaps the most surprising of all. In those days, with each passing day, people saw the marvelous and stupendous "miracles" present to them by science, stunned and full of natural amazement: new and efficient machines were appearing to facilitate arduous human tasks; new and extraordinary discoveries in medicine, physics and chemistry drew exclamations of astonishment and admiration; and new ideas and strange, even bizarre, philosophical concepts appearing to accelerate the development of consciences that were still dulled by the doldrums in which they had been immersed for millennia, and which had always been restricted in their freedom of action and creation– attributes immanent to man and derived from the peculiar and uncommon natural need that creatures have to observe, analyze, understand, transform, and create– characteristics that have been gifted to them since the beginning of time by the infinite goodness and supreme wisdom of the Creator...!

Fortunately, after countless years of slavery and torture, under the merciless guarantor of blind faith and the imposition of empty and innocuous rituals, that only catered to external form–absurd and even cruel practices! – arbitrarily instituted by Christianity, which, filled with extreme pride and boasting that it was the sole and exclusive heir to the

Christian legacy, had in reality always shown itself to be oblivious and indifferent to the true designs of Creation, man was finally free...! How much struggle has been expended, and how much sweat and blood has been shed, so that, millimeter by millimeter, the lights of knowledge could advance in this world of darkness and ignorance...! If religion commanded even the kings of the earth, what can we say about the ignorant people...! Until then, in matters of faith, no one else had the authority to pronounce except the "representatives of God on Earth", and science and philosophy were imprisoned and tightly gagged, having to restrict themselves only to what God allowed... Thus, Christianity, instead of enlightening and liberating souls, enslaved them, thus evading te most sacred of all the Spirit's conquests: free will...!

However, those who think that Christianity and Christendom are the same thing are deeply mistaken! In fact, they have very little in common. The dust of centuries has constant and inexorably settled on the clear truths brought by Christ. An avalanche of rubble, considered to be "articles of faith", has been deposited on the immaculate and very clear Gospel Message, to the point of making it lose, in principle, the real content that it had when preached and, above all, fully experienced by the distinguished Jesus...!

Much of the essence of Christianity had apparently been lost over time, vilified and squandered for the sole purpose of serving the immediate interests of a spurious and indecent minority who set themselves as the "spiritual directors of humanity..."! However, Jesus himself, profoundly aware of human passions and vices, had referred to this when

He predicted that there would be necessary to restore things to their proper values later on, and promised to send the Comforter, the Spirit of Truth, to Earth, since at that time people would not be able to bear all the knowledge that surrounded the Greater Reality...[2] Minds would have to mature first, before the existence of the World of Spirits and the consequent Laws that regulate life here and beyond could be revealed... All in good time... The Law of Progress itself takes care of this and, despite all the "temporal power" of which the fallible and precarious earthly institutions self-constitute, it, the Law of Progress surreptitiously goes about its work, silently and constantly, even in the absence of those who are supposed to carry God's will on their lips...

Tupi Paulista, Summer of 2008

Eusébio Sintra

---

[2] Saint John, 14:15-17 & 26.

Chapter 1

Clash of Ideals

Cautiously, the boy pulled the lace curtains away from the window, his dark brown eyes intently scanning the street below. In his right hand, he carried a cocked pistol, which he kept prudently pointed upwards.

"I think they're gone, Lulu," he mutters.

"When will it end?"– says the woman, as if she was letting off steam, letting herself sit down heavily in the red velvet armchair. Then, groping in the pockets of her pink silk peignoir, she took out her cigarette case and nervously lit a cigarillo.

"Come, sit here!", she gently invites him, as she takes a long puff of blue–gray smoke. The young man, full of care, disarms the pistol dog, keeps it in his waistband and goes back inside.

"Would you like one?" – she asks, offering him her cigarette case. Lieutenant Berg strikes a match, lights the cigarette and quietly takes a long drag. Then, little by little, he lets the smoke out, some of it through his mouth and part through his nose, while his gaze roams over the ceiling covered in paper with little blue, yellow and red flowers.

"I don't know how you can stay so cool!" – Lulu says, looking him in the eyes.

"This time, they almost caught you! What if I had not been at the window, watching the street? Where would you hide from those crazy people who were chasing you?"

"Oh, I am used to it, my dear! " he says, looking her into the eyes. And, with a slight smile, he continues:

"Surely you cannot imagine what a battlefield is like!"

Lulu just shrugged and looked at the ash from her cigarette which had stretched out into a faint whitish, twisted tip, about to collapse at any moment. With extreme care, she raises her hand and deposits the cigarette ash in a heavy glass ashtray she kept on the arm of the armchair. She took one last drag of the cigarette, which was almost completely consumed, squeezed her eyes shut as the smoke burned and then smashed the end of the cigarillo against the bottom of the ashtray, putting it out completely. Then she took a white cambric handkerchief from her pocket and carefully wiped her watering eyes.

"Do you want something to drink? It is still early; the girls are asleep..."

"No...! " says Berg, standing up.

"I did not come looking for fun... It is just that your door was my salvation today...! And, bowing elegantly, he kisses the matron's hand and continues:

"*Merci beaucoup, mon amie*[3] I will come back another time!

---

[3] Thank you very much , my friend…, in French

"Take care!" – she exclaims, giving a slight smile to her withered and discolored lips, when he was already very close to the door.

"*Au revoir!*[4]" – says the Lieutenant, turning slightly. Then he opens the door and goes out. He goes downstairs and, full of caution, first spies the street, exposing only a small part of his face. Everything seemed to be back to normal–the troublemakers were gone.

"Bunch of idiots!" – mutters Berg, setting off down the sidewalk, mingling with the passers–by hurrying in both directions.

That morning of March, the air in Paris had risen a little more sharply than usual. Lieutenant Wilfred Berg had left the house to take a leisurely stroll along the Boulevard des Champs– Elysées. He had chosen to wear his uniform because he intended to pass by his regiment later to meet his commander, General Emmanuel–Théophile du Servey. However, wandering alone through the streets of the city center in a Republican uniform was foolhardy, to say the least!

The aristocrats were unforgiving! If they looted a revolutionary soldier alone, they would hunt him down without mercy. As soon as he turned a corner, leaving the Rue du Commerce, where he had been looking for a famous jeweler, he had the misfortune to come across a pack of thugs who, identifying him as an enemy, immediately set about chasing him, shouting like crazy and firing their pistols left and right.

---

[4] Good bye!, In French.

And Berg, accustomed to such skirmishes, did not let himself be caught out. He took off at a run, zigzagging through the passers-by and, much better prepared than his pursuers, he quickly got ahead of them and entered the Rue de Saint-Sulpice, until he came across the cries of Lulu, who, from the top of her window, invited him to climb up, thus making it easier for him to escape the mad pursuit.

It was early in the morning and Berg checked his pocket watch: eleven hours and fifteen minutes. He stopped and thought for a moment. He had made an appointment with the General at two o'clock; if he got a coach, he would have time to go to Montmartre. He needed to see her and, who knows, maybe could they have lunch together? He was worried about her condition. When he had left her at her front door the previous afternoon, she had been crying. It was almost convulsive, deep crying, full of long sobs. An intense knot then settled in the boy's throat, and he swallowed thick saliva several times, trying to swallow the sorrow that was beginning to lodge in his chest. His relationship with Céleste-Marie deteriorated day by day.

"I feel her getting worse and worse" – the bride's mother had told him a few days before, when the two of them had caught a glimpse of each other in Place Pigalle, and here I am giving her another of Dr. Périgot's prescriptions.

"However, I feel that she is not getting any better, on the contrary, I see that her health is getting worse as time goes by!"

"You have to have faith, Marie-Louise" – he had told her, more to encourage the disconsolate mother than to instill in her the belief that her daughter could be cured of the illness that afflicted her.

"Faith". Berg murmured and smiled bitterly as he walked lightly down the sidewalk, deftly dodging the bumps of the oncoming passers–by.

"Poor Marie–Louise..." – he thought, full of regret.

"I do not think I was the least bit convincing in suggesting that she should have faith, even if I have not been believing in anything else lately."

Before long, he was in Place de la Concorde and approaching a rental car.

"To Montmartre!" – he orders the solicitous driver, who replies with a respectful nod.

The car sped along the cobbled streets, and Lieutenant Berg was thinking. What to do? He had fallen in love with Céleste–Marie when they were both teenagers. He had gotten used to her and could not imagine living without her loving presence. When his regiment returned to Paris after its long and terrible forays into the war (France was constantly involved in wars!), before even seeing home again, it was invariably to Céleste–Marie's house that he went first! His mother would never forgive him for such rudeness!

"You will see the other one first, will you not, you little rascal?" – his mother would say to him, burning with jealousy of Céleste–Marie. His mother and his fiancée did not get along well. They were always exchanging barbs, the kind of excessive attachment that women sometimes show. Berg was actually amused by all the jealousy shown by his two women, as he used to refer to his mother and fiancée.

When the carriage pulled up in front of number 23 Rue Constance in Montmartre, it was almost noon. Wilfred Berg pulled his cap over his head and, after looking at the sober facade of the house, pushed open the heavy iron gate with its high bars and entered.

"I did not think you would come today..." – says Céleste–Marie, offering her face to her fiance who kisses her respectfully.

"Maman left early; she did not tell me where she was going....

"I just stopped by to see how you were..." – he says, caressing the girl's face with the back of his hand.

"You made me worried yesterday.... you have been crying your eyes out..."

"I have my reasons!" – she exclaims, almost harshly, and suddenly sulking.

"In fact, you have been giving me such reasons!"

"*Oh, ma belle!*"[5] – he said, getting up from the armchair he had been sitting in, and taking her by the wrist, he continued:

"I think you are fantasizing.... What reasons could I be giving you to act like this with me?"

"Yes, you are giving reasons, Berg!" – she exclaimed, trying to break free of the hand that was holding her tight.

"I find you are distant! You are not the same anymore!"

"Oh, I think it is all just a load of hooey in your head, Céleste–Marie...! I think you should know that people

---

[5] Oh! My dear, in French.

change.... We are not teenagers anymore, you and I...! You see, we have grown up, we are both adults...! I am almost thirty, and you are over twenty–five...! It is natural that I am different...! You have changed too..."

"Do you know what I think?" – says the girl, after thinking for a few seconds.

"I think you have had enough of me...!"

"Oh, silly you!" – he exclaims, drawing her to him and hugging her tightly.

"How could I get tired of you?" – and, pulling a small bright red velvet bag out of his tunic pocket, he held it out to Céleste–Marie.

"Look what I have brought for you!"

The young woman's eyes suddenly sparkled. She picked up the bag and nervously opened it, scrutinizing its contents with her fingertips, full of anticipation .

"They are beautiful!" – she said, looking inexpressibly at the small, shiny objects in her open palm of her hand; but, unable to conceal the enormous disappointment that invaded her at the gift.

"I do not think you liked the earrings…" – he says, highly disappointed by the young woman's reaction.

"If you do not like their design, you can exchange them for others that you like…".

"No! That is not it!" – she exclaims harshly, and then, throwing the little red velvet bag on a *guéridon*[6], she lets herself sit, disconsolate and very sulky, on the sofa.

"Why are you acting like that, Céleste–Marie?" – asks Berg, sitting down next to her on the sofa.

"Do you not realize that you are hurting me deeply?"

"And you?" – she exclaims, staring at him steadily with a look of strange brilliance.

"Do you not always hurt me?" – and now she continues, her eyes wet with tears.

"I was not expecting earrings, Berg! I expected an engagement ring! I cannot tell you how much I want that...!"

The young man hugs her tightly, movingly. Then she let herself be carried away by the intense emotion that overwhelmed her and wept profusely.

"I'm sorry, darling" – he murmured, stroking her hair.

"I did not know you wanted it so badly..."

"I know I will end up losing you, Berg!" – she said, looking him in the eye, her voice broken by almost convulsive weeping.

"You live too far away, exposed to constant danger, and I cannot stand it any longer! When you go off to war, you do not know the distress I feel, knowing that you are in the middle of that hell...!"

"Oh, my love!" – he exclaims, taking her in his arms and kissing her passionately.

---

[6] A *gueridon* is a small, often circular coffee table supported by one or more columns or sculptures of human or mythological figures.

"So that is it!"

"I would like an engagement ring from you!" – she said, taking his hand and kissing it tenderly. And she continued, without looking at him, while caressing his hands with tender affection.

"And I would like you to resign from the army...! You are rich... I am rich! Why do you have to get into so much trouble? I get tired of seeing all this blood spilled so carelessly! Tell me, on what grounds are the French killing themselves these days? For the most absurd and childish reasons imaginable, right? First, they killed themselves for the republic! We have gotten the republic back! Have they stopped killing each other? No, now they are killing each other for the return of the monarchy! And, not satisfied with killing each other, they went to Africa to conquer others in terror! Violence and more violence! Oh, when will it all stop?" Then she turns her face and looks him steadily in the eyes, and continues, her voice full of supplication.

"Look, let us get married and live in the country! Mom has a lovely country house in Orly! Why do we not go and live there? We can be happy and have our children in peace, away from all that disgrace... Paris disgusts me!" And, resting her head on his shoulder, she continued:

"Oh, Berg, I dream about it so much!"

The young soldier thought for a moment. Sometimes, he really wanted to throw it all away, to retire to a corner with Céleste–Marie. But the world was in such turmoil, so many were taking place overnight.... What security was there now in France or in the whole of Europe? The old regime[7] had collapsed; there had already been an unsuccessful attempt to establish a republic with the Revolution[8]. However, what had actually become institutionalized in the country was chaos, corruption, lawlessness, rioting… How could he just sit back and let things happen? No, it was not his way. He was a political man; his family had always been given to politics; but, he was beginning to get tired of it. When would lasting peace finally come.?

"You are right, *mon amour*…"[9] – he said, stroking her dark, wavy hair down to her shoulders.

"You are absolutely right! We are all tired of so much bloodshed; but, if definitive peace is not established, what security will we all have? What kind of life will we bequeath to our children?"

"I don't know if I want to pay such a high price for future generations to live better than us…" – murmurs Céleste–Marie, with a long sigh.

"Ultimately, I think that men are wrong, not the regimes they set up! If men were good, institutions would be good, whatever their character, republican or monarchical, do you not think?"

"Yes, *ma belle*, you are right…! As long as men are not sufficiently educated and, above all, if they do not reach a consensus through the exercise of legitimate reason, there will

---

[7] Reference to the French monarchy, deprived of power by the Revolution of 1789.
[8] Revolution of 1789.
[9] My love! In French.

only be chaos...!.," and, changing the subject, he continues with a mischievous smile.

"Look, are you not going to ask me to lunch...? I am starving..."

"No...!" – she says laughing.

"You are rude! How dare you invite yourself like that? Your mother did not teach you any manners, did she?" And she burst out laughing.

"Ha! Ha! Ha...! Ha...! Ha...!

How good it was to hear Céleste–Marie's laugh! Crystal–clear laughter, innocent laughter... Poor thing! Berg looked into her eyes. He loved her, but he was afraid: his great love was going mad! Lately, Céleste–Marie had been moving between lucidity and the tinges of dementia with extreme ease....

"Tell me, Céleste–Marie..." – said the young man, taking her hand.

"Do you not want to go to the regiment with me? We can have lunch in the Cité! What do you think?"

"I would love to...!" – she exclaims, getting up.

"Wait two minutes, I will do my make–up and we will leave!"

While he waited for his fiancée to get ready, Wilfred Berg thought: He had to make up his mind. He could not leave Céleste–Marie like this, waiting for him forever. They were getting old, and a stand had to be taken. But what about her illness? He could get married, yes, and he would remain in the army; they could have children; she would take care of raising them, and perhaps she would even be cured of her illness. What if she did not heal? What if the illness was, in fact, irreversible? There were strong indications that it was! If Céleste–Marie got married and had children, it could get worse...! Perhaps she did not know how to deal with and solve the problems that would inevitably arise in running a household.... He urgently needed to see Marie–Louise, his fiancée's mother. He needed to have a serious discussion with her about the issues that were tormenting his soul.

"*Allons–nous, M'sieur le lieutenant?*"[10] – Céleste–Marie interrupts his intimate musings. And gracefully, she turns around, showing herself off to him, highly conceited.

"*Comment te paraît–il?*"[11]

"*Magnify, ma belle!*"[12] – he exclaims, after blowing a whistle of admiration.

"You look exquisite!"

The city center was buzzing. It was spring and the sky was spectacularly blue. Céleste–Marie was parading proudly, arm in arm with her Lieutenant in his impeccable blue uniform.

"How about Le Boulanger, darling?" – he suggests.

"*Parfait!*"[13] – she replies, opening a smile that showed the tips of her white, well–kept teeth.

Céleste–Marie was happy. She chewed slowly, savoring the food, while looking at Berg.

---

[10] Do we go, Sir Leutenant? In French.
[11] What do you think? In French.
[12] Wonderful, my dear! In French.
[13] Perfect! In French.

"What are you thinking about?" – he asked, realizing that she could not take her eyes off his face.

"I was thinking how handsome and elegant you are!" – she says, laughing.

"I think you are exaggerating..." – he says, smiling proudly. It was a delight to be adored by Céleste–Marie! He continues, tenderly stroking her hand:

"You are beautiful!"

"But that makes me suffer terribly, Berg!" – the young woman exclaims, apparently ignoring the compliment he had paid her and then, suddenly feeling extremely sad, she continues:

"Paris is full of cheeky little girls!" – and she continues, pretending to soften:

"Besides, I know that when you are off duty, you often go to Chez Lulu...."

"Oh, soldiers need a bit of fun sometimes!" – he says, blushing a little.

"Don't you agree? We need to forget the hardships of the battlefields! And besides, the whole National Force knows Lulu Fontainebleau!

"Debauched!" – she exclaims, pinching the back of his hand.

"No, it is not debauchery, *ma petite!*"[14] – he observes seriously.

---

[14] My Little one! In French.

"I can tell you without a shadow of a doubt that there is no wiser or more experienced person in the whole of Paris than Lulu Fontainebleau!"

"What kind of things could a woman like that know?" – asks Céleste–Marie, full of spite.

"Only if it is the tricks of the trade!"

"Oh, you are so wrong, my dear!" – he says laughing.

"Not even the top brass of the army can escape her wise counsel!"

"You are not going to tell me that she also understands military strategies?"

"Strategies of life, *ma belle*!" – he says seriously.

"Lulu Fontainebleau was educated in the school of life! In the difficult art of living!"

When Berg and Céleste–Marie arrived at the barracks, it was a little after two o'clock.

"The General must be waiting for me!" – exclaims the young man, hurrying forward.

"And we are late!" – and, looking sideways at his fiancée, with a pretended air of reproach, he continues:

"If my boss spins me, you will be the one to blame! You stopped in front of all the shop windows on the Rue du Commerce!"

"Oh, you are exaggerating!" – she said, trying her best to keep up with his long strides down the corridor that led to the barracks' Administration.

"And if you are scared shitless, leave the General to me! Have you forgotten that he and my father were very close friends? I cannot tell you how much the General du Servey likes me!"

"Oh, I forgot how close you and your family were to the General and his wife Constance!" – he exclaims, and continues ironically.

"Apart from the very annoying Robert, their son."

"Oh, you are jealous of Robert!" – she says, laughing and pinching his ribs.

"You fool! Have you forgotten that Robert and I have never had anything to do with each other and, what is more, he has already married to Amélie Rochefort and is the father of two adorable little children?"

Soon they were standing in front of the door to General Emmanuel–Theophile du Servey's office. Before knocking, Berg fixed his cap and straightened the collar of his tunic. He looks at Céleste–Marie, who approved with a broad smile and a mischievous wink. Then, resolute, the young soldier knocks on the door with a closed hand.

"Oh! Berg and Céleste–Marie! What a nice surprise you are giving this old heart!" – exclaims the General, getting up from his desk.

And, after shaking his young friend's hand effusively, he turns to his companion:

"How beautiful you look, *ma petite*... Long time no see!"

"Yes!" – Céleste–Marie exclaims, allowing herself to be hugged by her old family friend.

"We have not seen each other much since Dad left, General!"

"And Marie–Louise?" – asks the old soldier, once everyone is settled on a spacious leather sofa.

"Maman is fine..." – answers the young woman, and she corrects herself:

"Relatively well, I mean! Since Dad died, she has never been the same.... I often notice her sad and sulking in the corners..."

"Such is life!" – exclaims the General with a deep sigh.

"Such is life...!" – and, turning to Berg, he continued:

"We have gotten news for you, my boy! The High Command has just recommended your promotion! We will certainly have the ceremony soon."

Berg's eyes light up. Céleste–Marie, however, does not hide her disappointment. Tinges of sadness run through her eyes.

"The army keeps taking him away from me"– she thinks.

"And I do not know if I will have enough strength for this fight! I presume I will lose this battle..."

"I do not think you are happy about the news, *ma chérie*!" – the General's voice interrupted her thoughts.

"Well, I guess Berg will not have any more excuses not to walk you down the aisle!" – and, winking mischievously at the boy, he went on, deliberately calling him by his new rank:

"What do you say, *Capitaine* Berg?"

"I think you are right, *mon general*" – says the young man, kissing the girl's hands lovingly.

"If she wants me!"

"Oh, she will... I'm sure she will! Women always want to get married!" – says the General, laughing. He got up and walked over to a sober dark wooden cupboard, opened the door and took out a bottle of wine. Then, turning to Céleste-Marie, he asks her:

"Help me with the glasses, *ma petite*! We must celebrate!"

After a warm toast, they sat back down on the leather divan, sipping from their glasses of wine. A short silence then fell between the three of them, who seemed to be deep in thoughts.

"You can both imagine that last night I witnessed a strange phenomenon at the home of the Marquise Adele Souvigny!" remarked the General, breaking the silence that had formed.

"I think you have heard of these spinning tables, haven't you?"

"I have already been to one of these sessions, at the house of Colonel François Henri de Mont-Parmis last winter, sir" – replied the young man.

"What I saw was impressive, my friends!" – continued the General.

"There was a strange phenomenon that I never thought could happen! The little table simply danced, suspended in the air, with such impetus to the point of madness!"

"And they say it speaks!" – remarks Céleste-Marie.

"Yes!" – agrees the General, highly enthusiastic. And he answers questions that were put to him with the greatest ease!

"Did it happen with such intensity?" – the young man is amazed.

"At Colonel of Mont–Parmis's house, the little table only hovered in the air for a few moments, nothing else! And no matter how long they insisted, no more phenomena occurred that night. But even though it did not have the intensity you have just reported, General; it still really impressed me! However, sir, do you really believe that there is no fraud in such manifestations?"

"At first glance, I don't think so..." – replies the General.

"I assure you that we have taken every precaution to avoid any hoaxes, but...

"That is true, you never know!" – agrees the young man.

"Presumption is an art that has been cultivated for millenia! Let's not forget that!"

"Yes, and no matter how quick our eyes are, who can unmask a simple circus illusionist in his magical art?" – observes the girl thoughtfully.

"They are so clever..."

"I agree with you, *ma chérie*!" – says the General.

"However, as I have already told you, we took every precaution beforehand, before the phenomena took place: we thoroughly scanned the room for trap doors, invisible silk threads, possible pulleys hidden in the ceiling or behind the curtains...But, the search was fruitless! No evidence of fraud! I think I can assure you that there was not the slightest possibility of any form of deception having taken place!"

"You said that the table answered questions, sir?" – asks the girl.

"What kind of questions did it answer?"

"All kinds, my dear!" – the General answers emphatically.

"From the most serious to the most infamous and puerile vexations you can imagine! And without hesitation!"

"I would like to see such things!" – exclaims Céleste-Marie. And, after a moment's thought, she continues:

"But how can a simple *guéridon* speak? I cannot understand it! How come the ones in my house do not speak?"

"Oh dear, they don't speak like that, like we do!" – the remarks the boy, laughing. And, after exchanging a brief, meaningful glance with the General, he continued:

"The tables telegraph! They use a code of knocks! Can you understand that?"

"How could it happen to the telegraph?[15]" – she asked, still a bit confused.

"Exactly...!" adds the young man.

---

[15] In 1844, Samuel Morse's invention of the telegraph revolutionized the transmission of information and made it possible to send news over long distances. The events recounted here took place from 1850 onwards, the year that marked the beginning of the ostensible manifestations of spirits, which initially took place through the famous "spinning tables" in the salons of Paris, These events caught the attention of Allan Kardec, who found in them not the frivolity of those who entertained themselves with such phenomenology, but the starting point from which serious research and later discoveries about the reality of communicability between spirits and incarnates would begin, and from there the foundations of the Spiritist Doctrine would emerge.

"They follow a code, very similar to the one used by telegraphists, and answer questions in the form of knocks, rising into the air, rotating on their own axis and systematically tapping one of their legs on the ground, making a noise."

"Unbelievable" – exclaims the young woman.

"Yes!" – says the General.

"And they even answer questions posed by thoughts!"

"Do they read thoughts?!" – amazed Céleste-Marie even more.

"It certainly does!" – replied the General.

"I took the test myself! And the table gave me a completely accurate answer! It really impressed me!"

"I would like to witness such things!" – says the young woman.

"Oh, General, when are you going to the Marquise de Souvigny's house again?"

"Towards the end of the week! – replies the soldier. If you wish, you and Berg will be my guests! Oh, and if she is willing to go, you should also take Marie-Louise! I think she will have a wonderful time! Constance loves it, because the tables are sometimes very indiscreet and give away secrets that are kept under lock and key! Ha...! Ha...! Ha...! Ha...! Ha...! " – the General bursts out laughing, and continues:

"You have to see the problems faced by certain ladies and young men in our society! I addition to some ladies who passed themselves off as modest ladies, and men who have always been considered venerable gentlemen! And, as you can well imagine, the little table unmasked everyone![16]

"Really?" – Céleste–Marie was astonished.

"So, they tell us such closely guarded secrets?" – and glanced sidelong at her fiancé's face. Suddenly an idea popped into her head: the chances to find out if her fiancé really loved her, or if he had not been cheating on her all this time?"

"What do you think is the origin of such phenomena, General?" – asks the boy.

"Actually, I'm not sure, Lieutenant, " – the old soldier replied.

"Sometimes I think that they are manifestations of forces that we are still completely unaware of. Other times, I describe these phenomena as possible hidden sides of electricity which, in itself, because it is invisible to the eye and because it provides an infinite number of phenomena that were hitherto thought to be impossible, usually generates a lot of questions in our heads and for which we have not yet to found plausible answers! In addition to electrical phenomena[17], there is also the magnetic phenomena!

---

[16] In the early days of spiritist manifestations, in the mid-19th century, through the spinning tables, in Parisian party halls and also in many other places in Europe, the character of the séances and of most of the spirits who manifested in them was consistent with the purposes they served: futility, vehemence and amusement only.

[17] From amber (Greek élektron) came the name electricity. In the 17th century, Otto von Guericke began systematic studies into electrification by friction. In 1672, von Guericke invented an electric charge-generating machine in which a sphere of sulphur constantly rotated, rubbing against dry earth. Half a century later, Stephen Gray made the first distinction between electrical conductors and insulators.

"Do you know that Mesmer[18] carried out a lot of research into animal magnetism in the past and this research, after being investigated by the Academy, came to nothing? I

During the 18th century, electrical machines evolved to consist of a rotating glass disk rubbed against a suitable insulator. An important finding was the capacitor, discovered independently by Ewald Georg von Kleist and Petrus van Musschenbroek. The capacitor consisted of a machine that stored electrical charges. It consisted of two conducting bodies separated by a thin insulator. However, an important invention of practical use was the lightning rod, made by Benjamin Franklin when he realized that the electrification of two rubbed bodies was caused by the absence of one of the two types of electricity in one of the bodies – resinous and vitreous electricity. In the 18th century, Luigi Aloisio Galvani carried out an important experiment in which electrical potentials produced contractions in the leg of a dead frog. This enabled Italian physicist Alessandro Volta to invent the voltaic pile, which consisted of a series of alternating copper and zinc disks separated by pieces of cardboard soaked in salt water. With this invention, a stable source of electric current was obtained for the first time. And from then on, research into electric current became more and more evident until the full application of electricity today.

[18] Franz Anton Mesmer was born in Well, Austria, in 1733. Creator of the philosophy of mesmerism, he is considered the father of animal magnetism. Before studying medicine at the University of Wicker, where he became a doctor, he studied philosophy, law and theology in Ingolstadt. He was a constant visitor to occult circles, where he gained a great deal of alchemical knowledge. He studied the life and work of Dr. Paracelsus (Phillippus Aureolus Theophrastus Bombastus von Hohenheim, 1493-1541) in depth. Paracelsus' therapeutic approach was based on the belief that there was a correspondence between the outside world – the macrocosm – and the different parts of the body – the microcosm. "De Influxo Planetarum In Corpus Humanum" was his thesis, which described the influence of the planets through a universal fluid with magnetic powers on living matter. He also described animal magnetism which, according to him, existed in two opposite forms and tended to emanate from the right and left sides of the human body. He also explained that the cure of illnesses consisted of restoring the altered balance or harmony between these fluids. Based on these theories, Mesmer built his therapeutic technique, using eye fixation and the application of passes with the hands.

still think that Mesmer's theories were given short shrift! You know how it is! Envy goes hand in hand with many of those gentlemen who call themselves "wise"!"

"And most of the time, they are not really wise at all...!" Berg points out playfully.

"You are right, dear...!" nods the General. "In the end, they sacrificed Dr. Mesmer and his theory out of pure envy...!

The afternoon was quiet and the three continued their conversation, which now took a different course. Politics came up as always. Now, Céleste–Marie was quieter than she expected. Her eyes merely jumped from her boyfriend to the General and then back again as the heated conversation continued, debating between the arguments about the monarchy and the fragile republic that persisted in not being definitively established....

"Do you know that Mesmer conducted a series of investigations on animal magnetism in the past, and that such research, after being examined by the Academy, gave no results...? I still think that they paid little attention to Mesmer's theories...! You know how it is...! Envy goes hand in hand with many of these gentlemen who are "wise"...!"

"And they usually have nothing of real wisdom!" – remarks Berg jocularly.

"You are right, my dear!" – agrees the General.

"Deep down, they sacrificed Dr. Mesmer and his theory out of sheer envy!

The afternoon fell quiet and the three of them continued their conversation, which now took different turns. Politics invariably came up. Céleste–Marie was now more silent than opitionated. Her eyes only flicked from her fiance to the General and then vice versa, while the heated conversation continued, debating between the theses on the monarchy and the fragile republic that stubbornly refused to take root...

Finally, the conversation stopped; they died of exhaustion, and Berg and Céleste–Marie said goodbye to the General. Outside, the afternoon waned and the lamp–lighters hurried past with their long sticks slung over their shoulders. The couple took a rental car and quickly got lost into the mists of the city, which was beginning to flicker with a light that was already half–softened, deadened and yellowed, and which had already lost its battle with the inflexible darkness of the night....

Chapter 2

Hearts in love

François–Armand approaches the immense mirror with its wide gilded frame in the ballroom and adjusts the collar of his dark blue tunic. He then runs a pair of excessively critical eyes over his entire image relected in the crystal and approves the whole thing with a slight smile. He was impeccable! After the thorough examination, he carefully adjusts the cap on his head and takes a final look.

"*Où vas–tu ainsi tout tôt?*"[1] – asks his mother who was entering the room at that very moment.

"*Chez Sylvie, maman*"[2] – he replies, jovially.

"How did you know that the Rousseletes were in Par? – asks his mother. They were not in Champagne!"

"Oh, *maman*, I have my informants... Have you forgotten?" – he said, approaching Amandine and kissing her tenderly on the forehead, continues:

"*Au revoir!* And for today, do not count on me for anything else, huh?"

---

[1] "Where are you going so early?...", in French
[2] "To Sylvie's house, Mom...!", in French.

"Oh, go on, you naughty boy! When Sylvie's in town, you do not care about anyone else, do you? What is more, I think you will snatch her while she is still asleep in bed... Do you not realize that it is still too early?"

"If she is still asleep, I will wake her up with kisses, *maman*!" – he replies and bursts out laughing.

"Ha...! Ha...! Ha...! Ha...! Ha...! Do you not understand that I am proposing to surprise her?"

"Oh, look at the manners! Watch your manners!" – Amandine admonished him, struggling to follow him as he left the house in long bstrides.

"Restrain yourself! If Colonel Rousselet catches you fooling around with his daughter, he can kick you out!"

"Nonsense, *maman*!" – he said, laughing, as he descended the gray granite staircase that led to the vestibule of the house.

"The Colonel adores me and wants me to marry Sylvie! You are the one who is gnawing jealous! Ha...! Ha...! Ha...! Ha...! Ha...! "

"Am I jealous?!" – exclaims the mother. And showing a great deal of annoyance at the young man's audacity, she continuous, pointing a threatening finger at him:

"Look here, you naughty boy, if you got married tomorrow, I would thank God! That is the only way I would get rid of you and finally have peace in my mind!"

"You are just saying that *maman*! – he says, already in the small courtyard outside the house.

"Deep down, you are afraid of losing me, aren't you?"

With eyes filled with tenderness, Amandine follows him as he disappears into the street, after turning around one last time and sending her a long kiss through the air, laughing happily. Her chest heaving, she let out a long sigh and went back inside.

"Yes, I'm losing him" – she thought as she sat on the turquoise velvet divan in the living room. The immense house was plunged into a heavy silence and she suddenly felt the weight of loneliness and was scared. She then looked at the wall and her eyes fixed on the huge painting with its wide gilded frames, where her husband's figure was depicted, almost life–size, and masterfully painted in oil. In the portrait, Colonel Louis–Henri Rounet had serious and noble features in his dark blue uniform.

"Yes, I'm losing him" – she thought as she sat on the turquoise velvet divan in the living room. The immense house was plunged into a heavy silence and she suddenly felt the weight of loneliness and was scared. She then looked at the wall and her eyes fixed on the huge painting with its wide gilded frames, where her husband's figure was depicted, almost life–size, and masterfully painted in oil. In the portrait, Colonel Louis–Henri Rounet had serious and noble features in his dark blue uniform.

"God in heaven, Louis–Henri!" – she thought, staring at the portrait. Her eyes filled with tears as she gazed at the beloved figure depicted there. The elegance, the majestic loftiness, the hand resting on the hilt of the sheathed sabre, the medals on his chest, the golden pennants, the blue, white and red chevrons....

"I have a feeling that my life, from now on, will be terrible, *mon amour!*" – she continues, talking to her beloved image.

"First of all, I have lost you, my darling, to the wretched war at such an early age...! Now, I am losing my other love to young Rousselet. Our boy's heart already has another owner! For me, only the memories will remain! From now on, I will live on memories!" – and poignant sobs broke the heavy silence.

An hour and a half later, the young cadet François–Armand Rounet stood in front of the old dark granite house, the residence of Colonel Hippolyte–Antoine Rousselet. His heart was pounding as he pulled the string of the bell, which sounded its shrill clang.

"Ah!" – uttered the butler who had come to open the heavy entrance door, when he saw the young man who was anxiously waiting in front of the gate in his impeccable dark blue uniform. Then, arming himself with purposeful phlegm, the servant walked slowly down the front steps and, approaching the gate with its hugh, black bars, run his eyes up and down the boy with a pair of cold eyes and said, in an extremelly affected voice:

"*Mademoiselle se trouve–elle encore a dormir, M'sieur!*"[3]

"Oh, I know!" – François–Armand exclaimed, not caring a bit about the coldness shown by the pernicious butler.

"If you don't mind, I will wait until she wakes up!"

---

[3] "The little lady is still asleep, sir...!", in French.

"*S'ainsi vous plaît– il!*"[4] – said the butler, shrugging and opening the gate for him. Settled in the living room, the young cadet began to wait for his girlfriend, who was still asleep in her room. Next to the wide door that gave access to the living room, standing as still as a statue, the butler remained impassive, staring inexpressively into the void, clad in his impeccable white silk livery with light blue collar and cuffs, neatly ironed.

"Is Madame Edith not at home?" – the young man asked the butler, after a long moment of absolute silence.

"No, M'sieur," – replies the pedantic butler, laconic.

"And the Colonel? Did the Colonel leave so early too?"

"*Parfaitement, M'sieur...*" – the other replied dryly.

"His Lordship left the house, accompanied by his wife, very early in the morning, as soon as dawn broke."

"Do you know where your employers have gone?" – asks the young cadet, getting up, already bored of the monotony of waiting, since it was not his style to sit still for more than five minutes.

"I think they are walking in the countryside, *M'sieur*. Madame Edith loves the countryside!"

"Hmm! I know!" – exclaimed the boy, glancing slightly at the butler's emaciated face. Then, with both hands, he lifted the flaps of his dark blue tunic and sat down again, right on the edge of the sofa and continues, more to irritate and spike the discourteous servant:

"Pierre, are you not going to serve me anything?"

---

[4] "If you wish...!", in French.

"Oh, what would you like, gentleman?" – exclaims the other, pretending to be ready, as if to apologize for the alleged rudeness he was committing towards his visitor.

"*Vin...? Du liqueur...? De la brioche...? Ou qu'il sait d'une pièce de tarte à la creme suisse, par hazard...?*"[5]

"*A liqueur, s'il vous plait!*"[6] – says the young man, shaking himself on the bright red velvet divan and, relaxing, crosses his legs, chivalrously.

"*Amande... Poire... Cerise... Choisissiez la saveur, s'ilvous plait, M'sieur!*"[7]

"*Cerise!*" – exclaims François–Armand after pretending to be thinking seriously for a moment.

"*Je voudrais bien de la cerise!*"[8]

Soon, the butler brought him a tiny crystal goblet containing the ruby–red liquid on a rich polished silver tray. Once the drink had been served, Pierre returned to his old post and closed himself off in his usual muteness. In the meantime, he watched what the other man from the sidelines. The young cadet deftly picked up the tiny crystal glass by the stem, using his index finger and thumb to pinch it; then, he brought the glass close to his nostrils and sucked in the bouquet at length, as great connoisseurs of drink do. Then he carefully studied the color of the liquid against the light from the window; then he held the tiny glass for a few seconds,

---

[5] "– Wine?... Liqueur?... Cake? Or perhaps a piece of Swiss custard tart?..."', in French.

[6] "– A liqueur, please...!", in French.

[7] "– Plum... Pear... Cherry... Choose the flavor, please, sir...!", in French.

[8] "– Cherry...! (...) – I would very much like cherry...!", in French.

looking at it intently The butler followed his gestures and wondered inwardly:

"Imbecile, fool! Where have you seen drinking liqueur at this time of the morning?" Meanwhile he had a slight jolt: the young man was calling him.

"Pierre!" – says François–Armand and hands him the glass, untouched, without taking a single drop.

"Thank you, Pierre!" – continues the young man, looking him in the eye and, giving him a very cheesy smile, continues:

"You would not believe that I would be crazy enough to drink at this time of the morning, would you?" – and bursts out laughing:

"Ha...! Ha...! Ha...! Ha...! Ha...! "

Pierre was amazed. It seemed as if the madman had read his mind. And as he presented him with the silver tray and took back the untouched glass of liqueur, he realized that the wretch was looking at him and laughing with delight! Oh hate! Deep down, the servant felt himself burning with rage: that wretch was mocking him! Oh, you wretch!

He then had an unnamed urge to slam the tray into his face, without mercy, until he disfigured him, until he killed him with so many blows!

"Ah, Pierre!" – the butler heard the unfortunate man's voice calling him as he stood on the threshold of the door, leaving the living room towards the scullery.

"Tell me, are you still in love with Sylvie?"

Pierre almost collapsed. What was the wretch saying? How did he know?! He had hidden it so long! And did the bandit not know?

"*Par... Par... don..., M'sieur!*" – stammers Pierre, without turning around. He was blushing up to his ears, he did not have the courage to turn around and face that wretch!

"*Qu'est ce que vous avez dit?*"[9]

"Oh, do not play dumb, you poltroon!" – listens to his reply. Now he was very close, right behind his back. And, circling him, he got right in his face and went on, serious:

"Do you think I have not understood everything, you idiot? That you are in love with my girlfriend? But, look, huh? You dare touch her with a finger and you will see the weight of my sword!

Pierre felt faint. He almost let the silver tray slip out of his hands. But how did that slimeball know? He had never told anyone that! He watched himself all the time so as not to betray himself! Yes, he loved her... He loved her with a passion! But, he did not want them to know! But alas, the tramp knew! What a disgrace! He had been taken so much by surprise! He had really betrayed himself! Whoever he truly wished would never find out about his secret, which he had thought he was keeping under lock and key, already knew! Lightly, he had discovered everything! He had set him up! And he, Pierre, had fallen for it! The other had taken advantage of the element of surprise and caught him off guard! Wretch! Miserable!

---

[9] For... For... give, sir...!"(...)..."What did you say?, in French

Oh, that pest did not know, that is for sure! He had no way of knowing! He hardly ever stayed in Paris! Did he not live all over the world, following the wars? He only suspected! Nothing else! The smart boy had set the bait well, and he, Pierre, had unwisely taken it! He had not prepared himself in time for such an eventuality! Now, however, when he had reacted so boldly in this way like, he was sure! Ah, you infamous wretch!

"Look, you disgusting bastard!" – François–Armand continued, pointing a threatening finger at him, just an inch from his nose.

"I will kill you without mercy if you dare! If you even hint at her, you will see! – and he sits back down on the sofa.

Pierre could not move. He felt pinned to the ground! His ears were burning like fire. And now? What if that demon told her? What if she knew everything?

"Go, slug!" – hears the wretch's voice.

"Come on! – get aou of my sight view!"

"Yes... Yes, sir!" – the butler finally manages to stammer and, pulling himself together, disappears, almost tripping over his own feet; so out of control was he.

"Idiot..." – mumbles François–Armand, smiling and enjoying himself very much when he sees him leaving in a huff. At this moment, the young cadet's eyes lit up. From above, in the dormitory wing, he hears a familiar voice:

"Pierre! Pierre! Where have you been? Bring my *petit déjeuner*![10] Come on, you lazy bastard...! You want to starve me, huh?"

The butler returns from the pantry almost at a run and eagerly loaded the tray with the breakfast which, to be served so promptly, had certainly been prepared well in advance, so that the young lady would not have to wait for it for a single minute.

However, as soon as the helpfull servant began to climb the first steps of the wide gray granite staircase that led to the upper floor, he felt he was being held by the flaps of his lab coat.

"Oh, you're not going up to her room, you worm!" – François–Armand exclaims, between his teeth, with a heavy, threatening frown.

"But, *M'sieur*!" – exclaims the butler, exasperated.

"The lady is calling for me, and it is my duty to answer her!"

"Oh, you love answering to the lady, I suppose!" – observes the boy, full of irony, and, moving closer to the trembling butler, catches him by the collar of his coat and continues:

"Come on, give me the tray!"

"*Mais, M'sieur*!" – protests the butler, resisting.

"This is my task! It's my duty to do it!"

---

[10] 10. Breakfast, in French

"Oh, you love fulfilling such a task, don't you, smart guy?" – exclaims the young cadet, holding on tightly to the tray that the other man insisted on not handing him.

"Come on, let go off the tray or I will hit you in the face!"

"*M'sieur*!" – shouts the butler, dragging him away, filled with fury.

"You have no right to do that! This is not your house, and I do not obey your orders!"

"Ah! You dare to confront me, you idiot?" – sneers François–Armand.

"Do you want to bet that I have enough influence here to demand that your bosses throw you out on your ass?"

"Well, do it, sir!" – shouts the butler, getting even angrier.

"Do it and I will tell Monsieur and Madame that you intended to force your way into Mademoiselle's room during their absence!

"Would you really have the nerve to invent such a slander against me, Pierre!" – says the boy, staring at the other man's face with a terrible expression in his eyes, as he groped with his hand for the handle of the knife sheathed in his belt.

"You are forcing me to do this, sir!" – says the butler, undeterred.

"Pierre! Where have you been, you slacker? Look, I'm starving!" – insists the girl, calling for the butler.

Taking advantage of the servant's slight distraction when he heard his mistress's pleas, François–Armand, with a quick jerk, took the tray out of the other man's hands.

"*M'sieur! Non!*" – shouts Pierre, trying futilely to get back the tray that Armand–François had cleverly snatched from his hands. Then, deftly sidestepping the siege that the desperate butler had tried to put him under, he easily managed to outwit him and, in no time at all, he was already climbing the steps of the staircase, two by two, towards his young girlfriend's room.

"And do not come after me or I will tear your ears off with my knife!" – threatens the young cadet, already at the top of the stairs, ostentatiously placing his free hand on the handle of the rapier attached to his waist.

"Hold still, you fool, or you will see what I am capable of!"

Dejected, Pierre stands at the foot of the stairs and stares helplessly upwards.

"*Miserable...!*" – mutters the dejected butler, full of rage.

"Ah, bandit, you will pay me! Oh, yes, you will pay me!"

Already in the long, semi–dark corridor, François–Armand was tiptoeing along. He wanted to surprise her! He knew that Sylvie had not even imagined he was there! They had not seen each other for six months. He, on campaign, with his regiment; she, with her mother, in the country house in the *Champagne*. Edith did not like Paris; she preferred to live in the countryside, and her daughter accompanied her, especially when her father was away defending the country's borders.

The young man knew where his love's room was. His heart beating furiously in his chest, he approached the door and knocked gently with his closed hand.

"Come in!" – hears the beloved voice from inside.

The window was still closed in the room, and therer was a slight gloom. In the half–light, François–Armand looked at his young girlfriend sitting in a moss–green velvet armchair. Her eyes were half–closed and her legs were tucked up, her arms wrapped around her exposed knees and slipping carelessly out of the front opening of her pink silk peignoir. It was clear that she was still very sleepy. François–Armand entered the room and stood looking at her, full of tenderness. Oh, how he loved her! Without making the slightest sound, he placed the breakfast tray on a *guéridon* and, on tiptoe, walked over to her and stood in front of her, his face almost touching hers. She continued with half–closed eyes, dozing off, still full of sleep, and he brought his face closer to hers, more and more, ever so slightly, imperceptibly, and he could even feel the soft breath of her delicate, fragrant, sweet, breath.... His heart was beating so hard in his chest that it felt like it was going to explode into thousands of pieces. He could not resist. He brought her face closer and stole a kiss...

Oh, the surprise! The unexpected surprise! First, the fright, the amazement at the audacity!

"*Toi?!*" – she cried out in astonishment, after the natural reaction of trying to get away from the audacious fact. Then, the explosion of intense joy, of infinite happiness, when she recognized him!

"Toi, ici! Mais, tu est même plus fou que je pensais!"[11]

"I am crazy about you, my love!" – he exclaims, taking her in his arms and kissing her passionately.

And then there were many hugs and kisses until the passion calmed down.

"When did you get back to Paris?" – she asked, while eating her breakfast.

"Yesterday…" he replied.

11. *"You?...!" (…)"-You, here?...! But you are even crazier than I thought!"* in French.

"When my regiment returned, it was already late at night! And almost before I got home, still dusty and dirty from the roads, I first wanted to come here and meet you!" – he exclaims, laughing.

"I missed you so much!"

"And why did you not come?"

"Oh, the manners!" – he says.

"What would your parents say? It was after midnight!"

"Oh, so I was already asleep!"

"Besides…" – he continues:

"I was so tired that I could hardly get into bed and I slept until the morning, when I decided to come to see you first hand!"

"Are you still serving in the same regiment, under the command of your cousin?"

"Yes," – he replies laughing.

"Or do you think I should serve with your father, so that he can make fun of me until he gets sick? I prefer Berg to command me! You know how it is, with him, I have certain perks!

"And Dad would certainly have you peeling potatoes with the cooks, I presume! Ha...! Ha...! Ha...! Ha...! Ha...! "

"Oh, do you have any doubts, *ma belle*!?" – he observes, with a yellow chuckle.

"Oh, you are slandering Dad!" – she exclaims, pinching his cheek.

"You know he loves you and would never do anything like that to you!"

"But I will not risk my neck by asking to be transferred to the regiment he commands, no, my dear! You never know! Better not risk it!

The crystal–clear laughter of the two lovers spread through the house. Still awake at the foot of the stairs, Pierre heard their joyful hovering and was filled with hatred and spite.

"You bastard!" – he mutters through his teeth.

"Have fun with her! But, you cannot wait! Ah, you will see, you rascal, what I have in store for you!

In the bedroom, the couple continued sharing the girl's breakfast, between tiny pieces of bread and candied fruit sweets, which she alternately took into her mouth and gently into his, and often interspersed with light kisses and giggles of joy and pleasure, without once taking their eyes off each other.

"Come and see what I am doing!" – she exclaims, getting tired of eating and, standing up abruptly, she pulls him by the hand and leads him to a corner of the room. Then, resolutely, she pulls back the curtains and opens the window. The light of the early morning invades the room, brightening everything. An easel was covered with a cloth sptained with various shades of paint. Sylvie, with a quick gesture, uncovered the canvas and proudly displayed it:

"Look...!" – she exclaims, always beaming with joy.

"Study everything carefully and try to find out whose features they are!"

The boy squeezed his eyes shut tightly to adjust them to the intense light, then he opened them and looked carefully at the drawing.

"But this is me!" – he exclaimed and, turning to her, proselytizes, very exmotional:

"Oh, *ma petite!* You are portraying me!"

"Yes, it is you!" – she says proudly.

"This is the only way to quench the intense longing that consumes my so! I have been working on a portrait of you for a few months now!

"Oh, *mon amour!*" – he exclaims, embracing her, his eyes welling with tears, deeply moved, and continues:

"But how can you portray me so faithfully if you do not have me standing in front of you all the time, posing as a model? Look, I do not know anything about paintings, but I can imagine how difficult it is to portray someone without the model! But, you can do it!

"Yes!" – she says, always very proud of her work.

"Even *M'sieur* Pichon, my master painter, does not understand how that happens! However, I know: I have you so present in my mind and in my heart, that I know you by heart! I have memorized your features, down to the smallest detail!

"Oh, my love!" – he says with emotion and, drawing her to him, kisses her passionately.

"Tell me: did you like it?" – she asked, disentangling herself from his arms and looking him in the eyes, she adds:

"It is already in the final details! Then, I will hang it on that wall, right in front of my bed, tolook at you every day when I go to sleep, and when I wake up the first image my eyes will see in the morning will be your face!

He embraces her passionately after that tender revelation.

"Look, why do we not go to the cité!" – he suggests, taking her by the hand and making her sit down next to him on the edge of her bed.

"We could have lunch together at Place Pigalle... It looks life it is going to be a beautiful day today!"

"Oh, I would love to!" – she says, her eyes lighting up with an intense glow.

"Then go! Wait for me downstairs, while I do the toilette!"

Shortly afterwards, François–Armand came down the stairs, swollen and almost bursting with happiness. His head was in the clouds and almost ran over the butler who was still standing at the foot of the stairs.

"Get out of the way, cripple!" – he growls, when he sees that the servant is still standing in the same place, clogging up the passage.

Pierre jumped slightly, sideways, so as not to be run over by the boy who was coming at him, determined to give him a powerful blow with his shoulders.

"*Manant!*"[12] – murmured the butler between his teeth.

"What did you say, you filth?" – asks the boy, turning around and bringing his hand down hard to the other man's chest, he pushes him and continues, threateningly:

"Get back to the kitchen before I break your filthy snout! Come on!"

Pierre steps close to him, glaring at him with a pair of horrible eyes filled with intense hatred, but he does not leave. Resolutely, he stood at the doorway leding to the living room and remained there, as still as a statue. François–Armand walks past him and sits, as before, on the divan, and starts to wait for his girlfriend. Often, out of the corner of their eyes, they studied each other meticulously and threw mental darts at each other, full of mutual hatred and spite.

Within half an hour, Sylvie appeared resplendent at the top of the stairs, dressed in a light dress of white gauze, lined with purple silk. On her head was a black tricot hat, with long

---

[12] "– Rude...!", in French.

starched brims that highlighted her snow features enormously. Her lips, dyed an exuberant shade of ruby, were in perfect harmony with her zygomas, slightly reddened by crimson; on her feet, she wore delicate black lacquer shoes with fantastic high heels...

"*François! Ici suis–je! Alfons!*"[13]– she shouts, as she lightly descend the gray granite steps.

François–Armand jumps up and runs into the hall. Pierre, also excited, makes a point of running to the foot of the stairs.

"Stay there, you worm!" – he mutters through his teeth as he passes close to the other man and applies a formidable blow to his flank with his elbow.

"Uuhhh" – moans the servant, cringing in pain. He had not expected this unusual aggression.

François–Armand approaches the foot of the stairs and offers his arm to his girlfriend.

"You look exquisite, *ma belle!*" – he says, kissing her cheek.

"Pierre!" – shouts the young lady.

"What have you gotten yourself into?!" – the butler appears at the threshold of the large door, slightly bent over from the intense pain he was feeling as a result of the hard blow he had received.

"Oh, there is Pierre!" – exclaims François–Armand. Sweetening his voice as much as possible, he continued:

---

[13] "– François...! Here I am! Let's go...!", in French.

"How pale you look, good Pierre! But what happened to you, my friend? It is like you have seen a ghost!"

"Oh, yes!" – agrees the young lady, approaching and, taking pity on the young man who was still writhing in pain, asked:

"What happened to you, Pierre?! Are you feeling ill? Do you want us to call Dr. Durraine?"

"Non..., made... moi... selle," – the servant shouts, breaking out in a cold sweat. *"Je me suis bien.... Une légère malaise, je crois ...! Il ne faut pas de désespérer!"* [14]

"Oh, good Pierre!" – exclaimed the young man, tenderly stroking the butler's shoulder.

"Are you sure you are all right? Look, we will go in search of Dr. Eustaque Durraine!"

Pierre looked at him with a pair of horrible eyes. He really wanted to bit and tear off a piece of that hand that the cynical bastard was keeping amicably behind his back.

"No..." – says the butler, feeling completely humiliated because of that thug.

"I'm fine..."

"Eh, allors, très bien!" [15] – says the young lady, shrugging and, becoming cheerful again, continued:

"If you feel ill again, go back to your quarters! And there will not be anyone else in the house apart from Berthe! If you need anything, turn to her! Oh, and when maman and

---

[14] "– No..., la... la... la... dy...!" (...) "– I'm fine...! A slight indisposition, I think...! There's no need to despair!, in French
[15] "Eh, well done...!", in French.

papa come back from their walk in the countryside, tell them I have gone out with François–Armand and we will have lunch! Do not forget it, huh? *Au revoir!"* – and she runs to the door of the vestibule.

"*Au revoir, bon Pierre!*"[16] – exclaims the young cadet, winking at the weary butler.

"Bandit! Miserable!" – mutters the servant between his teeth, but loud enough for the other to hear.

At the door, Sylvie was waiting for her boyfriend. François–Armand kisses her tenderly on the dusty cheek, and then, without her noticing, he turned and laughed a scornful laugh at Pierre who, still bent over, was twisting more from the pain in his soul than from the phenomenal elbow he had received from that wretch, which almost broke a good pair of ribs...

"You are so kind to our butler!" – exclaimed the girl, snuggling up to her boyfriend's side, as he drerw her to him and hugged her tenderly.

"Oh, you know how it is..." – he replies, pretending to be very sympathetic.

"Pierre is all alone in the world, even though he is still so young! I really feel a lot of compassion for him!

"Yes..." – she agrees.

"His father, Gregory, served as our butler until his death, as well as his mother, Hélène, who has also passed away, leaving him all alone in this world! Poor Pierre...! Did you know that I grew up with him? Papa wanted to adopt

---

[16] "Good bye, good Pierre...!", in French.

him, to give him a military career, but Maman did not want to. She preferred to initiate him into the domestic arts.! It's so difficult to find reliable servants! The best thing is to raise them from a young age! And that's what she did with Pierre: she brought him up from a young age to eventually replace his parents when they were gone! And it seems she has guessed!

"Your mother is very smart!" – exclaimed François-Armand, smiling slightly with satisfaction. And he continues, sticking a very fine barb into the other man's character:

"And besides, I do not think Pierre would really be suitable for the army. I think he is too affected in his manners, full of gestures, do you not agree?

"Oh, François!" – exclaims the girl, laughing.

"Poor Pierre! I do not think he is affected as you say, no...! His parents and, above all, Maman have given him a very refined upbringing! Nothing more than that!" – and, wanting to spur her on, she continues, more with the intention of provoking her jealousy:

"I think he is handsome, contrary to what you say! He is a lot bigger than you, he is a lot thicker!"

"Yeah, right!" – replied the boy, flushing with sudden anger. And he continues, full of spite up to his ears:

"The little guy is much older than me! At least ten years!"

"Oh, you exaggerate! You know that Pierre will be, at most, only two or three years older than you!" – she said, barely containing her laughter at the boy's highly angry features. I did not know you were jealous of Pierre! – and she continues, lightly pinching his flank:

" Oh, you silly, I did not know you were so jealous of Pierre!

"Jealous, me?!" – he exclaimed, stopping and looking her in the eye, full of emulation for what she was saying about him.

"How could I be jealous of such a fop like that?" – and, frowning, he continued walking, almost dragging her, in long strides, along the square cobblestone sidewalk.

"You are walking too fast!" – she says, trying her best to keep up with his long strides.

"So, you will force me to break my heels!"

"We would better get a coach right away!" – he says, still rather upset.

"I thought I would walk a bit further with you, basking in the morning sun, but I see you prefer a car!"

"Come on, clear your face!" – she exclaimed, hugging him as they settled into the hired carriage that was speeding towards the center of the city.

"You got your ass handed to you for nothing! Did you not realize that I was playing with you? Do you not know that you are the only one in the world for me?

The boy squints at her, trying to keep down the anger gnawing at his soul; however, those piteous, honey-colored, slightly almond-shaped eyes have completely disarmed him, and he smiled at her and, in a flash, clasps her in his arms and kisses her furiously on the lips...

The Cité was glistening in the spring sunshine when François–Armand and Sylvie alighted from the hire car at Place Pigalle. Arm in arm, they set off along the promenade, under the shade of the lush almond trees. High above, the sun was still beautiful, spreading its golden darts, flooding the whole world with radiant light...

Chapter 3

A Trip to the Countryside

Edith–Aurore Rousselet climbed out of the carriage in front of her husband and, opening her arms, took a long breath of the fresh morning air. In front of her was the open field, full of lavenders bursting with purplish–blue flowers. The perfume that spread through the air was intoxicating, almost dizzying.

"*Oh, combient j'adore la lavande!*"[1] exclaims the woman, inhaling the air greedily.

"I think you will get dizzy if you keep smelling so much lavender like that!" – says her husband, laughing and coming up behind her, he hugs her tenderly.

"Oh, you are exaggerating, Hippolyte!" – she said, laughing, as she tenderly hugged him tightly from behind.

"You know how much I prefer the country to the city... I hate crowds! Parisian hustle and bustle makes me sick! I feel much better in the peace and quiet of the countryside... It is you and your daughter who love the movements, the parties, the gliter of the city halls!

---

[1] "Oh, how I love lavender...!", in French.

"It's because you were born and raised in the countryside, *ma chérie*, amidst the cows, the geese and the hares! Ha...! Ha...! Ha...! Ha...! Ha...! " – he laughed.

"Ah, and you mock me!" – she says, pinching the back of his hand.

"Do you have the nerve to call me a provincial like that?"

"Why are you surprised? You know perfectly well that I have always liked provincial girls!" – he says laughing at her.

"Did I ever hide this fact from you? I love your country accent rough, bordering on rustic....It really enchants me! It is so peculiar, so different from the pedantry of Parisian ladies...! And, by the way, isn't that why I married you? And why I chose you as the mother of my children? I love you, above all, for your simplicity...."

"It was..." – she agrees. And, breaking free from his arms, she walks a few steps into the flowery field and continues:

"Did you know that I was crazy about men in uniform?"

"Really?" – he asked, laughing, and begins to follow her through the lavender field.

"So, that is why, at that ball when we met for the first time, you could not take your eyes off me? Was it me you were looking at or my uniform?"

"Fool!" – she exclaims and laughs.

"I said men in uniform! I looked at you, at your eyes as green as emeralds! I was enchanted by them!"

"Oh, Edith... I love you so much!" – exclaims Colonel Rousselet, taking his wife by the hand and forcing her to lie down in the flowery field. He then lies down next to her, wraps his arm around her and kisses her long and tenderly on the mouth. Then they both lie on their backs looking up at the clear blue sky.

"I love you very much too, Hippolyte!" – she murmurs.

"We have been so happy! God has been so good to us that even though you are not always by my side, as I would like, and apart from the fact that you are always exposed to extreme danger, I am happy nonetheless! I know that you will never die in war! I feel it! You will die an old man in my arms."

"Oh, how can you be so sure of that?" – he exclaims, laughing.

"Do not tell me that, as well as besides being a beautiful country woman with a charmingly harsh voice, you are also a Pythoness!"

"Pythoness, me?!" – she said, sitting down on the tufts of lavender that had crumpled under their weight and become a soft, fluffy vegetable mattress. And, laughing at the joke he had played on her, she exclaimed amused:

"I wish I were!" – then, turning serious, she continues:

"But, joking aside, what I feel is real! You know, *mon chéri*, women usually have a sixth sense, and I have a feeling that one day you will leave this life of a soldier and we will move to the countryside for good, you and me!"

"And Sylvie?" – he asked, looking at her seriously.

"Will our treasure not go with us?"

Edith–Aurore's eyes were fixed on the purplish–blue lavender that waved in the fresh breeze of the radiant morning and she gave a sad smile.

"I don't know..." – she murmured, and her eyes filled with tears.

"I have never told you before, but sometimes I feel that our little girl will not live with us!"

"Oh, of course, maybe she will not live with us!" – he exclaimed, sitting down too, and tenderly touching her face with his fingertips.

"Surely she will get married and live with her husband, starting a family!"

"No!" – she retorted.

"That's not how I feel! I know what you said would be the obvious, the natural thing to say, because she is lost in love with Amandine's son. However, every time I hold her, every time I touch her, I feel as if she is slipping away from me, as if I am letting her go and as if I am losing her, like a hand full of fine sand slipping through my fingers! And as much as I try to hold her tighter and tighter, I feel like I am losing her! In fact, I do not even know how to express these things to you!"

"Oh, it's all nonsense in your head!" – he exclaims, drawing her to him and wrapping his arm around her. "Take your mind out of this nonsense, will you?" – he continues, stroking her back and kissing her tenderly on the hair.

"Our daughter is crazy about François–Armand!" – he continues, trying to cheer her up.

"You will see: they will end up getting married much sooner than you think, and they will give us half a dozen grandchildren!"

"Oh, you are too much!" – she said, removing her head from his chest and, looking him in the eyes, continued:

"If *ma petite poupée*[2] continued to live even if she were far away from me, I would be satisfied...." – and having a deep sigh, she continues:

"Even without giving me grandchildren"

"Oh, come on! Let us go!" – says the Colonel, tenderly stroking her hair. And then, purposely changing the subject, he continues:

"What did we bring the canvas, easel, paints and brushes for? The day is beautiful, the landscape magnificent! Are you not going to paint? Is it not that what we came for?"

Edith–Aurore looks at the landscape of purple flowers, her eyes highly desolate.

"Not today, *mon chéri*..." – she says in a sad voice.

"Not today..."

"What would you like to eat?" – François–Armand asked his girlfriend who was looking around in amazement, not missing a single detail of the luxurious *patisserie* where they were sitting around one of the little tabes wuth a white marble top.

---

[2] "My little doll", in French.

"*Une grosse tranche de tarte à fromage! Et des pommes de terre rôties et des...*"³ – she replies, still undecided about what else to order.

"Oh, eating like that, you will get as fat as a whale!" – he exclaimed, laughing at her voracious appetite.

"Rude!" – she exclaims, pinching the back of his hand.

"And what are you going to eat? A whole roast rooster, I presume!"

"Oh, you want me to turn into a pig, do you?" – he asks, laughing.

"I think I will just eat the roast potatoes, that is all. I want to stay in my current shape.... Or else, my sergeant will kill me with so many heavy exercises when I go back to the front! That happens, my dear! We come home and bury our snouts in the food! You have no idea what is like in the army! When you are in the army, you are forced to stay in shape by eating what the state provides!"

"Ah, is it?" – she is amazed.

"I thought you led a life of kings there!" – and she continues ironically:

"Now I understand less why you want to go to war! If not for the food... Then, why is it ? Women? I know you do not have them there.... Money? Not either, because Dad's salary is a pittance! If it were not for the person I am fortune he inherited from Grandpa... So, why do men love to go to war?"

"A desire for adventure, my dear!" – he replies.

---

³ "A thick slice of cheese pie...! And roast potatoes and...', in French.

"Did you know that we men are born adventurers? It's all just the unstoppable desire to fight! The incessant search for new adventures and the irresistible desire to always be in danger are ingrained in our blood!"

"I think you are born troublemakers!" – she says, laughing.

"You do love it, it is a good party! I even think men invent wars when they are bored enough! To amuse themselves, they kill each other! Pure lack of fun... And I think that when they invent things that really amuse men, wars will be doomed to disappear!"

"You know you are right..." – he says, marveling at his girlfriend's philosophical tirade.

"Who have you been reading lately?

"Leibniz!"[4] – she replies.

"Men have the ability *to think about action and know why they act.*"

"Hum! I see..." – he says. It was clear that he did not know anything about the subject. In fact, since leaving the Lycée and joining the army, he has not read anything else. He simply asked:

"And what else does Mr. Leib... Leib... say? What?"

"Leibiniz!" – she adds.

"He admitted a series of efficient causes to determine human action within the causal chain of the natural world.

---

[4] Gottfried Wilhelm von Leibniz (Leipzig, July 1, 1646 – Hanover, November 14, 1716) was a German philosopher, scientist, mathematician, diplomat and librarian.

This series of efficient causes concerns the body and its actions. However, in parallel to this series of efficient causes, there is a second series, that of the final causes. The final causes could be considered as an infinity of small inclinations and dispositions of the soul, present and past, which lead to the present action. There is thus an immeasurable infinity of reasons to explain a singular desire. In this sense, all the choices made become determinants of action. According to him, there is no such thing as arbitrariness or action isolated from context. The notion of free action also seems to fall by the wayside, but this is not the case Leibniz believes in free action if it is, at the same time, contingent, spontaneous and reflected"

"*Ula–lá!*" – the young man is amazed.

"You are really enjoying the lessons at the Lycée des Arts!"

"And you, would not take advantage of them?" – she asked, full of irony.

"No!" he replies, laconic.

"I slept all the time during Philosophy lessons! And during Latin, too! Ha...! Ha...! Ha...! Ha...! Ha...! I thought it was all so boring!"

"Oh! The men!" – she exclaims.

"The men!" – and continues, ironically:

"I guarantee that, in fencing lessons, you were the first!"

"That is for sure!" – he confirms, puffing out his chest with satisfaction.

"I was unbeatable!"

"Tell me, François..." – says the young lady, suddenly becoming serious.

"What was the first time you killed a man?"

He stops himself at once. From playfulness to absolute seriousness. For a moment, his eyes were lost in the void. They were certainly searching for memories, rummaging around in the depths, in the recesses of the soul.

"It was horrible!" – he mutters, his eyes fixed on nothing.

"It was really horrible, the smell of blood!

"How did you kill him?"

"The bayonet... a sharp blow, tearing deep into the guts... He was young, just like me..." – and he swallows dryly a few times, as if to indicate that those memories were always accompanied by intense discomfort. Then he continues, his voice filled with sudden emotion:

"You know, Sylvie, when we shoot down an enemy soldier from afar with rifle fire; that is one thing; but sometimes the battles go hand-to-hand, and then we have to draw our bayonets, attach them to the end of the barrel of our guns and face the enemy, face to face, and measure forces with him! And to fight, fiercely, chasing each other, like two beasts catching up! And always be the first to strike the fatal blow, at the right moment, taking advantage of a split second in which the other falters, falters in their own defense! There will never be a second chance! It is always fatal! It is something indescribable, cruel! You cannot imagine what it is like to feel the iron penetrate another person's body, to feel them tremble.

The weapon brings to our hands the agonizing spasms of the victim, who is shaking with intense pain, as their flesh is struck by the sharp metal! You feel the other person's pain in yourself within seconds! You see him staring you in the eyes and asking you with his gaze why! Why, Sylvie? Then, their eyes quickly became opaque, losing their shine, and pallor invaded his features! It is the implacable embrace of death! You had to see their despair *in extremis* stamped on their gloomy features!" – the young man remained silent for a moment, overcome by emotion. Then he continued, his voice full of bitterness:

"The first time this happens to us is really terrible! However, the dark baptism of fire is usually followed by a hardening of the emotions! No more of what you felt the first time happens afterwards: you get used to it! Everything in life is trivialized; even these bestialities become commonplace...! All that remains is the furious outpouring of the intense animality contained in the chest! It is the waterfall of human ferocity pouring insanely over each other, with the strongest and most skillful always winning! Battles do not spare the weak, the unfit! Only the strong survive...! And as time goes by, a sort of enjoyment develops, a grim pleasure in killing, more and more! You have no idea what madness a battlefield can become! The intense smell of fresh blood spilling over and over again, the nauseating smell of the flesh roasted by the cannons and the deafening noise of the dismounts, the neighing of the horses, the savage cries of the soldiers, intoxicated by the intense madness that is affecting them there, combined with the cries of extreme pain and despair of the wounded who fall, are truly frightening!"

"Wars!" – Sylvie murmured, taking the boy's hands and squeezing them tightly.

"Will they one day be outlawed from this world?"

"I do not know, *ma petite!*" – he said, looking into her eyes, still overcome with great sadness, motivated by those terrible memories.

"But, deep down, you should know that I also would like the wars to end for good!"

"Ah!" – she exclaimed, cheering him up.

"Look! They are already bringing us food! Never mind those memories! Let's enjoy the menu, which looks very good!"

François–Armand just smiled at her. Sylvie was too wonderful! She never allowed herself to be sad for long! She was happy! She loved being happy!

"I think you are right, *ma belle!*" – he finally says, infected by her joy.

"Why the sad memories?"

Outside, the afternoon was drawing in. The sun was still beautiful, covering everything with its radiant golden light.

"Where are we going next?" – she asks, while tasting the first piece of her tarte à fromage.

"Where do you want me to take you?" – he asks, looking at her full of passion.

"Boating down the river!" – she exclaims, coming alive.

"*Le jour se trouve–il parfait par une soirée de bateau à la Seine!*"[5]

"Perfect!" – he exclaims, delighted.

"As soon as we have finished lunch, I will take you for a boat trip on the river!"

It was after five o'clock when the Rousselet couple returned home.

"Did you have a nice walk?" – asked Pierre, as he opened the door to the lobby.

"The countryside was magnificent, Pierre!" – exclaimed Edith–Aurore, letting herself sit down heavily on a divan in the living room. As she untied the knot of the light green silk scarf around her neck, she asked:

"And Sylvie! Where is she?"

"Mademoiselle left first thing in the morning in the company of Cadet Rounet, Madame!" – replied the butler, without hiding the hint of jealousy that had been gnawing at his soul throughout the day.

"And they have not come back yet!"

"Did they even say where they were going?" – asked the Colonel, handing his wife one of the two glasses of wine he had picked up from the tray that the butler had gone to get from the pantry earlier.

"Not in detail, *M'sieur le Commandant*..." – replies the servant.

"Only that they were going to the Cité."

---

[5] "The day is perfect for a boat trip on the Seine!," in French.

"Oh, well!" – Edith–Aurore said, after sipping lightly from her glass of wine.

"If she is with François, fine! Is there anyone in the world more trustworthy than him?"

"Certainly not, *ma chérie*..." – agrees the Colonel, laughing and sitting next to her on the divan, his glass of wine in hand.

"If Sylvie is with François–Armand, she will be well–protected! And woe betide the idiot who dares to touch her hair! Ha...! Ha...! Ha...! Ha...! Ha...! He guards her like the most faithful mastiff ever! You know..."

"I do know!" – exclaims Edith–Aurore, laughing.

"Do you know any greater passion than this?"

"Only mine for you, *ma belle!*" – he says, winking at her mischievously.

"Oh, where did you learn to lie with such skill?" – she jokes, laughing.

Just then, the front door to the vestibule opened with a bang.

"Come in, *mon chéri!*" – the young lady's voice is heard.

"Papa and Maman must have returned from the country by now!"

"Oh, my dears..." – exclaimed Edith–Aurore, getting up and running to meet the young people who were rushing in. And after kissing them both on the cheek, she continued:

"Your skin is toasted by the sun! Where have you been all day?"

"Oh, Maman!" – says the little girlo, now throwing herself into her father' arms, who hugs her warmly and kisses her on the cheek.

"You have no idea! François–Armand took me for a walk in the Cité!" – and she continues, almost choking on her words with excitement:

"First, we had lunch at Oiseau–Mouche in Place Pigalle! Then, we took a boat trip on the river! Oh, it was so romantic... The sun was fantastic!"

"And you have been rowing up and down the Seine all this time?" – asked the amused Colonel amusedly to the young man standing quietly beside him. It was clear that the boy was a wreck, tremendously exhausted by the excessive effort.

"Oh, yes!" – he replied.

" Sylvie did not want to leave the boat anymore! I'm a wreck!"

"If you let yourself be carried away by her wild desires like that, one of these days she will end up killing you, my dear!" – remarks the Colonel, laughing.

"Sylvie is tireless!"

"Sylvie is adorable, *mon Colonel*!" – the young man corrected, looking at the young lady who was hovering happily on the divan, next to her mother, gesturing vivaciously as she told her the details of her outing.

"Will you have dinner with us, François?" – asked Edith–Aurore, taking advantage of an rare pause in her daughter's chatter.

"Oh, of course he will eat with us, *Maman*!" – hastens to answer Sylvie, for her boyfriend.

"The way he rowed today, he must be starving!"

"If you do not mind..." – says the young man gazing into the girl's eyes. He was delighted that he could stay with her a little longer!

Standing against the wall, as still and mute as a statue, Pierre watched, out of the corner of his eye, the young couple who, were now sitting close together, holding hands, on a divan, chatting animatedly with her parents. Deep down, the butler was consumed with rage when he saw the tenderness and affection exchanged between François–Armand and Sylvie. Despised and full of hatred, Pierre ruminated in his mind:

"Damn you! Bastard! Wait there, in the good graces, and the first chance I get, I will kill you without mercy! Wait for me, you filthy worm!"

"Pierre!" – calls Edith–Aurore.

"Come on, get ready to help Berthe with the dinner, because *M'sieur* Rounet is starving! Did you not hear that he rowed all day to take Sylvie up and down the Seine in a boat? Do you think rowing a boat is a joke? Come on, I will not allow any delays at dinner!"

"*Parfaitement, Madame!*" – says Pierre and, bowing slightly, leaves the living room.

Before he left, however, he casts an ill–concealed look of hatred at the little couple who were gazing into each other's eyes, and thought, gritting his teeth with rage:

"You bastard! I'm going to add arsenic to your soup tureen, you rogue! Wait for me! And why has not a cannonball split you in half yet?"

It was past ten o'clock when François–Armand said goodbye to Sylvie at the door to the looby.

"Oh, the day flew by!" – exclaims the girl, in the boy's arms.

"Yes, *ma belle*!" – he agrees, hugging her even tighter.

"When I am with you, time passes so fast!"

"Will you come tomorrow?" – she asks.

"I will get you out of bed again!" – he exclaims, his eyes shining.

"How nice!" – she says.

"Now go quickly! I want to go to sleep next, so that the night passes quickly and the morning comes soon!"

"You are sending me away, aren't you?" – he says, wrapping his arms around her tighter.

"I am!" – says the girl, laughing.

"And control yourself, Pierre is there, standing by, watching over us."

The boy stretched his neck and checked: through the short corridor that led from the front door to the vestibule, he could see that the butler was standing in the doorway of the living room and was certainly spying on them.

"I will kill that bastard!" – mutters the boy, highly annoyed by the butler's indiscretion. And, looking into the girl's eyes, he asks:

"Is he doing this on his own, keeping an eye on you, or are your parents recommending this?

"My parents love you and trust you with their eyes closed, *mon chéri*!" – she replies. And she continues, amused:

"Fool, do you not realize that Pierre is jealous of me? He has me as a sister..."

"Sister?!" – he remarks, full of irony.

"I know..." – and he goes on, very mocking!

"Sister! That is where you are completely wrong! That idiot is jealous of you because he loves you madly, *ma belle*! Or can you not see that ?

"Oh, I really think that you see things where they do not exist!" – argues Sylvie.

"Pierre and I were bought up in this house like two brothers, since we were children! We were both born and raised here, always together! Everybody knows that! You are the only one who stubbornly thinks otherwise..."

"Oh, how naive you are! How innocent you are!" – he exclaims, shaking his head in disbelief.

"And God forbid that this should bring us trouble!"

"What kind of trouble are you talking about?" – she asks seriously.

"If you are implying that Pierre has ever mistreated me or said something indecent to me, you are completely wrong! He has always acted like a perfect gentleman! Do you not realize that he is treated like a member of the household? That Maman and Papa look after him like a son? And until now, he has always fully lived up to the trust we have placed in him! Papa even wanted to send him to the Army..."

"I know!" – he interrupted her abruptly.

"I know this story backwards and forwards! And I do not want you to come and applaud that asshole now! I do not trust him and that's it!

"Oh, you are just picky about him!" – she laughed, realizing that her boyfriend was getting carried away.

"In fact, I think you and he are spying on each other all the time... And I thought you treated him well!"

"I do not know!" – exclaims the boy, now disentangling himself from her arms and moving a little further away, he looks at the dark street as he continues:

"There is something strange about that little guy's behavior! His posture intrigues me! I find him arrogant, too pernickety for a simple servant! Do you not see that, Sylvie? It seems to me that he feels too humiliated as a servant, as a simple butler! And when none of you, his bosses, are aroundis so rude to me... You had to see how insolent he is!"

"No kidding!" – says Sylvie, laughing at her boyfriend.

"So you and him are very good actors, excellent actors in fact, since you have been fooling me all along! Maman and Papa do not even suppose that you and he cannot stand each other! Imagine, then, when we get married and you come to live here with me!"

"I do not know if we will live in this house once we are married, *ma belle*!" – he said thoughtfully.

"We'll still have to sort this out...! Maman is a widow and maybe she needs both of us more than your parents. But if we choose to live in your house, I will have to kill that bastard first!"

"Oh, how radical you are!" – she says, laughing and, drawing him to her, kisses him on the cheek.

"You do not have to become a murderer! All we have to do is demand it and Papa and Maman will send him away! That is it! We have solved your problem! Now, come on, clear your face... I do not like seeing you like this, fretting over quirelas!"

"They are not quirelas, *mon amour*!" – he exclaims, hugging her tightly.

"I shudder at the thought of some idiot casting his lustful eyes on you! I confess to you, full of bitterness: Pierre is just one of them! If he leaves here, I will find a replacement for him straight away, believe me? When I am away, my thoughts are never far from you! I cannot, nor would I ever want to! Erase or remove your image from my mind! In between, I suffer intensely knowing you are here, without my eyes watching you every step of the way! In my crazy fantasies, I see myself losing you and I feel devastated! Then I fall into heavy sobs because of the impotence of not being able to run immediately to where you are, to see if you are well, that no evil is lurking around you, taking your peace of mind by surprise! Oh, you cannot imagine how deeply that hurts my soul and how much it makes me suffer!

"You suffer because you are jealous of me!" – she says.

"But you know that I love you enough for you to trust me with your eyes closed! There is not and never will be a place for another man in my heart! I swear it! You let yourself be tormented by jealousy for nothing, my darling, and you suffer without any need to suffer!"

"I know that deep down it is all just a sick fear of losing you, my love!" – he says, looking into her eyes.

"Oh, if that ever happens, I know that I will die soon!"

"You will not lose me, my love!" – she said, smiling a beautiful smile that showed the tips of her white, slightly rounded teeth.

"I swear eternal fidelity to you! Even if I die...and I do not intend to do that any time soon!" – she exclaims, playfully.

"I will be waiting for you in eternity! I promise! I will not fall in love with any other angel there!" – and she continues, joking:

"Even if, as they say about the appearance of angelic beings, I find another one more handsome than you! I swear I will wait for you!"

"Oh, you mock me!" – he says, smiling.

"But I meant what I said! You do not know how much the possibility of losing you one day hurts me!"

The night went on a little longer. And a little longer still, the two lovers stood at the entrance to the vestibule of her house, whispering to each other vows of love and eternal fidelity. Then, irresolutely, he left her and walked away, slowly disappearing into the darkness of the street. She watched him disappear, swallowed up by the darkness of the night, as he sent her a long, final kiss through the air. Then, the young woman, her eyes shining and fill with deep reverie, entered the house and went to sleep. She was going to dream of her love…

Céleste–Marie walked over to the window, still groggy from sleep, and pulled aside the heavy dark blue velvet curtains. Then she opens the pair of panes and looks down at the street below. The bright spring sun hurt her retina, and she squeezed her eyelids shut and opened them several times to adjust her vision, still dulled by the darkness of the room, to the intense brightness of the rising day. Although the morning was well underway, few passers–by were walking along the cobbled streets.

"*Oh, malheurs! Disgrâce!*"[6] – exclaims the young woman, suddenly shaking her shoulders, ostentatiously and irritably, as if she wanted to get rid of something that was bothering her deeply. Leaving the window, she turned back into the room and threw herself on the bed. A deep sigh of discouragement was heard. Then there was a soft knock on the door.

"Come in!" – says Céleste–Marie, without moving.

"Oh, there you are, prostate on the bed again!" – exclaims her mother, walking over to her daughter and sitting down next to her, tenderly stroking her back.

"You have just got up and you are already throwing yourself back on the bed? You need to react, my darling! Have you taken the medicine I brought you yesterday?"

"No…"

---

[6] "Oh, misfortune! Disgrace...!", in French.

"Oh, why are you acting like that, Céleste–Marie?" – says the mother, getting up nervously and going over to the window, taking a brief peek at the street below and then looking back at her daughter, who is lying face down on the bed, her face buried in the sheet. Marie–Louise shook her head sadly and continues:

"You have to react! How can you be cured if you do not take your medicine?"

The daughter does not answer. Her face is still sunk in the sheet.

"Come on, turn around, look at me!" – orders her mother, returning to sit by her side on the bed.

"I need to talk to you!"

Céleste–Marie let out a deep sigh and slowly turned around, but did not look at her mother's face. Instead, her eyes are fixed on the white plaster ceiling, decorated with a few floral details and arabesque in gold relief. Her gaze was almost fierce, and Marie–Louise shivered.

"Good heavens!" – she thought, as she studied in detail the terrible expression in her daughter's eyes. "What could it be that is tormenting my little girl?"

"Tell me, *ma petite*..." – Marie–Louise ventured to ask:

"What is tormenting your soul? Why do you not trust me and open your heart to me? Look, maybe I can help you..."

"No one can help me, Maman!" – exclaims Céleste–Marie, getting up abruptly from the bed and, sitting down in front of the dressing table to study her features in detail. After a few moments of detailed examination of her face, she turned to her mother:

"Do you not realize that I am getting old? What a passage of time... Ah, Maman, I so wish he would marry me, that we would start a family soon, that we would have our own children!"

"If this is all that is troubling your soul, be patient! Berg loves you, I am sure of it, and if he has not married you yet, it is because of the contingencies of life! Do you not realize what France has become lately? What have our men done except die in war defending our borders? Is that not what happened to your father? Is that not what happened to all the men in our family? Where are our men? Dead, *ma chérie*! They are all dead! Killed by the stupid war! There are no more men in this country, Céleste–Marie! The war killed them all!"

"And it will end up killing Berg too!" – murmurs the young woman, her eyes filled with tears.

"Sooner or later, Maman, the war will kill him!" – and she bursts into sobs of intense weeping.

"Oh, *ma petite!*" – exclaims Marie–Louise, hugging her daughter and trying to console her.

"Not everyone will die in the war! Berg has survived!"

"You know, Maman?" – says the girl, between sobs:

"Sometimes I think that Berg has not married me yet so he will not leave me a widow.... If I am not a widow, I will have a chance to get back on my feet..."

"*Berg has not married you for another reason yet, my darling!*" – Marie–Louise thought to herself as she tenderly stroked her daughter's hair.

"*For another reason that is much more serious than that, and I know what it is....*" and she lets out a deep sigh. Then, with her fingertips, she gently lifts her daughter's face and, looking deep into her suffering eyes, says to her:

"Look, why do you and I not go to the Cité? Yesterday I had a quick peek at Le Bon Marche[7] and saw some silk fabrics that you cannot even imagine...."

"Really?" – the girl seemed interested, and her eyes suddenly opened in a different way. She laughed and stood up. She took her mother's hand and said resolutely:

"Let's go!"

It was female magic at work. It was feminine magic invading her, combined with the magic of love that mothers invariably have to give.... The magic of love that makes up for the infinite number of deficiencies that almost every soul in this world possesses, almost all of them, in fact, with very few exceptions...

---

[7] Le Bon Marche is the name of one of the most famous department stores in Paris, France. It is also considered to be the first department store of its kind in the world. Its founder was Aristide Boucicaut, who created it in 1838, at first as a small store, but which grew to become the first fixed-price or department store to exist by 1850. And after undergoing a series of extensions and additions over time, it still operates today as one of the largest and most luxurious department stores in the world, located at 24 Rue de Sèvres in Paris, France.

Chapter 4
Turning Tables

Céleste–Marie and her mother were sitting in a boulangerie having a light snack after walking around all morning looking at the stores.

"Oh, I feel very tired!" – cries Marie–Louise.

"I am glad you have had enough of the fabrics we bought!"

"I have had enough too, Maman!" – said the girl, wiping away a few drops of sweat that have gathered on her forehead.

"It's so hot, even in the morning!"

"Oh, the juice will certainly cheer us up!" – Marie–Louise remarks, also wiping the sweat from her face with a delicate white cambric scarf.

"Let us stay in the shade for a while and we will cool off!" – and, looking around, she exclaims:

"But, look! Is it not Constance du Servey, the General's wife, the one who just sat at the table in the corner with the young lady?"

"I think she is..." – said Céleste–Marie. And after steadying her vision, she continued:

"Yes, they are: General du Servey's wife and his daughter Josephine! I know them very well!"

"Look, why don we not go and say hello?" – invites Marie–Louise.

"We were such good friends when your father was still alive! Constance is a very fine lady!"

"Yes, she is!" – agrees the daughter.

"Elegant and very cultured... I would love to talk to her... Let's go!"

"Constance du Servey!" – exclaims Marie–Louise, standing in front of the General's wife who was talking to her daughter in a very low voice.

"Madame Coty!" – exclaims the other woman, her face lighting up with surprise and, getting up, she embraces Marie–Louise and kisses her gently on the cheek.

"Long time no see! How nice to find you here!"

"This is Céleste–Marie..." – Marie–Louise introduced her daughter.

"You remember her, don't you?"

"Oh, of course!" – says the General's wife, embracing the young woman and kissing her on the cheeks as well, she continues, always very affable and kind:

"How are you, my dear? I remember you perfectly from when you were still a little girl; your father was still alive and our families met more often! Your fiancé is my husband's commanding officer, isn't he? But sit down with us!" – she continued effusively, pointing to her daughter who had remained seated:

"I am sure you remember Josephine, my little girl, don't you? We went out shopping, but the heat is unbearable, isn't it?"

"Yes, it is!" – agrees Marie–Louise. And she continues the conversation:

"It has been a long time since we have seen each other, hasn't it? I think that since Guillaume–Philippe left, we have spoken very little to each other."

"Oh, poor Guillaume–Philippe..." – exclaims Constance.

"They were such good friends, your husband and mine! France has lost a great soldier!"

"The wars, Constance!" – says Marie–Louise with a deep sigh.

"Always the terrible wars taking our husbands and our children!"

"If not!" said the other woman. She continued, her eyes suddenly clouded with great sadness:

"I also lost Jean–Claude, my youngest boy! Remember? He was barely nineteen years old, and the damn war took him!"

"How sad, *ma amie*!" – Marie–Louise condoled.

"But take comfort: you still have Robert left, your other son.... He is a doctor who does not care about wars, isn't he? He is much smarter and wiser because he is trying to save lives and not take them like the others do! Your son is married, isn't he?"

"Yes, he is married to Amélie, Captain Rochefort's daughter..." – replied Constance. She continued, her eyes lightening up suddenly:

"And he has already given us two grandchildren: Jean-Henri and Isabelle-Antoinette!"

"Oh, how good! It is life is continually renewing itself! Too bad Jean-Claude left so soon! I remember him well: he was a handsome boy! Strong and healthy!" – remarks Marie-Louise. Then, nodding sadly, she continued:

"But that is the way it is: there is not a single family in the whole of France that has not lost a loved one in the war! Every home has this wound that never closes! The loss of those we love is an insurmountable pain!"

"You are right, *ma amie*!" – agreed Constance. And turning to Marie-Louise's daughter, who was silent, meditating, as was her wont, she asked, taking her hand:

"And you, Celeste-Marie? When are you going to get married?" – and smiling slightly, she continued:

"Or has Lieutenant Berg not made up his mind yet?"

"Berg only thinks about the war, madam..." – says the girl, her eyes lost in the void.

"Even more so now that he has been promoted to Captain...."

"Really?" – exclaims the General's wife in surprise.

"And has Emmanuel-Theophile not told me anything yet? He must have forgotten! So, Berg is a captain now, huh? When he becomes a General, I guarantee he will marry you, *ma chérie*!" – Constance jokes.

"And it will only be a few ranks before he does! I always thought Berg would have a brilliant career in the army!"

"Yes... replied Céleste–Marie, laconic.

What she really felt was like sending the army and everything else to hell! But she held back, so as not to be rude to the General's wife. After all, that fine and elegant woman had always treated her extremely well.

"What I really admire about Lieutenant Berg is that, despite being half–French, he is only French on his mother's side, because his father was German, he opted for French nationality, declining his paternal family, which is very wealthy and descended from the princes of Bavaria!" – observes Constance.

"Wilfred loves France because he was born here, madam!" – Céleste–Marie clarifies.

"His German relatives have never forgiven his father for getting involved with a French woman! You must know very well how much the Germans abhor the French! For them, such a mixture is simply inconceivable! Berg would never be accepted by the German side of his family!"

"To me, it is just pure envy of France on the part of the Germans!" – Marie–Louise remarks.

"They do not forgive us for the fact that Paris is considered the capital of the world!"

"Should it be Berlin?" – asked Constance's daughter ironically, entering the conversation for the first time.

"Dad always says that the French and the Germans will never be friends! This disagreement between these two people is historic!"

"Our borders with Germany have never been well defined!" – Constance remarks.

"I think there will be a lot of bloodshed before things settled down! But let's not talk about wars !" – says the General's wife suddenly, trying to raise spirits.

"Our husbands and sons are going to war and we are being left in Paris, aren't we? Ha! Ha! Ha! Ha! Ha! Ha! And I totally agree when they say this is the center of the world! What nicer place could there be, ladies? Answer me with truthfully!"

"Yes! You are absolutely right!" – agrees Marie–Louise, laughing at the other woman's good-natured tirade.

"By the way…" – continues Constance:

"After your husband's death, I saw you very rarely in the salons of the city! Are you still in mourning after all this time? How many years has it been? I think more than eighteen, don't you?

"Twenty years…" – replies Marie–Louise.

"And you're right: after he left, I lost the fun of things in the world! Everything was suddenly lost to me…"

"But there is so much news out there, my dear!" – exclaims the other woman.

"The world is moving on! If your husband is dead, that is no reason to bury yourself alive with him! By the way, have you heard about these spinning tables? No?! They are all the rage!"

"Really?" – observes the other without showing much spirit.

"Yes! And they talk! Can you imagine the tables talking to us? They answer the questions we ask them!"

"Do they talk?" – Marie–Louise is amazed.

"But how can they talk if they do not have a mouth?"

"Oh, *ma chérie*!" – the General's wife laughs at the expression of astonishment on her face.

"Force of expression: in fact, the little tables telegraphed!"

"Telegraph?" – Marie–Louise was even more confused, to the point of disbelief.

"Yes, through beats, like the telegraph!" – Constance explains.

"Oh, I still cannot understand you properly!" – exclaims the other woman, still very confused.

"I will explain it to you more clearly, my dear: a few people sit around a *guéridon*, they hold hands and, a most curious fact, the table magically rises a few feet above the floor and starts spinning like crazy! And at the right intervals, in the middle of the vortex, it rapidly tilts over and hits the floor with one of its feet, emitting an audible thump which, added to a succession of other thumps, begins to form words and, consequently, whole sentences!"

"Incredible!" – exclaims Marie–Louise, stunned. Now I understand: they use a code, just like the telegraph!

"And, as I have already told you, they answer questions that are put to them!"

"Really?! – and what questions do they answer?" – asked Marie–Louise, still unable to grasp the real basis of what the other woman was telling her.

"What can a lowly table know?"

"Oh, they know so much!" – replied the woman, highly amused. And she continues, with a chuckle indicating a hint of malice:

"Very interesting things indeed!"

"Your husband, the General, told me and Berg about this news when we were with him last week…" – said Céleste–Marie, entering the conversation.

"He also seemed to be very interested in this spinning tables…"

"Yes, he is!" – remarks Constance, very enthusiastic. Emmanuel and I have not missed a single session of spinning tables, held at the home of Marquise Adèle de Souvigny!"

"And when will the next session be?" – asks Marie–Louise.

"Always on weekends…" – replied Constance.

"And by the way, I know you know the Marquise de Souvigny! Look, if you wish, you can come with us to the next meeting!" – and, by way of confidence, she said to her, almost in a whisper:

"The last time we were there, an unexpected surprise, happened, *ma amie*! From what everything seems to me that there was a communication signed by the Emperor![1]

"What are you saying?!" – amazed Marie–Louise.

"His Majesty died in 1821, if I am not mistaken, and now we find ourselves in the spring of 1850! How can this happen? He is dead!"

"That is where the mystery lies, Marie–Louise" – remarked the other, full of amazement! They have read Napoleon's statement, full of warnings about the Germans!"

"But you did not tell me that such things had to do with the dead!" – exclaims Marie–Louise, also filled with astonishment.

"Nor did I know, *ma chérie*!" – explained the other.

"Neither I nor anyone else who was there thought that such a phenomenon was produced by the dead!"

"Oh, such revelations seem so illogical to me, do you not think?" – remarks Marie–Louise, full of inner cogitations.

"How can the dead speak through a *gueridon*?"

"Many of those present did not believe the message…" – explains the other.

"However, my husband thinks that there is a lot of logic in what the Emperor said. He agrees that the Germans

---

[1] Reference to Napoleon Bonaparte, in French Napoléon Bonaparte, born Napoleone di Buonaparte, (Ajaccio, Corsica, August 15, 1769 – Saint Helena, May 5, 1821) was the effective leader of France, from 1799, and also Emperor of that country, adopting the name Napoleon I, from May 18, 1804 to April 6, 1814, a position he briefly retook from March 20 to June 22, 1815.

cannot be trusted, and that the current peace treaty between the Austro–Hungarian Empire and France will not stand; it will be short–lived! And he joked:

"Dogs and cats never got along..."""

"I don't know..." – Marie–Louise mumbles, thoughtfully.

"On the other hand, the world is changing, shaking enormously... Look at how quickly things have been changing since you and I were little girls!"

"If they change!" – agrees the other woman.

"Today we can travel lightly and safely from Paris to Moscow on a train at sixty kilometers per hour! Who would have imagined such a feat thirty years ago?

"Unimaginable! What about the telegraph?" – continues the other.

"We know the news so fast! As soon as something happens in Berlin or London, the telegraph can transmit it to us in no time! That is why, if those who have already died suddenly decide to communicate with us, I do not doubt it anymore, my dear! I do not doubt it anymore! Do we not cross the Atlantic to America today on very fast steamers that take a few weeks at most to make the crossing? It used to take sailboats months..."

"All right, Constance!" – exclaims the other.

"You have convinced me! Next Friday, we are also going to the Marquise de Souvigny's house! I want to see for myself what these tables really say!"

For a little longer, the women stayed in the boulangerie to have a snack and cool off from the intense heat that was invading Paris that spring morning. When the afternoon began to fall, they said goodbye and returned to their respective homes.

"Are you really going to check out those little tables, Maman?" – Céleste–Marie asked to her mother, already in the rental car that was taking them back home.

"Why not?" – Marie–Louise replied.

"I think you and Berg should go too. You live cooped up in that room of yours! You will end up getting moldy..."

"Oh, Maman!" – exclaims the girl laughing at her mother's jocular remark. Then she tenderly wraps her arms around her mother's neck and continues:

"How good is to see that, despite everything, you still maintain your unsurpassed humor!

Marie–Louise just looked at her daughter and returned her smile, tenderly. They both had to get it right. They had to get their lives back on track, at any cost...

The ballroom of the Marquise de Souvigny's mansion was literally filled with people bustling about in a hubbub of voices, laughter and little squeals of delight. The couples Constance and Emmanuel–Théophile du Servey, Céleste–Marie and Wilfred Berg, as well as and Marie–Louise Coty were also in the midst of the almost half a hundred ladies and gentlemen, richly dressed and displaying expensive jewelry and props, and hovering animatedly on the large red velvet divans, in the countless carved wooden chairs, in the chaises longues or even talking, arranged in small circles of three or four, standing up, sipping champagne from long goblets of fine crystal, and smoking fragrant cigarillos, embedded in long, exquisite ivory cigarette cases, set with delicate gold or silver filigree.

There was a general sense of excitement on all their faces: you could tell they were looking forward to something that would give them unparalleled pleasure.

When the chime of the great hall struck nine o'clock, Adèle de Souvigny got up from the couch where she was sitting and, ostentatiously clapping her hands, drew everyone's attention.

"*Dames et Messieurs!*" – she exclaims, raising her voice.

"It is time to start our session!"

"Let's get closer, my dear!" – invites Constance to her friends.

"You need to be very close to appreciate the phenomenon!"

The hostess then moved towards the center of the room and approached a small, rounded table made of carved wood, which was supported by a single rod which, in turn, opened up into three small legs, giving it perfect balance.

"Please come closer to form our chain!" – and invites a few people to sit around the table, occupying chairs placed in a circle.

"*Monsieur* Deville! *Madame* le Sanson! *Mademoiselle* Durreine! Marquis de la Rochelle! *Inspecteur* Lalande! *Général* Cartier! *Capitaine* Fourtin! *S'ilvous plaît...! Assiez–vous!*"[2]

---

[2] "Please...! Sit down!", in French.

The people who had been invited by name, sat down on the chairs and joined hands, forming a large circle that encompassed the table in the center. Madame de Souvigny was in charge of everything, standing up and, agitated, walking from one side to the other, as if she were directing a great show. The audience huddled in a thick circle, craning their necks and standing on tiptoe to better follow the unfolding phenomenon.

"Mr. Marinet... *Attention!*" – orders the hostess to a gentleman who settles into his chair and, with a pencil and a large notebook in hand, makes his way over.

Then something truly fantastic happened to those dozens of pairs of eyes which, highly anxious, did not miss a single detail of the events taking place there. A few minutes after those who formed the circle around the little table had joined hands, the small piece of furniture began to rise, mysteriously into the air! First, there was a small jolt, and the little table as if it were swinging from side to side like a pendulum, then it started spinning, slowly at first, but in a very short time it was spinning with incredible speed. The people in the audience looked at each other in amazement. How could what they were seeing be possible?

"Oh...!"

"*Mon Dieu!*"

"*Quel mystère!*"

"*Fantastique!*"

"*Ce–là c'est chose du diable!*"[3]

---

[3] "This is a devil's thing...!", in French.

"No!"

"*Sssh! Ecoutons!*"[4]

"Silence, gentlemen! Please, be quiet!" – shouts Madame de Souvigny.

Mon'sieur Deville...! Madame le Sanson...! Mademoiselle Durreine...! Marquis de la Rochelle...! Inspecteur Lalande...! General Cartier...! Capitaine Fourtin!.. S'ilvous plaît...! Assiez–vous...![5]

"A lot of silence and attention is needed! Now for the questions!" – and, after a slight, purposeful silence, she raises her voice and continued, asking a question:

"Is anyone there?"

The little table spins, even more dizzily, and one of its feet hits de floor, producing a peculiar, rhythmic sound. Marinet, with pencil and pad of paper in hand, concentrates and writes down the letters, one by one, that emerge from the code of knocks that the table produces in its spin. It is a long wait; he process is time–consuming, but the anticipation is enormous. Finally, the table stops knocking.

"Collignon!" – exclaims Marinet, reading the writing.

"*Oh, c'est Collignon, le pirate!*" – exclaims a lady, laughing with extreme pleasure. And, highly excited, she continues:

"*J'adore Collignon* Hi! Hi! Hi! Hi! Hi!"[6]

---

[4] "Sssh...! Let's hear it...!", in French.
[5] "Please...! Sit down!", in French.
[6] "I love Collignon...! Hi...! Hi...! Hi...!Hi...!", in French.

"Ask him about Victor... Oh, please, ask him about Victor!" – shouts a beautiful young woman, standing out from the crowd and almost running to the side of the circle.

"Where is my Victor, Collignon? Why do you not come to see me anymore?"

The table started spinning again and the succession of knocks continued. Marinet, very attentive, deciphered and wrote down the code on the paper. After a while, the little table quietened down and the message was read out, to the great expectation of everyone:

"Victor is having fun with a beautiful Opera dancer! He loses himself for a pair of lush legs, my dear! He has made an excellent bargain: he has exchanged those withered reeds you are carrying under your skirts for the other girl's fillings!"[7]

General laughter erupts in the audience.

"*Collignon c'est fenomenal*...! Ha! Ha! Ha! Ha! Ha!"

"*Oh...! Que tristesse!*" – exclains the girl, letting herself be overwhelmed and her eyes. Welling up with tears.

"*Oh, malheurs...!*"[8]

"Look, if you wish, I will comfort you, Isabelle!" – shouts a young hustler from the crowd.

"Since that bastard Victor does not want you anymore!"

---

[7] It is important to remember here that, at first, this phenomenon was considered fun and, consequently, did not bring anything serious, starting with the spirits that commonly participated in it.

[8] "Oh, how sad...!" (...) "What a misfortune...!", in French.

"*Imbecile toi!*" – murmurs the girl between her teeth and, passing close to the boy, glares at him with a pair of hate-filled eyes and leaves the room stomping.

"Ask him about Otile!" – shouts someone from the audience.

"She thinks she is pregnant and does not even know who the real father is! Ha! Ha! Ha! Ha! Ha!"

The little table spins again and, with peculiar regularity, gives the answers. Moments of great anticipation. After the long, steady trot, the little table stops in mid-air. The communication was over. Joseph Marinet first read the writings quietly and meticulously and then, raising his voice, asked for silence and read, to the intense expectation of the audience:

"The child's father is Frédéric-Alphonse Paligny!"

The young Paligny was standing there, in the middle of the audience, and was taken aback by the revelation. Outraged, he stood up and shouted furiously:

"It is a lie... This is a blatant hoax!"

"Now Frédéric!" – exclaims another boy, full of irony.

"Let us go! Why would the pirate lie? Come on, man, confess!"

"Come on, confirm everything, Frédéric!" – remarks another boy.

"Everyone was already suspicious of you!"

"You are all imbeciles!" – says Frédéric-Alphonse, pouting himself enormously. That idiot Collignon, if he even exists! – has just thrown this disgusting slander in my face, and you all prefer to credit his words to mine!"

"Oh, the table never lies, Frédéric!" – remarks a matron, laughing mischievously.

"If it says you were the child's father, it is because you are!"

"Let us proceed gentlemen!" – the hostess tries to put an end to the discussion.

"And you, Frédéric, do not let yourself be softened by such things! We all know all this is just a joke, don't we? We are here for fun, nothing else! No more useless agonizing! Nothing should be taken seriously!"[6] – and, turning to the table, orders:

"Collignon, get out of there now! Give way to someone else, come on!"

The table swings slightly in the air and then lands completely on the floor.

"Well done Captain!" – said a satisfied Adèle de Souvigny.

"You're a good boy!" – and, after a few deliberate minutes of silence, she continues:

"*Qui est là?*"[9]

The table rises a foot above the ground again and swings from side to side. Then it spins around and hits the floor with one of its feet, telegraphing. Minutes of intense anticipation. Finally it stops and remains suspended in the air.

---

[9] "Who's there?...", in French.

"René Descartes!" – Marinet's clear voice is heard.

"Oh, mais quel étonnant plaisir, Monsieur Descartes!" [10] – broken the Marquise de Souvigny, being highly satisfied, and now taking full control of things, she continues:

"Et alors, qu'est–ce que avez–vous à nous dire?" [11]

The table started to trot again, and Joseph Marinet, very attentive, did not miss a single one of the knocks that the little piece of furniture emitted in its rapid rotation. Long, expectant minutes, and finally the little table stood, swaying slightly in the air. Marinet focuses intently on the writing first, then he sniffles, clear his throat, and his voice sounds loud and clear in the absolute silence of the room:

"Français! Attention! Do not rejoice too much, you lovers of freedom, because the New Republic –the greatest desire of the Great Revolution [11]–is still just a newborn baby! And I am sorry to tell you, with a heavy heart, that it is in danger of dying in its cradle! So, beware of your overconfidence! Be on the lookout, for those who love to wear crowns on their heads are already conspiring!" [12]

---

[10] "Oh, but what an astonishing pleasure, Monsieur Descartes!", in French.

[11] "So, what do you have to say to us? ", in French.

[12] In fact, the words of the spirit René Descartes here could be taken as prophetic, because the February 1848 elections, which created the Second Republic, established universal suffrage, but the June 1848 elections, marked by the workers' revolt, threw the Republic back into conservatism. The Second Republic only lasted until 1852, when Louis Napoleon Bonaparte, under the title of Napoleon III, proclaimed the Second Empire (1852-1870).The French empire then expanded, particularly in Southeast Asia and the Pacific. The Second Empire is remembered for its material prosperity, the development of industry and trade, but also for a foreign policy that was both idealistic and efficient, which ended with the disastrous Franco–Prussian War of 1870-1871.

When the message was read out, a strange silence, permeated by sudden unease, overtook the audience, which until then had been very cheerful and lively. The terrible episodes of the February Revolution of 1848[13] were still fresh in the minds of everyone there. Was the great philosopher right? Was it really him? Everyone knew that the Republic was fragile. The crowned heads and the proud aristocracy, so outraged by the bourgeoisie, would never forgive the rebels who had already systematically dislodged them twice! They then looked at each other with suspicion and accusation. There were supporters of both regimes: bourgeois and aristocrats! There was no doubt that the communicating spirit's words caused significant discomfort for everyone.

"*Eh, bien!*" – exclaims Madame de Souvigny, clapping her hands. The situation needed to be turned around very quickly, because this could trigger the antipathy that was soi common between republicans and monarchists, which that was taking place in the streets and parks of the city. Had not skirmishes between the troublemakers from the two factions been happening almost every day? And, raising her voice, Adèle de Souvigny, pretentiously addressed the spirit:

"*Merci beaucoup, M'sieur Descartes!*[14] We are very grateful to you for the warning! But what has to be will be!" – and, signaling to her butler, who was standing by, she gave him the go–ahead, and a small battalion of servants then

---

[13] R eference to the February Revolution of 1848, which deposed Louis Philippe I; the king was forced to abdicate in favor of his grandson Philippe d'Orléans, Count of Paris, and take refuge in England. The revolutionaries, however, refused to recognize his successor and, in the same year, proclaimed the Second Republic of France (1848–1852).

[14] "Thank you very much, Mr. Descartes...", in French.

entered the hall, carrying silver trays containing rich crystal goblets, literally bubbling with the golden Champagne they contained.

"Let's drink a toast to France and freedom, *mes amis!*" – shouts the hostess, and with that, she ends the night's session of the turning tables....

"Impressive!" – exclaims Marie-Louise Coty, shortly afterwards, to the group of friends who, sitting on chairs in a small circle, were sipping from their glasses of Champagne. And, turning to General du Servey, she asked:

"Tell me, Emmanuel, do you really believe that there will not be the slightest possibility of fraud occuring in such phenomena?"

"Oh, I can swear to you, *ma amie!*" – replied the General smiling.

"The notary, Jean-Charles de la Chapelle and I carried out a thorough examination of the place a few days ago! You can be sure that there are, in fact, no hidden wires or trapdoors or any other paraphernalia that promoting such a phenomenon!"

"And to what do you actually attribute such things?" – asks Céleste-Marie.

"All of this has really confused me! What would Monsieur Descartes be doing here? Did he not die more than two centuries ago? How can those who have already died speak?"

"Oh, *ma petite!*" – exclaims Marie-Louise.

"Did you not hear what Madame de Souvigny said at the beginning of the session? It is all just a joke!"

"I do not know, no!" – Wilfred Berg replies.

"Jokes? You heard what the General said earlier: there is nothing hidden promoting the phenomenon! How can you explain the fact that the table hovers in the air and spins like a spinning, without any apparent force propelling it? You see, all of this is contrary to the most elementary principles of physics!"

"There are no mysteries for me!" – remarks Constance du Servey.

"I am convinced that it really is the souls of the dead who are back here to tell us what really exists after death! We will soon know everything...!"

"I do not know, *ma Cherie*!" – the General shouts.

"I think you are jumping the gun! You're showing yourself to be too gullible! I am in favor of research. It is necessary to study the phenomenon seriously! In particular, I think it all has a lot to do with animal magnetism! Mr. Mesmer[15] has left vast studies on the subject; however, to date, he has not been credited! On the contrary: the Academy has always persecuted him, branding him a charlatan, a cheap hoaxer!

"To me, it is not but pure envy!" – remarks Constance.

"Poor Mr. Mesmer had the misfortune to be German and not French! If it had been the other way around, you can

---

[15] Franz Anton Mesmer (Iznang, May 23, 1734 - Meesburg, March 5, 1815) was a Swabian physician and magnetizer. In 1779, after unsuccessfully trying to have his system examined at all the universities, he published an analytical account of the new science in Paris: Memoir on the discovery of animal magnetism.

be sure that the course of animal magnetism would have been different!"

"Oh, always very practical, my dear Constance!" – says the General, laughing. He continues:

"You know, deep down, I think you are right, *ma belle*! It may have been nothing more than the old Franco–German rivalry!"

"In today's world..." – notes Berg:

"If things do not come from France or England, little credit is given to them! It is as if intelligent men only exist in these two countries!"

"You do not know, my dear, how the French and the English cannot stand each other!" – says the General. He continued, making a broad gesture with his hands:

"In reality, jealousy is a disease that affects everyone, without exception...."

"And the whole of humanity ends up losing a lot as a result! – exclaims Marie–Louise. "How many geniuses of the past have been ostracized and even murdered out of sheer envy?"

"You are right, *ma amie*!" – remarks Constance.

"What you say is biblical. Was it not envy that led people to the first fratricide? Cain killed Abel out of sheer envy..."

"I think that rivalry is an attribute of humanity!" – says Céleste–Marie.

"Were it not so, there would be no reason for so many wars! Jealousy, greed, envy... All of this leads to disharmony, a lack of peace...."

The group of friends remained chatting animatedly for a while longer. Then, as did most of the guests of the famous Adèle de Souvigny, they left the luxurious ballroom of the palace on Rue Lecourbe and returned to their homes, their minds still buzzing with excitement at the strange phenomena they had witnessed on that pleasant spring evening....

Chapter 5

Sorrow and Resentment

Pierre, the young butler of the Rousselet family, raises his eyes and stares longingly at the white-columned mezzanine above. Then he begins to climb, carrying Sylvie's breakfast tray with extreme care.

"*Oh, mon Dieu!*" – he thinks, as he climbs the immense gray granite staircase, his chest heavy with anxiety.

"I love her, so much, and every day it becomes a maddening torment for me to have her so close and not even be able to touch her! I feel consumed by intense passion! Oh, cruel misery! How long will I endure such martyrdom?"

Once upstairs, foot by foot, he walked down the corridor, which was still dimly lit, and with his eyes filled with intense sadness, his thoughts were filled with self-pity:

"Woe is me, I am just a lowly servant of the house! I know she does not take me for a man, but just another one of those who are here, for the sole purpose of serving her, of fulfilling her needs and desires!" – and as he approaches the door to Sylvie's room, he stops: he does not knock immediately. His eyes suddenly change: from sad, they flash with intense hatred.

"All she can think about is him, the infamous man!" – and, gritting his teeth with rage, he had the urge to throw the tray containing the girl's breakfast to the ground and shout at the top of his lungs all the spite that was consuming his soul. However, making a painful effort, he restrained himself and tried to pull himself together and find the phlegm that, whatever the cost, he would always show. Was that not how servants were supposed to act? Was that not how his mistress had told him all these years?

The servants must be undead, soulless zombies; just hollow, empty corpses with nothing inside.... Ah, wretched life! Why did he not just run out of there and tell everyone and everything to go away? Was he not b free? He was alone in the world, but he was free! Then, sadly he shook his head and smiles bitterly and pathetically, with the breakfast tray in his hand, in the semi–darkness of the corridor, in front of her room! Ah, I was not free at all! He was a prisoner, a miserable slave to those bright eyes, those honey–colored hair, that smile that was like the most beautiful of spring suns! How could he leave if he was her captive? How could he live away from his love? Then the image of the other man, her fiancé, appeared in his mind. Again, he was filled with intense rage.

"Ah, you usurping wretch! If you had not shown up here, she would have certainly looked at me!" – and, perking up, he smiles:

"I am not ugly... I think I am even more handsome than you, who have a nose like... like that... curved like a hook!" – and he almost laughs, when he remembers that his rival did not have a nose as straight and correct as his.

"You are just a little younger than me! That is all, nothing more!"

Pierre Durand, finally, lets out a long sigh, shook his head slightly, as if to clear his head of the turmoil that was going on his mind, and, pushing himself up, knocked gently on the door with his knuckles.

"*Entrez!*"[1] – he hears the soft voice from inside, and his heart pounds even harder.

"*Bonjour, mademoiselle!*"[2] – exclaims the butler kindly.

"Did you sleep well?"

"Like a stone, *mon bon Pierre!*"[3] – she exclaimed happily, sitting on the white satin sheets of her large bed. And, making quick gestures with her hands, she continues:

"Pass me the tray, I am starving! And I am in a hurry! François is about to arrive, and I'm still in bed! You know what an early riser he is! He always ends up arriving before the agreed time and, as Maman and Papa are certainly not at home, you will have to make room for him while I finish getting dressed and, as I now know what really happens when there is no one else around, you and he will end up fighting! You definitely cannot stand looking into each other's face, can you? How did you manage to hide from me the fact that you could not stand each other for so long? And I thought you liked each other, that you were even friends! In front of me, you always treated each other with such kindness, but behind me, you were fighting like a cat and dog! Ha! Ha! Ha! Ha! Ha!"

---

[1] "Come in...!", in French.
[2] "Good morning, Miss...", in French.
[3] "My good Pierre...!", in French.

– she bursts out laughing and continues, without giving him a moment's respite, while the boy, haggard and blushing to the ears, fumbles around trying to serve her the breakfast on the tray:

"Tell me, Pierre, why are you so jealous of François?" – and, looking at him with a a pair of eyes full of mockery, she burst out:

"François–Armand is fully convinced that you are madly in love with me!"

"Par... Pardón, Sylvie!" – Pierre stammers, without the courage to face her even once. And always crestfallen, he mutters:

"*Je quitte!*"[4] – and leaves the room, almost running.

"*Pierre! Halte!*"[5] – she shouted, laughing her ass off at the way he had reacted to her words.

"Come back here, you fool! Let us go talk!"

"Damned! Wretched!" – mutters the butler through his teeth, almost running down the stairs.

"It was him, the bastard, who told her! Damn him! A thousand times damned!" – and waving his head, full of despair to the core, said softly:

"Now she knows!

Just then, the gate bell went off. Pierre stopped and tried to pull himself together. His features were highly decomposed by the strong emotion; a mixture of anger and

---

[4] "I quit!", in French.
[5] "Pierre! Stop!", in French.

intense shame. She had been hurt enormously because she had mocked his feelings. How embarrassing, my God!

How was he going to face her from now on? The doorbell rings again, nervously. Pierre had a jolt. He had to answer the door.

"It must be the wretch who has arrived!" – he mutters, full of hatred, as he hurried towards the vestibule.

Then, slowly and imperceptibly, he opens just a tiny crack in the doorway and peeks through it. Yes, it was him. The unfortunate man was there, in front of the gate, all decked out in that ridiculous uniform! And he was jumping up and down with impatience at the delay, in getting the door opened.

"Stay there, you idiot, just a little longer!" – muttered the butler, and laughed, enjoying himself enormously, as he spied on the other man through the tiny crack in the door.

François–Armand became more and more irritated by the delay in getting the door opened. He rang the doorbell again, and this time quite vehemently, indicating his impatience.

"Pierre!" – he heard the voice of Berthe, the cook, calling him from the pantry.

"Where has Pierre gone? Pierre! Did you not hear the doorbell, you deaf man?" – continues the cook, calling for him.

Fearing that he would be pilloried for deliberately teasing his visitor, Pierre opens the door once and for all and goes down to the gate.

"*Bonjour, Cadet Rounet! Comment allez–vous?*"[6] – said the butler, with a strong hint of irony in his voice. Then, barely holding back a laugh of complete satisfaction and almost bursting with intimate joy at seeing the other man on the verge of fury, he let him in at the gate and continued. with a slight bow.

"*Entrez, s'il vous plaît, Monsieur*"[7]

"You did it all on purpose, didn't you, you cheek bastard?" – François–Armand exclaimed, moving ahead of the butler who was slightly behind him and trying his best not to burst out laughing.

"*Pardon, Monsieur?*" – says Pierre, pretending not to understand.

"You know very well what I am saying, you imbecile!" – exclaims François–Armand, tremendously irritated.

"You made me wait outside on purpose! But I am going to complain about you to your bosses! You will see! I will have you thrown out on the street!"

"They are not at home, *Monsieur le cadet!*" – exclaimed Pierre, leading the other into the living room.

"You'll have to make your report later!"

"And Sylvie?" – asked the boy, trying to swallow down the anger that was rising more and more at the cheeky butler's petulance.

"Is she at home at least?"

---

[6] "Good morning, Cadet Rounet...! How are you...?", in French.
[7] "Come in, please, sir...!", in French.

– *Mademoiselle* does the *toilette, Monsieur*!" – replied Pierre, trying to maintain a deliberate phlegm, because he knew that this would irritate the other man even more. He continued, with a strong accent of irony in his voice:

"*Il ne faut pas de désespérer!*"[8]

"*Désespérer moi?!*"[9] – exclaimed the other man, reddening with rage and rising from the couch on which he was sitting, he lunged at the other with his fists raised and delivered a formidable punch to his stomach. Pierre, overcome with pain, groans as he tries to defend himself against the other man's furious attack. Just then, Sylvie entered the living room. François–Armand, noticing the young lady's arrival, quickly bent down and groaned, as if he had been the one struck by the blows.

"Pierre!" – screams the girl.

"You brute! Why are you hitting François–Armand? Oh, you poor thing!," – she says, covering her boyfriend with kisses.

"That brute has hurt you, hasn't he?"

"But... But..." – stammered the butler, pressing down hard on his belly with his hand.

"Sylvie...! He hit me! Did you not see?!"

"Oh, you are slandering François, aren't you?" – she replied, hugging her boyfriend, who was still pretending great pain in his belly, and leading him to sit down on the sofa. Then she continued, turning to the astonished butler.

---

[8] "There's nothing to despair about!", in French.
[9] "Despair...!", in French.

"Come on, get out of here! Go to the kitchen to help Berthe! And when Maman and Papa come back from their morning stroll, I will tell them everything! I want to see how you get out of this!"

"But, Sylvie!" – the poor butler tries to defend himself, still in pain from the blow he had received.

"Go on, come on..." – she exclaims, unyieldingly.

"You behaved like a brutal savage today, attacking poor François like that! Shame on you, Pierre! That was truly unforgivable!"

Defeated, the butler slowly made his way inside the house. Before leaving, however, he looked at the brazen man who was holding on to the girl. François, then, without his girlfriend noticing, smiles with satisfaction and gives the other man a meaningful look, as if to say:

"Here you go, rascal, your change..."

"*Oh, mon petit!*" – exclaims the girl, now alone with her boyfriend.

"How pitiful! You and he are acting like two children!"

"You caught me off guard, you coward!" – says the boy, still feigning severe pain in his abdomen.

"And he almost killed me with his powerful fists! Oh, Sylvie, you had to see such savagery! He came at me like a bolt out of a blue, surprising me! And he punched me mercilessly! I did even not have time to defend myself! The bastard has a right hand as strong as a mule's kick!"

"Hmm! I know!" – she said, now looking at him out of the corner of her eye. She was beginning to get suspicious of the boy's poltroonery. So, he was taken by surprise? Was he not so used to skirmishes on battlefields? Then she decided to put him to the test and said:

"Darling, I think I forgot to lock my jewelry box. I will leave you for a moment and go up to my room to find out. I will be right back, okay?"

The boy acquiesced with a long, deep sigh of pain. The girl pretends to go into the bedroom, but stops a few steps away, having barely hidden herself from the boy's view. Then, foot by foot, she returned to the living room and, leaning against the doorframe, spied on François–Armand. When he was alone, the boy stopped bending over under the action of the supposed abdominal pain and, rubbing his hands together with glee, laughed out loud. He often looked towards the door where his girlfriend had come out and, shaking his head, laughed non–stop.

"What a scoundrel!" – thinks Sylvie.

"And is he not a first–class pretender? And all because he is jealousy of the other guy! Poor Pierre, I think I have been unfair to him!" – and she deliberately lingers for a few minutes until she introduces herself to the boy who, on hearing her footsteps, returns to his old position, feigning deep pains in his belly.

"Did I take too long, darling?" – she asked, taking a seat next to him on the sofa, without showing that she had plundered him pretending to be in pain. And, looking at him as he squirmed, she asked:

"Oh, does it still hurt a lot? From the gasps of pain you are showing, it must have been very serious! We would better take care of it right away!" – and, getting up, she said resolutely:

"I will send Pierre in search of Dr. Eustaque Durraine without delay! Do you not think it could be fatal? You said Pierre's punches are like mule kicks, didn't you? Do you not know that mule kicks are very serious? What if those kicks blew you up inside? No, *mon chéri*... I think the doctor should come and examine you straight away, without further ado! In the meantime, you should lie down in the guest room and rest while we wait for the doctor! Let us go... Do not argue with me! I care very much about your health! Imagine if you died for lack of care! No one would forgive me for such negligence!"

François–Armand looks at her in terror. No, not that! Surely the doctor would soon realize that he was lying! There was not even a mark on her belly, not even a welt! None at all! He had to act quickly or he would be lost in front of her! And he thinks fast.

"Oh darling, I am used to such aggressions!" – he lies.

"Do you forget that I am involved in battles? I have been getting kicked by all sorts: mules, horses, donkeys! Look, even from camels! Are you not scrabbling around Algeria now?[10] Did you know that there are camels there? A few cheap

---

[10] In the midst of the colonial expansionism of the 19th century, France invaded Algeria in 1830, and the Algerians resisted the invaders throughout, fighting bravely for the first four decades; however, they ended up remaining under French rule until the European spring of 1962, when a plebiscite was held on July 1st, in which six million Algerians voted in favor of independence. Algerians voted in favor of independence and only 16,000 against it. Algerian politicians then took power in Algiers and most Europeans left the country.

punches from your wretched butler will mean nothing to me! I will be back on my feet in no time! Look, I am starting to get better! The pain will go away soon! Soon, I will not feel anything anymore!"

"Oh, what a handsome poltroon you have made of me, your naughty boy!" – the girl thinks, looking him in the eye.

"Oh, if I didn't love you so much! I would give you a good spanking! That is what you deserve for acting so childish! But I know you do it out of love! And love always excuses everything!" – but she did not want him to know that she had discovered his deception. She did not want to upset her love.

"I am glad you are getting better, *mon chéri!*" – she exclaimed, letting nothing of what was on her mind show. And she continues with the farce.

"Your color is beginning to return to normal! You were so pale that I was startled by your appearance! You looked like a ghost!"

François–Armand was amazed. Had he managed to fake it that far? Wow! He had been so convincing that he had even gone pale! What a thing! He really should have pursued a career in the arts instead of the military! Certainly, he would have been an excellent actor!

"Tell me, my angel, where do you want to go today?" – he asked, eager to get off the subject. He suddenly realized that Sylvie might be mocking him.

"Oh, how about a visit to *Monsieur* Pichon, my painting teacher? I have not been to his classes for a few days! You know that while you were away in Algeria, Maman and I spent a few days in Champagne, in our country house. I have some doubts about light and perspective and I want to resolve them with my master!"

"You command and I obey!" – he exclaims, smiling.

"But first, we are going to pass through the Cité! I want to see the city, the people, the gardens, the parks! You know, my regiment spent six long months in North Africa, in the middle of the scorching desert, where the landscape is just an endless succession of white dunes! Just sand and more sand! You cannot imagine how much we miss the simple sight of green! That color rests us and calms our hearts! Until then, I had no idea how important greenery is for our minds! The sameness of that landscape makes us despair! And the heat! It calcinates our brains and there is not enough water! The desert is hell, Sylvie! During the day, the sun is inclement and the heat becomes unbearable; at night, it is bitterly cold!

"I can only imagine what the French feel in such an inhospitable and cruel land!" – remarks the young lady.

"We are so used to the friendliness European climate!"

"You are right, my love!" – he exclaims.

"And, as well as the climate, which is hurting us enormously, there are the terrible clashes with the opposing troops! Did you know that most of the fighting's takes place in the desert, under the scorching sun?

"Really?" she wonders.

"So, you are fighting in the middle of the dunes?"

"Yes!" – he replies.

"Enemy attacks happen by surprise! When you least expect it, a rain of Algerians, armed with muskets and long scimitars, come at you from the top of the dunes, as if out of nowhere! And how well they know the desert! Unlike me, for example, who finds everything the same there! Just dunes and more white dunes; an ocean of sand and more sand, nothing else!"

"And how can they know the desert so well if there is almost nothing to refer to?" – puzzles the young lady.

"What mystery is behind this?"

"I am as intrigued as you are, *ma belle*!" – he says.

"We French still use compasses, but they have nothing visible to show them the way! At night, I know that they follow the stars, but during the day..."

"Yes, it is really a mystery!" – she observes.

"I wonder how are the caravans guided during the day?"

"I would like to know too!" – he exclaims.

"And when I find out, I swear I will tell you!"

"Tell me, *mon chéri*..." – she continues, full of curiosity:

"When you are in the desert, where do you take shelter from the inclement weather? Does it never rain there?"

"We take shelter in tents woven from wool!" – he replies, and continues to explain:

"Wool is the best insulator, also for the heat! However, there is no need to worry too much about rain, because I think it hardly ever rains there! At least, during the time I was there, nothing! Not even a drizzle! Just the inclement sun cracking our heads open from the heat during the day, and the intense, shiver–inducing cold at night! But, what hurt us even more than the sum, the heat and the cold, is the wind! You do not know what hell sandstorms are!"

"Really?" – she wonders.

"Is it windy in the desert?"

"Sometimes, yes…" – he explains.

"The wind usually blows harshly, blowing clouds of sand into our eyes, mouths, clothes and shoes! It is very exhausting! So, we have to cover our faces with a scarf and leave only our eyes open! And even then, we have to squeeze them very tightly so that they do not get clogged up with sand and cause us terrible burning and tearing! And even worse is when you are eating and suddenly the storm comes up! You do not know how much sand I have eaten with my food! And surely you can appreciate how much pain it is to chewing food that contains a few grains of sand! But imagine that, with the food completely taken over by sand! It is hopeless!"

"Oh, darling, I did not realize how difficult life is for soldiers in the desert!" – she exclaims, yakking pity on the boy.

"So, you live in constant stress!"

"If we live!" – he says.

"And then there is the most important fact of all: the preservation of our lives, because the enemy does not give us truce! They rebel all the time! You do not know how obstinate these Muslims are!"

"I think I understand their obstinacy, *mon chéri*!" – she replies.

"Has France not invaded their country, taking away their freedom to govern themselves? What would you do if they suddenly invaded our land and came to enslave us? Would you accept everything passively?"

"Come on, Sylvie!" – he retorted, annoyed.

"Those Algerians. Are just ignorant bastards... You should see the filth they live in.... They are like pigs... They do not even value themselves! They are nothing but a sub–race!"

"Oh, I think differently from you, *mon chéri*! – she retorts.

"I believe that all people should be free! And they should live their lives as they please! Do you not think that Algerians live in filth precisely because of the lack of water there? You said yourself a moment ago that it never rains in North of Africa! If it does not rain, surely their access to water must be very, very limited, which in itself would not justify the same standard of hygiene that we Europeans are used to!

"I do not know!" – he replies, almost harshly.

"But I did not say that it does not rain all over their territory! There are parts of Algeria, especially near the coast, where it rains, and even snows in the highest places!"

"However, I assume thar this will have to take place in a restricted area!" – she observes.

"In the rest of the country, the inclement drought certainly prevails!

The boy just stares at her, defeated. That was the end of his arguments. Sylvie was definitely against the colonization of foreign lands. However, she continued to look him firmly in the eye, as if to challenging him to counter–argue.

"We would better leave the Algerians and their terrible land there!" – he said at last, after moment's thought. He knew his girlfriend very well and knew in advance that he would not be able to sway her one millimeter in her opinion of the domination that France had been arbitrarily o imposing on Algeria for decades, based solely on political and commercial interests. And then, he continued, with a smile, indicating that he was accepting his inevitable defeat:

"I would rather talk about more pleasant things than continuing discussing those horrible people!"

She looks at him with a pair of honey-colored eyes, full of mockery, and thinks:

"You always end up running away, don't you, you naughty boy? I knew you could not take it!" – and laughed, satisfied. Outside, the day was progressing, full of light. It was the power of spring inviting people to leave their homes, to see the sun, the light, the birds, the flowers...

"Were you not going to see your master painter?" – he asks, looking her in the eyes and falling deeply in love with her.

"I was going to..." – she replies, opening a beautiful smile, full of tenderness.

"So, come on..." – he says, holding out his hand.

A little more, and they were both walking down the cobbled street, holding hands, looking at each other and laughing happily. They were just laughing happily, immersed in each other's eyes... Nothing more... High above, the sun kept them company, dazzling the world with an infinity array of brilliant rays...

Céleste–Marie had just woken up, but was still in bed. Her eyes were gradually getting used to the semi–darkness of her bedroom. As happened almost every morning, she had no desire to leave the bed; her limbs were numb and every muscle in her body ached.

"*Disgrâce...! Malheurs...! Oh, vie misérable et inutile!*"[11] – she murmurs softly.

"*Ah, se viendrais ma mort aujourd'hui! Combien je serais heureuse!*"[12] – and she sighs deeply.

Céleste–Marie could never have guessed, but a shadow was systematically clinging to her body, enveloping her like a disgusting octopus wrapping its dreadful tentacles around her.

"Oh, silly!" – whispered the obsessing spirit, projecting the words into the girl's mind.

"You really are an idiot! Do you not realize that he does not love you? If he did, he would have married you years ago...! He is just taking advantage of you! And when he has had enough, he will throw you away like an empty bottle! Ah, he does not love you! He does not love you! Leave him! Leave him while there is still time! This guy does not deserve you! Do you think he does not have someone else? You have already noticed that he is quite strange and distant, haven't you? Let us go, you fool, get on with it! Tell him that you do not want him anymore, that you have had enough of him! Come on! Give him his change first! Do you not realize that he

---

[11] "Disgrace...! Misfortune! Oh, a miserable and useless life...!", in French.

[12] "Oh, if only my death today! How happy I would be...!", in French.

never leaves Chez Lulú, having fun with the girls in that shameless pimp? He does not hide it from you that he often goes there! And if he is going now, imagine after betrothed to you: he will leave you alone to look after his children, and he certainly will not leave that den of perdition!

Céleste–Marie stirs in her bed. Those strange conversations invading her head, inexplicably and invariably, every day, aggravated her enormously. She loved Berg. She knew she loved him, but why did she keep martyring herself with those kinds of things that came to her mind?

She could not control herself any longer. She had fits of rage against herself, trying to get rid of those thoughts that were hurting her so much; however, she found herself unable to get rid of them. Such mental colloquies pursued her relentlessly!

"You are lying to me!" – the girl exclaims, pushing away the voice that was talking to her.

"Berg does love me! And he is going to marry me soon!"

"Oh, how gullible you are!" – she hears in response. And a loud laugh follows:

"Ha! Ha! Ha! Ha! Wait and see if I am not right! The scoundrel will leave you in the lurch! The war is just a pretext! In fact, he has had enough of you, of your whining! You yourself know that he does not have to go to war! He is rich and an only child! He will not have to share his inheritance with anyone when his mother dies, who, by the way is already old and broken, and who will certainly pass away soon! Your beloved will inherit a fine fortune, my dear… It would be enough for you and him to live lavishly and carefree until the end of your lives! However..."

"Oh, you are lying to me!" – replies the girl, exasperated.

"You lie to me! Berg will never leave me!"

"Oh, I told you, wait and see!" – replies the insistent voice.

"Time will tell if I was not right!"

Céleste–Marie stirs insistently in her bed. In addition to the torment, she was feeling at the thought of that voice invading her head, she felt like she was being tied down, restricted in her movements, because a strange weight was on the back of her neck, her back, her arms and legs. She shook and twisted all over, trying to get rid of the discomfort, but it was impossible, as the strange, intolerable sensation stuck to her body. This exasperated her, making her irritable and constantly tired[13]. Sometimes she would clutch her head with her hands in despair, loudly asking it to leave her, to get out of there, a fact that had caught the attention of her mother and fiancé and, consequently, the sad realization that the girl was possibly suffering from some sort of mental alienation.

---

[13] The character presents a typical picture of obsession, a situation in which an inferior spirit, taking advantage of the weakness of character or conscious or latent guilt of an incarnate enemy of theirs and who then uses this to torment their victim – invariably their tormentor in the past – resorts to such tricks, He takes advantage of his invisible condition and thus seeks revenge for aggressions or betrayals once imposed on him by the victim of today, thus bringing him unspeakable suffering, as well as masking symptoms of various illnesses, including the most diverse mental abnormalities known to man.

"Oh, go! I am begging you!" – Céleste–Marie moans, pressing her ears with her hands.

"Leave me alone!"

"You have no cure!" – the voice continues to hammer at her head.

"Do you know why Berg does not want you? Because you are crazy! You are crazy! Your illness is incurable! There is only one way out for you: kill yourself! Why do you not get it over with? Peaceful and eternal rest awaits! Would you not prefer it this way? No pain, no fear, no constant insomnia, no endless sadness, no false promises of marriage! Just the serenity of eternal sleep, of infinite tranquility! Come on!" – said the voice in a softly and tenderly.

"You already have the poison! Drink it now! Did you not leave it there? Come on, courage! All you have to do is put out your hand and open the little drawer in the bedside table! The little bottle is there!"

Céleste–Marie lifts her head and looks at the small piece of furniture next to her. The little drawer, the polished brass handle. She reaches out slowly and pulls. The drawer opened and, at the bottom, in the middle of a series of colored cardboard boxes, was the bottle of poison!

"No! It's a sin!" – she murmured suddenly, shrinking down and sitting on the bed.

"God punishes those who take their own lives! Those who commit suicide go straight to hell!

"Oh, what nonsense!" – comes the insistent voice, countering.

"There is no hell! Death is the freedom of being! When we die, we will all be free! It does not matter how we die! The destination will always be the same: freedom, the end of pain and suffering!

Céleste–Marie looked again at the bottom of the drawer that remained open. Suddenly, she began to tremble. An immense knot rose in her throat. Good heavens! She was tired of all this! With a leap, she left the bed and, bewildered, began to walk around the room, which was still semi–dark because the window was still closed.

"Oh, my God!" – exclaims the girl in despair.

"I cannot take it anymore!" – and keeps walking around the room in circles.

Then she turned to the open drawer and looked again at the bottle of poison: small, made of translucent glass, with a golden metal lid! The greenish liquid, the elixir of death...

"Just a few drops, diluted in water or wine, and death will be sudden, inexorable!"– the old Jew had assured her, in that exotic, poorly–lit apothecary's shop on the Rue d'Anjou.

"But you see, Mademoiselle..." – the old apothecary had warned her:

"Once the poison has been administered, the effect will be swift and fatal! There is no antidote for it!"

Céleste–Marie shivers as she remembers the conversation she had with the old herbalist. She looked at the bottle once more, then slowly closed the little drawer in the cabinet and sat down on the bed. Her muscles were in tatters, her body ached intensely. Her head began to feel dizzy, her eyesight darkened and she fell backwards onto the bed.

Everything starts spinning dizzily and she loses consciousness. Beside her, a grotesque shadow stared at her mockingly.

"Not this time!" – the spirit mutters, visibly annoyed.

"But I know how to wait!" – and, with a smile full of mockery, he continued, consoling himself:

"Patience is a virtue I know how to cultivate extremely well, my dear..."

Then the shadow, walking with extreme difficulty, sat down in an armchair and looked intently at the girl who was struggling in an anguished crisis of hysteria.

"You will still be mine, my darling!" – he says, full of spite.

"You did not want to love me in the past, but you will be mine now!" – and laughing sadly, he continues:

"Elsewhere, you made me suffer like a dog but now it is my turn! Do you really think I will leave you go for that bastard? No! I will have you in my arms no matter what! And it will only be a matter of time, nothing more..."

Outside, the morning was radiant, in stark contrast to the gloomy situation in which poor Céleste–Marie found herself. Finally, exhausted by the tremendous emotional strain she had suffered, she went back to sleep in an agitated sleep, full of poignant moans indicating that horrifying nightmares were robbing her of her right to a peaceful sleep, which would allow her body to rest and recover. Essential and necessary conditions for the soul to live fully in this world.

Chapter 6

In Champagne

François–Armand and Wilfred Berg's leave from the regiment had expired. The fifteen days off, at home, with family and friends, were gone in a flash, and both boys had to return to the front, to resume their difficult lives in North Africa, where France, with great difficulty, maintained its iron colonial grip on Algeria. Sylvie and her mother were hastening their preparations to return to the country house, since her father's leave had also expired and he had to return to his post in command of one of the desert patrol garrisons.

"The house is empty again, *ma petite!*" – Edith–Aurore exclaimed to her daughter, who was helping her pack.

"Without your father around, life is no longer any fun for me…"

"You really love Papa, don't you?" – asks the girl.

"Yes, I love him as I always have, ever since I met him!" – the mother replies, with a twinkle in her eye.

"And I do not know if it is because, in reality, we spend most of our time away from each other!"

"Do you think, then, that if you and Papa had lived together all this time, things would have been different?"

"I do not know, Sylvie!" – the mother replies.

"I might even think so, because if you added up all the days I spent with *ton Papa*, it wouldn't be very little time indeed. The army had him more, you know?

"I see..." – says the young lady thoughtfully.

"And do you think the same will happen to me, *n'est-ce pas?* François is also in the army!"

"Prepare yourself, *ma chérie!*" – exclaims Edith–Aurore, with a deep sigh.

"You can be sure that if you marry him, you will certainly be left to bring up your children alone, without their father!" – and smiling slightly, she continued:

"So, it was with you! You were still a little girl, only three or four years old... and when your father returned from the front, you did not recognize him at first. You took him for a stranger!"

"Really?" – Sylvie is astonished by such a revelation.

"Yes!" – the mother continues.

"And it took you a long time to accept him. Your father found your attitude funny, but at the same time, he felt hurt, because every time he came, he found you different, more grown up... He missed your daily development and that hurt him a lot! Deep down, I think he feared that you would end up forgetting him for good and that you would not love him anymore or that you would reject him once you were an adult!"

"What nonsense!" – retorts the girl, her voice laced with emotion.

"I love Papa and I will always love him, even if I did not have him by my side all the time!"

"It is the contingencies of life, my dear!" – says Edith-Aurore, with a long sigh.

"Someone has to pay the price, so that we can all have security, freedom... Deep down, I believe that your father did and still does everything for both of us, because he loves us too much! He joins his ideal companions to build a just, rich and strong nation!"

"And for defending such ideals, we all pay a high price, don't we, Maman? – remarks Sylvie thoughtfully.

"The two of us and the families of all those who gave their lives and are still giving their lives so that France can become greater and greater!"

"France gave the first great cry for freedom to the whole world, which was, and still is, oppressed by the powerful! And we paid the price for such boldness! Since the Revolution[1], we have never known tranquility in this country!

"Rivers of blood are pouring out unceasingly, and I assume that much more will be spilled before things settle down.! In the meantime, like your father, I also believe that the feeling of freedom, equality and fraternity will one day come to all people! That is what we are fighting for, Sylvie! That is what we have been dying for ever since! And we will not stop offering our blood as a holocaust until such things are commonplace and ordinary, not only in France, but throughout the world...! Enough of oppression! No more lies,

---

[1] Reference to the French Revolution of 1789.

no more inversion of values, no more privileges! Equal rights must be extended to everyone!"

"Oh, your speech will convince even the kings, Maman!" – says the girl, laughing.

"With such arguments, even the hardened aristocrats will want the Republic forever!"

"Oh, *ma petite!*" – exclaimed Edith–Aurore, also laughing and hugging her daughter.

"And I am proud to know that you are also a supporter of our ideals! If we are depriving ourselves of peace today, it is so that you and your children will have it in the future! We know that this sacrifice will not be in vain!"

"Oh, *Maman*!" – says the girl, affectionately responding to her mother's embrace.

"I love you so much!"

"I love you too, my darling!" – exclaimed Edith–Aurore, highly moved. And, changing the direction of the conversation, she continues:

"But now, let's go! We need to hurry! There is still so much to do and I intend to take the first train, early tomorrow morning!"

"Are you going to leave the house locked up?" – Sylvie asks.

"Yes! We will take Pierre and Berthe with us this time!" – and she continues, laughing:

"Will the two of us not just wander off? We will paint everything we see and we will walk around the countryside every day! So, we will leave all the housework to the two of them!"

"Oh, so are you going to give me painting lessons all the time?" – asks the girl happily.

"No!" – replied the mother, pretending to be serious.

"You know very well that my style and *Monsieur* Pichon are completely opposite! Let us not mix things up! He simply hates current trends and I particularly think that the world is not static. Everything in life is dynamic, everything tends to evolve! And why should arts in general be any different? I admire the undeniable value of the Neoclassics, of course, but the Romantics brought a new proposal to painting! I had a classical education, it is true, but I identify enormously with the Romantic ideal and I follow in their footsteps, especially when it comes to things of nature! I find an exciting and unparalleled challenge to try to copy his perfection of form! The excessive formalism of Neoclassicals was beginning to tire, do you not think? It is a pity that *Monsieur* Pichon's brush does not want to update itself..."

"He just does not want to get up to speed, and of course he is afraid that you will contaminate me with your style!" – remarks the girl, laughing.

"He is jealous of you, because he knows how much you love the Romantics[2] and he loves the Neoclassics![3]"

"And you, of course, follow in his footsteps!" – says Edith–Aurore.

"Oh, Maman! Deep down, I think you are the more jealous of the two!"

"Joking aside, ma petite..." – remarked her mother, becoming serious.

"I consider *Monsieur* Pichon to be one of the great masters of our time and you have the privilege of being his pupil! And you, like him, have the right to follow the school that best suits you! I like the Romantics style and you like the Neoclassics! What is wrong with that? Can you imagine if we all looked in one direction? How dull and anachronistic this world would be!

"Or we would all have a terrible case of torticollis, *n'est–ce–pas?*" – jokes the young lady.

"Oh, you are a slut Sylvie! Ha! Ha! Ha! Ha!" – Edith–Aurore bursts out laughing at her daughter's jocular tirade.

---

[2] Main characteristics of romantic painting: the approach to Baroque forms; diagonal composition, suggesting instability and dynamism to the viewer; valorization of colors and chiaroscuro and drama. Romantic themes; real events from national and contemporary history from the artists' lives; nature, revealing a dynamism equivalent to human emotions, and Greek mythology.

[3] The painting of this period was mainly inspired by classical Greek sculpture and the Italian Renaissance, especially Raphael, the undisputed master of balanced composition. The characteristics of this school were formalism in composition, reflecting the dominant rationalism, as well as the accuracy of contours and the harmony of color.

"On this point you have taken after your father! You definitely cannot take things seriously for long! Ha! Ha! Ha! Ha!"

François–Armand and Berg had been back on the battlefields in Algeria for a few days.

"Can I sit here with you?" – with his plate in hand, asked Cadet Rounet, approaching Lieutenant Berg who was also eating his evening ration, huddled on the soft sand in front of his tent, set up in a military camp on the edge of the Algerian desert.

"Oh, how nice of you to come!" – says the other, giving a slight smile.

"You are keeping me company! You do not know how bad it is to eat alone, especially in this hellhole..."

"Camp food is already awful, and having to eat it alone makes it even worse!" – exclaims François–Armand, also squatting down next to the other and, after making an extreme effort to swallow the rough, coarse piece of bread in his mouth, he swallowed it with extreme difficulty, he continued:

"Being the garrison commander has its disadvantages, doesn't it? Having to be alone at night, for example!"

"Yes..." – the other says, not very cheerfully.

"Or in the company of the Sergeant and the Corporal, who are not always willing to share their prose with anyone. Sometimes they are so exhausted that they would rather sleep than eat, like today... The march was so exhausting that they were simply exhausted!"

"Commanders get more tired than the soldiers because, as well as having to do what their subordinates do, they still have the responsibilities of commanding, leading the troops along the roads and employing the best attack and defense strategy..." – observes the young cadet.

"I can see that you are a lot more tired than I am!"

"We do have a great responsibility, François..." – said the other, putting aside the brass plate with the almost untouched food.

"Sometimes I wonder if it is time to stop, to stay at home! I was thinking about Céleste–Marie when you arrived. I am almost thirty, and she is already twenty–five. She keeps asking me to get married..."

"And why have you not married her yet?" – asked the boy.

Wilfred Berg looks longingly at the young Cadet's face. They were related. François was his cousin; their mothers were sisters. He liked him, despite the age difference; he thought he was mature, even though he was still young.

"Did you know that Céleste–Marie is ill?" – asks the Lieutenant.

"No... What's wrong with her?"

"She is out of her mind! – Berg says softly, looking at the whiteness of the desert sand which, undulating, is lost in the distance. On the horizon, the full moon appeared immense, round and opalescent.

"Really?" – amazed the other.

"I have not seen her for a while, but the last time I saw her, she did not seem to be..."

"Crazy?"

"Yes..."

"That is right!" – Berg says with a sigh.

"Now she is talking to herself, punching herself and lives locked in her room, lying on her bed!"

"God!"

"So, it is!" – Lieutenant Berg says, his voice filled with bitterness.

"Look at the situation I am in! She is pressuring me to marry her and keeps fantasizing about it, claiming that I stopped loving her, that I have another woman, and a whole host of other nonsense! Do you think I do not love Céleste-Marie? Yes, I love her, but faced with this situation, I do not know what to do! How could I marry her when I know she is getting worse every day?

"But what about the doctors?" – asks the young man.

"Did her mother not take her to the doctor?"

"She certainly took her to the doctor!" – replied Lieutenant Berg.

"Marie–Louise has taken her to the best doctors in the city, but the medicine has not done her any good! There is no improvement!"

"Oh, how sad, Berg!" – exclaims the young Cadet, deeply saddened by his friend's situation.

"I can see that you are really stuck!"

"I really do not know what to do!" – the other continues.

"She keeps asking me to marry her, but how can I marry her in such a situation? And if I marry her and get her pregnant, what will the consequences be? I feel that Céleste-Marie will not be able to be a mother! She cannot do it!

"Oh, and I know how much you want children!" – François-Armand observes.

"Like me, you are an only child, and your lineage will die out if you have no heirs!"

"Yes, and it is precisely for this and other reasons, François, that I have not married her yet! – Berg continues, highly embittered.

"I firmly believe that we will survive through our children. I see this as our perpetuation; we will remain eternal in our descendants! I do not know if it is pride, but I have always cherished this desire! And Maman dreams about it too! You do not know how much she longs for a grandchild!"

"And I also know how much Céleste-Marie loves you!" – says the boy.

"I do not know what she will do if you leave her!"

"Céleste-Marie will die, François..." – murmurs Berg, quietly, after pretentiously trying several times to swallow a huge knot that stubbornly clogs his throat.

"She will die of pain, *mon ami*..."

And then there was a long silence between the two boys. The night wind began to blow, gradually chilling the desert air. High up in the sky, the full moon walked slowly, spreading its silvery rays and lighting up the vast expanse of sand with magical, almost magical luminescence.

"We would better to go in." – invites Berg.

"We will soon freeze if we stay out here!"

"*Merci!*" – says the other, getting up. And he continues:

"But I am going back to my tent. I am tired and it is time to sleep... *Bonne nuit!*"[4]

Lieutenant Berg only replied with a slight shake of his head. He was too bitter. A knot the size of the world stuck in his throat. For a few more moments, he stared out at the desert night, which was brightening intensely in the moonlight. Then, slowly, he turned back to his tent. He was going to try to sleep...

The Paris train station, as usual, was buzzing that mid-spring morning. The intense coming and going of people, many of whom were arrivals, for the most part, were filled with intense chatter and were highly excited and dazzled by the brilliance of the City of Light, which at the time was considered to be the center of the civilized world. The other part of the population hurried to take the trains that left the capital of France, in search of nearby towns or even to the most distant stops, within the country istself or outside it, since the whole of Europe was interconnected, at a gigantic pace, by means of an extensive rail network and, for the first time in the history of mankind, distances were shortened and real crowds could travel fast, cheaply and safely to the most varied destinations!

These were the facilities provided by the advent of machines, making man's life easier, which until then had been difficult and full of obstacles! New horizons were suddenly opening up to the dazzled eyes of people who, until the dawn of the 19th century, were still closed to the restriction of short

---

[4] "Thank you...!" (...) " Good evening...!", in French.

distances, not knowing much beyond the space where they were born, due to a lack of fast, safe and efficient means of transportation, such as the arrival of the railways!

"*Vite! Vite!*"[5] – from under a mountain of bulky packages, Edith-Aurore exclaims, highly flustered, to her butler, who is bending over under the weight of very large luggage. "*Le train partira a tout moment!*"[6]

Behind them, and no less breathless than Edith-Aurore, came Sylvie and Berthe, both of them overstuffing a lot of bags.

"Whew!" – exclaimed Edith-Aurore, finally settling down next to her daughter in the first-class carriage. The servants traveled in the second-class compartment, as it was unusual for them to travel alongside their employers in the luxury car.

"Finally, rest!" – and let herself sit down heavily on the spacious and comfortable moss-green velvet upholstery.

"Now, just until Champagne! Oh, ma petite, I cannot wait to get there! Paris bores me!"

"It is because you were born there, Maman!" – says the little girl, smiling.

"You were brought up free, running around the countryside's, in the open! In the city, you feel trapped!"

"You're right!" – agrees the mother, as she looks into a tiny oval mirror, eagerly touching up the make-up that has been smudged by the effort of carrying luggage.

---

[5] "Hurry...! Hurry...!" (...) in French.
[6] "The train will be leaving any minute...!", in French.

"No matter how hard I try, I will never stop being a provincial! I like Paris, but not to live here! The city is growing too much[8], everything is congested! Do you not see how crowded the Cité is every day? Carriages and streetcars clog up the streets; there is no longer any freedom or tranquility to walk along the boulevards without the risk of suddenly being cut off by the wheels of a speeding car or the hooves of a mad steed! Accidents invariably happen every day!"

"You are right, Maman!" – the girl says.

"However, I believe that is the price we will pay for progress! The population is growing alarmingly!"

"Sometimes things scare me, Sylvie!" – remarked Edith–Aurore, her gaze lost in the landscape that was rushing past the train window.

"Paris is swollen with people, and despite the epidemics of cholera[7] that break out frequently and, above all, invariably attack the poorest, the population is going to increase every day! Extreme poverty is rife in the shantytowns of the infected mansards of the mansions of the Quai de Bourbon and in so many other places, even in the city center! Peasants leave their villages and come to Paris in search of the dream of a better life! But what do they find? Even more misery than they had in the countryside! Labor abounds; there are plenty of arms for industry and, as a result, poverty and crime increase! Who today, in their right mind, risks wandering around certain neighborhoods in the city, even in broad daylight? I really do not know where it will all end!"

---

[7] In the 19th century, Paris suffered from two major cholera epidemics, one in 1832 and another in 1849.

"Consequences of modernity, Maman!" – remarks the girl.

"As you well know, the invention of the telegraph quickly interconnected all the regions of the planet; with the railroad's distances are shrinking; new inventions and new discoveries in science appear every day. The world is crazy about novelties, and industry is rapidly taking over what used to be a way of life! Everything is happening so fast now that there is not enough time for things to settle down first! As the excellent *Monsieur* Baudelaire[8] says:

"*Le vieux París n'est plus (la forme d'une ville–Change plus vite, hélas! que le coeur d'un mortel).*"[9]

"You and Mr. Baudelaire are absolutely right, *ma petite!*"[9] – Edith–Aurore exclaims, marveling enormously at the philosophical tirades she had just heard. She continued, very intrigued by her daughter's words.

"But tell me, *ma Cherie*! Where did you learn such important things? You are still almost a child... How come you are messing around with creatures as important as Mr. Baudelaire?"

---

[8] Charles–Pierre Baudelaire (Paris, April 9, 1821 – Paris, August 31, 1867) was a French poet and art theorist.

[9] "The old Paris is no more (the shape of a city – it changes faster, oh, than a mortal's heart). ", in French, a quote from Baudelaire in his expressive work "The Flowers of Evil" and, to corroborate the above, the following excerpt from that book is transcribed: "Even before the physiognomy of the new has been configured, the old is crumbling everywhere. The 10th century was stigmatized by the persistent ambiguity of things and ways not yet being what they were supposed to be.

"Well, Maman, you forget that I am attending classes at the Lycée des Arts!" – replies Sylvie, laughing at her mother's remark.

"As you can well see, I am enjoying my Philosophy lessons very much!"

"I see you really are!" – her mother replies, almost unable to believe that she was facing a young girl of only fourteen discussing such profound matters.

"Tell me, Maman" – Sylvie asks, after a few moments of silence during which she noticed that her mother was looking at her sidelong, with an air that was still highly intriguing, while surely reflecting on the words that she, Sylvie, had said to her.

"How long do you plan to stay in Champagne?"

"For the rest of my life!" – said Edith–Aurore, without thinking. Then, realizing she had said something silly, she corrected herself:

"I mean, until summer comes and you have to resume your lessons at the Lycée..."

"Then we will not be staying long..."

"Yes, spring is already halfway over, and summer in Champagne is not that great! –

Observes Edith–Aurore thoughtfully.

"In that case, I would prefer the air of Paris! You know how it is, during the hot season, the city empties out a bit more, when many people seek the freshness of the mountains."

"But I will have a few days off in high summer too!" – the girl exclaims.

"Why do we not go to the Riviera? I would love to swim in the sea...!"

"The Riviera?" – Edith–Aurore exclaims, taking heart.

"Gosh! We have not been to the beach for so long! I think the last time we were there, you were eight or nine!"

"Seven?"

"Seven! And Papa was with us at that time! He was on leave from the front! It was the most delightful summer I have ever spent! Do you remember...?"

"If I remember?" – the girl exclaims, letting herself be contaminated by her mother's pleasant memories.

"We ate fresh oysters! Papa ate so many that he got sick!"

"Haha! Haha! Haha! Haha!" – Edith–Aurore bursts out laughing.

"And he had a bellyache like that!"

"Poor Papa! He never wanted to hear about oysters again!"

"Well done!" – continues Edith–Aurore, amusing herself to no end with those memories.

"I warned him that oysters are not to be trifled with! But he has shown himself to be such a glutton! Ha! Ha! Ha! Ha!"

"And he had to pay a terrible price!" – remarks the girl, also laughing.

"I still seem to see him half–green and in a cold sweat with terrible abdominal cramps! Ha! Ha! Ha! Ha! And taking over the toilet! Ha! Ha! Ha! Ha! No one could use it anymore, because your father took it over for good!"

"Poor Papa!" – says Sylvie.

"I think he has learned his lesson!"

"And how! After staying bed for three days, unable to leave the hotel room!"

"Only this time we will not have him with us!" – observe the girl, saddened.

"Yes!" – agrees her mother.

"And it will not be the same! Without your father making us laugh all the time with his antics, it will not be the same!" – and, after a few moments of deed silence, she continues:

"I don't think I would even want to go to the Riviera without him..."

"Neither do I, Maman!" – says the girl, her eyes welling up with tears.

"Neither would I!"

A heavy silence fell between them. It was the pain of longing that was taking a huge toll on their hearts. The train was running fast, cutting through the countryside and the plains, heading for the northeast of the country. In a few hours, they would be in the Champagne region, where they owned a country house on the edge of the Ardennes Forest, almost on the border with Belgium. However, the train would only take them as far as Reims; then the rest of the journey would have to be made by carriage. They would not arrive until late at night.

"Well, we will be on the train most of the day!" – exclaims Edith–Aurore.

"We will have plenty of time to chatter away!"

Sylvie just looked at her mother and smiled sweetly. How she loved her! Her mother and father had always been very dear to her, even though it was she, her mother, who had always been by her side. She had few and limited memories of her father from the past. He was always away at war. He came home so little! She remembers him imposing, in his dark blue uniform; the cap on his head, with the national colors, and also the golden chevrons on the shoulder of his tunic; on his sleeves, the shiny pennants and, on his chest, the gold and silver medals for merit and bravery in his performance on the battlefields and the polished brass buttons of his jacket, always impeccably ironed and without the slightest trace of creases or dents to spoil its perfect shape and fit to his body! How handsome and great, kept deep in her childhood memory!"

"What are you thinking about?"

"Papa..."

"And what did you think of Papa? Can I know or it is a secret? – says Edith–Aurore.

"Oh, of course you can know, Maman! – she replied with a smile .

"I remembered how handsome and elegant Papa was in his uniform..."

"If it was!" – exclaims Edith–Aurore, proudly.

"You would not believe how many little girls from all over the world were after him!"

"Really?" – remarks the young ladys, highly amused.

"Has Papa given you so much trouble?"

"It happened! And I could not take my eyes off him for a single moment! If I did not, one of those women out there might have taken him from me, do you not think?"

"If you say so! However, I never realized you were so jealous of Papa!" – remarks Sylvie.

"You have managed to hide it very well all this time!"

"Precaution, *ma chérie*! Precaution! You never know what is in a man's head!"

"Not even a woman's, *n'est–ce pas?*" – jokes the girl.

"Oh, you are a slut, *ma petite*!" – exclaims Edith–Aurore, laughing her head off.

"You are very funny indeed!"

When the train arrived in Reims, it was already past six o'clock.

"Let's get a car!" – remarked Edith–Aurore, barely concealing a stubborn yawn. It was clear that, like everyone else, she was very tired from the long hours of travel. And, turning to the butler who, dizzy and sleepy, was standing quietly beside the mountain of luggage that lay in a corner of the long platform of the train station, she ordered him:

"Pierre, go and hire a carriage! And make sure it is a big one or it will not fit us comfortably! We still have a long way to go!"

"Oh, Maman!" – says Sylvie, leaning on her mother's shoulder.

"I think we should spend the night in town! We are all so exhausted! And there is the danger of the roads! You know how frightening it is to travel at night through these dark woods! I am so scared!"

"Oh, do you not have faith in God?" – Edith–Aurore admonishes her.

"Nothing will happen to us, I am sure! And besides, we are in a quiet area! Even if we were in Paris! And our country house is not that far away! Just another two hours by car and we will be comfortably settled there! You will see!"

Before long, the four of them were settled in a large hired carriage that was speeding along the narrow path that snaked through the gloomy, endless black pine woods. No one said a word; they just dozed off, overcome by exhaustion and lulled by the jolting of the carriage which, was speedily overcoming the distance, taking them to their destination.

Two and a half hours later, the carriage was parked in front of the old stone building on the small country estate.

"Oh, we are here!" – exclaims Sylvie, waking up from a short nap and looking out of the carriage window.

"Finally!" – says Edith–Aurore, also opening her eyes from her slumber.

"Now, to rest!"

Extremely tired, they barely had a light meal and all went to bed. The journey that day had been exhausting, and no one was in the mood for conversation. Just bed and nothing else!

As soon as dawn broke, Edith–Aurore was up and about. In the centuries–old kitchen, the stone stove was smoking.

"*Bonjour, madame!*" – exclaimed Berthe, the cook, when she saw her mistress coming through the door, all happy and refreshed.

"Did you sleep well?"

"Like an angel, Berthe!" – she replies happily.

"Just like a beatific angel" – and, approaching the window, she peered out and continued, in a very good mood:

"Oh, how good it all does me! The smell of the countryside, the freshness of the woods, the mountain air! Hum, what a delight! It gives me such an appetite! And what are you preparing for breakfast?"

"Cinnamon rolls, tea, milk, butter, cheese, honey cakes, blackberry jam..."

"Oh, how nice!" – exclaims Edith–Aurore, taking a seat at the large oak table in the kitchen.

"I will have *le petit déjeuner*[10] alone; Sylvie is still asleep, and I do not want to wake her up now! You know how much she likes to get up a little later! – and, looking around, she asks:

"And Pierre? Where has he gone?"

"I sent him off early to the village in search of provisions and fresh meat!" – says the cook.

"I am thinking of making roast lamb for supper."

---

[10] Breakfast, in French.

An hour later, Sylvie got up. Her mother was reading a book in the living room.

"Oh, bonjour, *ma petite*!" – Edith–Aurore exclaimed to her daughter, who was coming down the stairs, step by step, still a little sleepy.

"How was it? Did you sleep well?"

"Yes, Maman!" – she replies, not very cheerfully.

"Oh, I can see that you are a little discouraged, *ma chérie*! – exclaims her mother, getting up and going to meet her, hugging her tenderly.

"Did you not like to come to Champagne?"

"No, it is not that, Maman!" – she replies, letting herself sit down heavily on a large leather divan.

"It is just that I dreamed about François..."

"Oh, and dreaming about your love has left you so crushed?" – remarks Edith–Aurore.

"Should you not be happy instead?"

"No, Maman..." – replied the little girl, full of sadness and holding her head in both hands.

"In the dream, François was crying and screaming for me, like a possessed man! And I could hear him clearly, but I felt lost from him, as if we were separated by an invisible barrier! I could see and hear him; I could even touch him; but, he could not see or hear me! Then, we were overcome with despair, because we could no longer find each other! We were lost, like in an impenetrable labyrinth, searching for each other! Oh, Maman, it was horrible..." – she said, hugging her mother, who was sitting next to her on the leather sofa.

"Oh, what nonsense, *ma petite!*" – exclaims Edith-Aurore, tenderly stroking her long honey-colored hair.

"It was all just a bad dream, a nightmare! Come on, clear your head! Forget it! Dreams are just dreams! Look, Berthe has prepared those delicious cinnamon cookies you like so much! I have already tasted them and they are simply divine! Go on, have your breakfast! Look, I am coming with you! Come on!" – and taking her hand by the hand, she gently pulled her along.

Shortly afterwards, and after a light breakfast, the two of them went for a walk in the countryside which, in the fullness of spring, was adorned with the immense variety of colors of the little wild flowers, their beautiful bouquets waving in the fresh morning breeze. And despite the fascinating scenery of the Champagne-Ardenne countryside, Edith-Aurore, often glanced sidelong at her daughter's face, who was walking beside her, and saw that she was sad, very sad.

"*Mon Dieu!*" – she thinks.

"I wonder why that strange dream upset my little girl so much, to the point of making her so down?" – and a slight shudder ran through her body from top to bottom. Would to God that nothing bad happened to her little girl. She certainly would not survive if she lost her. She loved her so much that she would not survive if such a thing happened! No at all!

Chapter 7

A Tragedy Strikes

Sylvie and her mother had been in the Champagne country house for a few days now. They had both got used to the simple, quiet life of the countryside again and spent most of their time, especially on sunny mornings, painting the stunning landscape that undulated in the distance, all tinged with the bright color of spring. In the afternoons, they would read or simply talk. Sometimes, they would go for a walk in the small village or, in the company of Pierre and Berthe, they would have convivial meals in the shade of the woods or ventured further afield to discover new and picturesque places. So, the days went by in a blur of peace and tranquility, without anything else coming to take them away from the safe seclusion they found in those quiet places of unparalleled beauty at the foot of the mountains.

However, on a certain late spring evening, when the summer heat was already setting in, Sylvie suddenly felt a strange and unusual feeling of unease.

"You are burning up, *ma petite!*" – exclaimed Edith-Aurore, very concerned, when she realized that her daughter was shivering with cold, even though the heat was making everyone uncomfortable.

"Have you cooled down?"

"I don't know, Maman!" – the girl replies, shivering with cold.

"My whole-body hurts!"

"It must be a cold!" – says the mother, full of care.

"I am going to the kitchen to order Berthe to make you some tea and a foot bath! And you, up to your room! Off to bed!"

"Oh, Maman!" – protests the girl.

"Here you go with your unnecessary worries! Just the tea! Not the footbath! It's not necessary!"

"Do not argue, Sylvie! Colds must be treated correctly from the beginning! If the doctors recommend staying in bed, drinking plenty of fluids and taking a series of footbaths, then so be it! What is more, we are not in Paris, consequently, we will not have the help of Dr. Eustaque Durraine! If you get any worse, I do not even want to think about it! What do we have in these wildernesses? No one, apart from the nearest help in Rheims, two hour's drive from here!"

"Calm down, Maman!" – observes the young girl, trying to reassure her mother, who was already getting too worried.

"You will see: it is nothing more than a cold! I have certainly caught some cold air! Nothing more than that!"

"Oh, is that so, *ma petite*?" – exclaims her mother, cupping her forehead with the back of her hand. She continued, distressed:

"No! I am sure the fever is rising! Oh, God in heaven!" – and went out, terrified, calling for the maid in loud cries:

"Berthe! Berthe!"

Shortly afterwards, Edith–Aurore returned, accompanied by the no less uneasy Berthe, who was carrying a steaming cup on a small tray.

"*Par Dieu, Mademoiselle!*"[1] – exclaims the maid, also filled with great concern.

"You are so flushed!" – and turning to her mistress:

"You are right, *Madame*! You are absolutely right to send Pierre to Rheims for medical help! You never know! By the time the doctor arrives, more than five or six hours will have already passed! What is more, as I was preparing the tea, I could see, through the kitchen window, that thick rain clouds were forming on the sides of the mountains! There may soon be a summer storm!"

"More of that!" – exclaims Edith–Aurore, extremely annoyed and, moving towards the window, she pulls back the curtains and scrutinizes, with highly worried eyes, the horizon that is opening up in the distance.

"You are right, Berthe, the sky is darkening quickly! A storm is coming soon! It is better to send Pierre off now, without further ado! And let him go on horseback!"

Shortly afterwards, the young butler was riding, with loose reins, a fine steed, through the winding, cutting through the darkness of the Ardennes woods.

---

[1] "By God, Miss...!", in French.

"Oh, *mon amour*!" – murmurs the young man, his chest tight with worry. Sylvie's reddened features came to mind, her eyes shining, her sweat soaking her clothes... He had seen her for a moment through the bedroom door when his mistress had called him and ordered him to go and see the doctor in Rheims. He was sure: the fever was mercilessly cooking his love! It could be a simple cold, but what if it was something worse? There were so many serious diseases everywhere, killing people of all ages, left and right! Had there not been a terrible cholera epidemic the previous year?[2] So many well-known people had died! But it was not just cholera, no! What about measles, smallpox, the plague and the flu? There were so many diseases attacking people and killing them mercilessly... In fact, no one was safe! At such thoughts, a shiver runs through his body, and he says softly:

"Oh, you will not die! You will not die! I promise to get you the doctor very quickly, no matter what it take! You will see! It will be nothing!"

Pierre looked apprehensively at the patch of sky that opened up at the top of the narrow path and noticed that heavy dark clouds were passing by swiftly. A tinge of worry crossed his dark eyes. If it stormed, things would get even worse.

The road would become waterlogged, the horse's legs would get stuck in the mud and it would be impossible for him to gallop without the risk of being thrown to the ground, and he could also fall victim. At the mere thought of this hypothesis, an intense shiver shook him.

---

[2] France suffered a tremendous cholera epidemic in 1849.

"Oh, my God...." – he prayed in thought. "Do not let such a misfortune happen, Lord! If the worst comes to her, I will also die of pain!"

At this moment, however, thick raindrops begin to fall. Lightning and thunder rumbled with great ferocity, added to the strong wind that began to blow impetuously, making the trees of the immense and endless forest ripple like waves of an ocean capsized by a violent storm! A tremendous downpour then fell on the poor rider, preventing him from keeping up the pace. Despite the fur cloak he was wearing around his shoulders and his wide-brimmed hat, the young man instantly felt drenched by a torrential downpour! He had to drastically reduce the horse's gait.

"God in heaven! What now?" – he murmured softly, as the water ran down his face and formed a spout that protruded from the tip of his chin.

"On this march, I should not reach Rheims until morning!"

And even though it was extremely difficult and the animal's legs were already sinking into the mud of the road, which was rapidly becoming muddy, Pierre was not discouraged. Despite that difficult walk, he continued tirelessly. The rain was hitting him hard in the face, often making him squeeze his eyes shut so as not to injure them under the impact of the thick drops that were falling without stopping for a single instant. It was difficult for him to breathe, as the water was invading his nostrils, suffocating him! Stop? Never! He would rather die than have to stop under one of those imposing black pines and wait for the rain to pass! But what if it did not? Thunderstorms in the mountains used to last hours.

Suddenly, Pierre felt afraid. What if he did not make it in time? What if Sylvie died first? The mere thought of never seeing her alive again, of never hearing her soft, delicate voice and her always beautiful, crystal-clear laugh terrified him! Oh, surely God would not allow it to be something serious! She was still so young, so beautiful! No, beautiful people like Sylvie should not die young, ever! It would be sacrilege!

High up in the sky, however, the rain showed no signs of letting up; on the contrary, the impetuousness of the wind and rain seemed to increase, buffeting even more the poor rider who was trying so hard to overcome the fury of the elements! The hours went by, time was ticking away and the distance did not get any shorter.

"God in heaven..." – murmurs the boy, on the verge of despair, as he scans with his water-dulled eyes, and even in the midst of the blackness of that horrible night, the position he was on the little path he was following.

"I am still so far from Rheims! I cannot seem to get anywhere!"

In fact, he had covered a few kilometers since leaving the house. The storm was slowing him down enormously; his horse's legs were stuck in the mud and the animal was already showing signs of exhaustion. The night was advancing and the storm showed no signs of abating. Finally, as nothing in this world seems to last forever, not even that terrible storm lasted forever. As dawn was breaking, the winds died down and the rain slowed down to a drizzle, but it was continuous, but it softened the situation of the poor rider, who was exhausted and soaked to the core! The weather had improved and consequently, the condition of the march had improved a little more and, at around three in the morning, Pierre's horse's hooves were finally clattering on the cobblestones of the streets of Rheims...

While Pierre fought frantically against the storm to get Rheims as quickly as possible, Edith–Aurore and the faithful Berthe fought with the weapons they had at hand to try to break the fever that was cooking poor Sylvie.

"Oh, Madam!" – exclaims the maid in distress.

"The fever will not leave her! Even with the strong cinnamon tea and crushed mustard seeds, we have managed to make our little girl's fever subside even a little!"

"Yes, Berthe!" – agreed the mother, overcome with extreme despair, while she tried to cool her daughter's temples a little with a damp linen cloth. The young girl was already starting to get delirious, under the terrible effects of the high body temperature that had been affecting her for several hours.

"We tried everything we could to bring her fever down, but we did not succeed. Now, however, we can only pray and beg God and Jesus to give us their support and protection!

"And this rain that never lets up!" – the maid exclaimed in agony, looking at the window through which the intense flashes of lightning could be seen.

"And Pierre, how will he fare under the storm?"

"Pierre is a strong and brave boy!" – exclaims Edith–Aurore.

"I know that he has a lot of affection for Sylvie and will do everything he can to get to the city as soon as possible to bring us a doctor!"

"May God hear you, Madam!" – exclaims the maid.

"And if you do not mind, I am going up to my room to light a candle for Sainte–Catherine! I will be right back!"

"Go on, Berthe! Go and beg Sainte–Catherine for our little girl! I m starting to fear for her life!" – said Edith–Aurore, her voice choked with tears, and a series of sobs overtook her.

"Oh, *Madame, il ne faut pas de désespérer!*"[3] – exclaims the maid, taking pity on the other woman's pain.

"God will hear our pleas.! You will see that our little girl will start to get better soon! Have faith!"

"Oh, Berthe! Berthe!" – exclaims Edith–Aurore, full of despair, hugging her faithful maid.

"I beg you to pray because I..." – and she feels suffocated by tears and sobs.

"I... am on the verge of despair! If Sylvie goes, I will go after her! I cannot bear such an ordeal!"

"Oh, do not think about such things now, Madam!" – admonishes the maid.

"It is time to have faith in God! Remember Jesus, the Sublime Doctor, the Healer of all Sorrows, the Comforter of

---

[3] "Madame, do not despair!"

the Afflicted! Let us kneel down right here, Madam, and say the rosary! Come!"

On her bed, Sylvie was moaning and writhing, overcome by the stupor of fever. The two women then knelt down beside the sick woman's bed and blessed each other, very sorrowful and overwhelmed by the extreme pain.

"Oh, dear Jesus!" – Berthe exclaimed, her voice shaking with strong emotion.

"Be merciful, Lord, to our little girl!" – and, clasping the beads of the rosary with her fingers, she repeated the words of the prayer taught to her by the great Nazarene Master: "*Notre Père qui êtes aux cieux, que votre nom soit sanctifié...* "[4]

Taken by faith, the two women prayed the entire rosary, hoping that God would hear their heartfelt prayers. However, nothing is known about the Creator's designs! The hours passed, the storm began to subside, and Sylvie showed no improvement. On the contrary, she only opened her eyes, tremendously red from the scalding fever, asking for sips and more sips of water, as her unrelenting thirst tormented her enormously.

"Oh, *ma petite!*" – exclaims Edith–Aurore, moistening her lips with a glass of water.

"What is wrong with you, my dear? What is the matter with you? It seems so strange to me! It is different from the colds you have had before!"

---

[4] This is how the Our Father prayer begins in French.

"Oh, Maman!" – stammered the girl, with difficulty. It was tremendously difficult for her even to articulate words, such was the tremor that shook her unceasingly.

"I do not know what is wrong with me! My body feels like it is bursting into flames! I feel like I am being boiled alive!"

"Oh, my!" – exclaims the woman, becoming even more desperate. "– and Pierre does not come back with the doctor!"

"Patience and faith in God, Madam!" – exclaims the maid.

"Pierre will be here soon! He has been gone so long!"

"The time, Berthe?" – Edith–Aurore asks.

"Look at the time!"

"It is past six, Madam! It has been more than ten hours since Pierre left!"

At this point, a few animal neighs are heard!

"Pierre returns!" – shouts Edith–Aurore, getting excited and becoming highly anxious.

Then they both run to the window.

"You are right, Madam!" – remarks the maid, steadying her gaze in the dim light that still pervades the morning.

" Pierre and the doctor are coming!"

"Go, run and open the door for them, Berthe! I will stay with Sylvie! Bring the doctor here without delay!"

Shortly afterwards, the bedroom door opened and the maid was back. A distinguished young man followed her, carrying a small black leather valise in his hand.

"*Madam!*" – says the doctor. And, bowing slightly before Edith–Aurore, he introduced himself:

"Jean–Luc Versonier, physician and surgeon, at your service!"

"Oh, *Monsieur le docteur!*"[5] – exclaimed Edith–Aurore, wringing her hands in intense distress. Then, turning towards the bed, she pointed to Sylvie.

"It is my little girl! She has been burning up with fever since yesterday evening!"

The doctor approaches the bed and attentivelly takes Sylvie's pulse. Then, with the back of his hand, he feels the temperature of her forehead. Then he pulled back the covers and, opening the black leather case, took out a primitive wooden stethoscope and, placing it on the girl's chest, listened long and hard to her heartbeat. Then he put the instrument back in its case and, pulling back the eyelid of the patient's eyes, he studied her sclera and pupil in detail. Then he took her temperature again with the back of his hand, again he felt her heartbeat with his fingers at her wrist, then he steadied his gaze and meticulously ran his eyes over her reddish complexion, her lap and the skin of her arm, and His frowns in a show of deep concern. Then he turns to Edith–Aurore and stares at her with steady eyes.

"So, Doctor?" – asks the mother, full of expectation.

"Can we talk alone, Madam?" – says the doctor.

"Oh, of course!" – says Edith–Aurore nervously.

---

[5] "Oh, Mr. Doctor...!", in French.

"The living room... *s'il vous plaît!*"[6]

"I must tell you, Madam..." – the doctor begins a short while later, alone with Edith–Aurore, sitting on the large leather couch in the living room.

"What your daughter has is serious! And, I emphasize: it could be extremely serious, if my suspicions are confirmed! Please answer these questions, Madam, just to confirm the probable diagnosis: the onset was abrupt, with malaise, fever, rigidity, vomiting, headache and back pain?"

"Yes..." replies the woman, with a slight wince.

"I think those are exactly the symptoms my daughter is showing..."

"And yet..." – the doctor continued.

"I also noticed intense reddness; in other words, abundant skin lesions on her face and extremities, with a centrifugal distribution..."

"What do you think that is, *Monsieur le docteur*?" – she asked, her voice trembling.

The doctor looks at her with very serious, grave eyes. What he was about to tell her would surely end her life instantly.

"I am afraid your daughter has contracted smallpox[7], Madam..." – he says, now lowering his eyes.

---

[6] "Please...!", in French.

[7] It is worth remembering here that when the events described above took place, i.e. in the middle of the 19th century, smallpox, like other infectious diseases, was still almost absolutely incurable and had no effective treatment or prevention and decimated people in terrible, constant and uncontrollable epidemics.

Dr. Jean–Luc Versonier did not have the courage bring to look her in the eye any longer. He had to give her the cruel stab, but what to do? He was almost absolutely certain that this little girl was inexorably condemned to death!

Edith–Aurore said nothing at first. Her eyes remained still and inexpressive, staring into nothingness. Had she really heard what the doctor had said?

"What did you say Sylvie has, *Monsieur le docteur*?" – she asked, her voice shaky and extremely weak, almost crying.

"Unfortunately, I think your daughter is suffering from smallpox, Madam..." repeats the doctor, squeezing her hand.

"No! Sylvie can never catch smallpox! You are wrong, doctor!" – she exclaimed and abruptly withdrew the hand that the doctor was gently holding between his own. Then she gets up slightly and walks around in circles, extremely excited.

"My little girl could never have caught such a disease! No! You are certainly mistaken! You will see it is just a slight feeling of unease! You know what is like: we are from Paris, and the abrupt change of scenery will have affected her! She is very fragile! You did not know! I am absolutely sure. It is just a cold!" – and, with a nervous smile, showing hints of insanity, she continued:

"No! Imagine what a foolish thing you have said! Not smallpox! How absurd!"

Doctor Jean–Luc Versonier looks at her, highly penalized.

"Poor woman!" – he thinks.

"Little does she know that her daughter is at high risk of not surviving... Few survive this terrible disease... And at the stage she is at, it will certainly be fatal to her. It is only a matter of a few more hours... It took her a long time to get medical help..."

"You must be prepared, Madam..." – he insists.

"Have you not traveled by train? You know how it is, trains carry all sorts of people... and there are always smallpox epidemics somewhere! I particularly believe that this disease, like some others, is highly contagious and you must all remain vigilant or you also will end up infected! There are some treatments for smallpox, but only in preventive situations, such as the one used in large hospitals, where tiny particles of dust from the dried crusts of pustules of patients who have survived the disease are inoculated under the skin. However, this is not so reliable, because the disease recurs, always reappearing more virulent than before! I do not think this is the way to cure it!"

"What are you saying?!" – exclaims the woman, on the verge of fury, looking him firmly in the eye.

"That we should relegate our little girl to her fate? That she should die of starvation, without any treatment, and without my care, if she has indeed contracted this horrible disease? Oh, doctor, forgive me, but I do not believe diseases are transmitted like that! What you say is supposition! Nothing has been proven yet..."

"We experiment, Madam!"[8] – observes the doctor.

---

[8] Microbiology as a science began to make real progress in the mid-19th century with the development of high-quality microscopes, along with improvements in sterilization techniques, the cultivation of microorganisms and cytological techniques. At this time, eminent scholars such as the French chemist Louis Pasteur (1822-1895) and the German

"And a lot is already known about this and other epidemic diseases! Transmission may occur from person to person through contact!"

"So, what do we do? There will not be time to transport her to Paris, I suppose."

"She would die on the roads, Madame..." – says the doctor, lowering his eyes.

"And what do you suggest?" – asks Edith–Aurore, highly distressed.

"Time is running out and surely my daughter is already very compromised by the disease!"

"Unfortunately, as I have seen, that is the case, Madam..." – agrees the doctor.

"If only she had received medical assistance from the beginning, we might have had the chance to have a few more weapons in our favor! However, we lost precious time, and the disease set in, tremendously voracious. The fever cooks her, inclement, and the pustules are already beginning to hatch. But as long as there is life, there is a chance..." – says the doctor, cheering up. And getting up, he continues:

"Let us take a chance! That is why I am here! In the meantime, I urgently need hot water for tisanes and poultices..."

"Berthe! Berthe!" – Edith–Aurore stressed voice is heard calling for the maid.

---

physician Robert Koch (1834–1910) developed studies that led to the establishment of the foundations of Microbiology as a structured and specialized experimental science.

Before long, the doctor was meticulously and patiently medicating the patient. The mother and the maid stood by the bedside, always attentive to the slightest request from the doctor. At the foot of the stone staircase, Pierre remained attentive. His heart was squeezing; his throat was clogged with a knot the size of the world. Deep sighs of intense regret could often be heard rising from the bottom of his chest. Deep down, the young butler blamed himself. Hidden behind the stairwell, he had overheard his mistress's conversation with the doctor. He was not that in the habit of listening to his bosses' conversations, but in that situation, where his love's life was at stake, he felt so desperate that he had to hear what the doctor was saying. He had been horrified to hear the dark diagnosis: smallpox! Good heavens! What if she died? Smallpox was a very serious disease! Some people survived it, but so many died! What if Sylvie could not bear it? What is more, if she did survive, that damned disease would leave its baleful mark forever, spreading throughout the person's body! What would become of her beautiful face, grotesquely disfigured by the horrible pustule's scars? Oh, he did not even want to think about it!

The hours progressed and the doctor fought with all the weapons he had against the terrible disease that was relentlessly devouring poor Sylvie's resistance. Drentched in sweat and writhing all over from the severe fever, the girl was delirious.

"François! François!" – she murmured, in the midst of a cruel fever.

"*Où c'est toi, mon amour? Le sordide diable, a monter son écoeurant dragon, poursuit moi!*"⁹

"Oh, Doctor!" – exclaims Edith–Aurore in great despair.

"The hours go by and no improvement! Look! Red spots are appearing all over her body!"

"*Mais c'est de la variole!*"¹⁰ – exclaimed the old maid in astonishment, only then realizing how serious Sylvie's illness was. In extreme despair, she raised her hands in the air and cried out:

"*Oh, mon Dieu! Oh, Sainte–Vierge! Oh, Jésus bien–aimé!*"¹¹

"Yes, Berthe!" – exclaims Edith–Aurore.

"Our little girl has smallpox!" And, also overcome with, she hugged the maid, who was already in tears.

"And now I understand that only God can save her!"

"So let us pray then, Madam!" – says the old maid, kneeling down and blessing herself, takes the battered rosary from her apron pocket and begins to unravel it with trembling fingers.

Edith–Aurore also fell to her knees, her eyes full with tears. And with a voice choked with pain, she accompanied the faithful servant in her dismayed prayer.

The hours progressed, the afternoon came, the night came too. And all this time, the doctor did not leave the

---

⁹ "François...! François...!" (...) "– Where are you, my love?... The sordid devil, riding his disgusting dragon, is chasing me...!", in French.
¹⁰ "But it's smallpox...!", in French.
¹¹ "Oh, my God...! The Holy Virgin! The beloved Jesus...!", in French.

patient's bedside, assisting her and giving her the medications known at the time. However, as the evening progressed, Sylvie's condition worsened.

"I have nothing more to do, Madam!" – exclaims the doctor, crestfallen, totally exhausted by the long hours of tension and apprehension during which he had tried, by all means known to him, to defeat the disease that was stealing the life of the delicate honey–eyed maiden.

"I am sorry, but I really have nothing more to do for your daughter!"

Edith–Aurore looks at him in terror.

"No!" – she cried out, falling to her knees before the young doctor and, taking his hands, begged him, bathed in tears.

"*Par Dieu, non! Je vous demande, s'il vous plaît, ne quittez pas!*"[12]

"Oh, madam!" – replies the doctor.

"I have done all I can and it would not cost me anything to stay. However, I am exhausted, hungry, and urgently need to rest! I have been treating your daughter for more ten hours non–stop..."

"Oh, doctor!" – exclaims Edith–Aurore.

"I beg you, as a mother! Stay, please! I will offer you a bed to rest on while Berthe quickly prepares dinner for you! Please, doctor! I beg you! Things could change! I have faith in God! Please!"

---

[12] "For God's sake, no! I beg you, please don't leave!", in French.

"All right, Madam!" – replied the doctor, after thinking for a moment.

"Besides, it is already dark, and it would be fearful to go out on the roads at such late hour! All right! I will stay at your house, but I must tell you: your daughter will hardly see the dawn of a new day! I leave you with no illusions! Better prepare for the worst!"

Berthe led the doctor to one of the spare bedrooms and then went down to the kitchen to cook him some dinner. Surely he would be the only one in the house who could swallow any food.

Edith–Aurore approaches her daughter's bedside and tearfully takes her hand.

"Oh, *ma petite!*" – she says, her eyes transfixed with pain at the intense suffering of her beloved daughter.

"If you leave me, what will become of me? *Et ton Papa?* My God, he will not be able to bear losing you! Oh, dear God! – she continued, overcome with extreme despair.

"Save my little girl, Lord! *Oh, Dieu, sauvez ma petite poupée!*"[13]

Realizing that her hand was being squeezed tightly, Sylvie opened her eyes in the midst of the tremendous numbness that was overtaking her.

"Ma.. man.." – she whispered.

"*Je... meurs...*"[14]

---

[13] "Oh, God, save my little doll...!", in French.
[14] "Mo... mother..." (...) " I... am dying...", in French.

"No! You are not going to die!" – Edith–Aurore cries out in despair.

"I will not let that happen! No, for God's sake, no!"

"Yes..., *ma... man*..." – the girl continued, with extreme difficulty. Her eyes watered so much. They contained tears both from the fever and from the pain of realizing that she was leaving this world, still so young, still so full of illusions in her heart...

"And your love? How would your love feel knowing she was dead?" – François–Armand's face then appeared beautifully on her mental screen and she smiled amid in the midst of all that pain.

"Fran... çois, *ma... man*... Tell him... that I thought of him..."

"Oh, I will! I will, *ma petite*!" – exclaims the woman, covering her daughter's flushed cheeks with countless kisses.

"But what am I telling you? You will tell him yourself! What nonsense we are both saying!! You are not going to die! You are not going to die!" – meanwhile, at that point, the little girl's rolls her eyes, disappearing.

"No! Sylvie! Sylvie!" – her mother shook her violently and screamed.

"Berthe! Pierre! The doctor! Hurry!"

The young girl opens her eyes again and looks longingly at her mother. She was no longer crying; only deep sadness flooded her face. Then, slowly, the glow of that beautiful gaze flickered and went out for good, like a flame in the wind!"

When Pierre and Berthe entered the room, followed by the sleepy doctor, Edith–Aurore was unconscious, hugging the corpse of her daughter...

Three days later, at the very busy Paris station, a train arrived from the north–east of the country; in the cargo compartment was the coffin of a young girl who had died of smallpox in a remote country house in Champagne-Ardennes.

"I will personally see to the release of Sylvie's luggage and coffin, Edith!" – exclaims General du Servey, hugging the poor mother condolingly.

"As soon as you telegraphed me, I told my friends who are already waiting for your poor girl's wake!"

"Oh, what a disgrace! What a disgrace!" – exclaimed Constance, the General's wife, also hugging poor Edith–Aurore, who was bursting into tears.

"How could this happen to your little girl?"

"Oh, it all happened so suddenly, Constance!" – the other replied, sobbing.

"I called a doctor in Rheims, but he could not do anything! Oh! My little doll is gone, in the midst of terrible suffering!"

"That what this disease is all about!" – exclaims the other.

"If it does not kill you, it leaves those horrible marks forever!"

"The army took care to warn your husband, Edith..." – says the General.

"However, as you can imagine, it is impossible for him to arrive in time for the wake. It is a long way to go"

"Oh, I know he will not make it!" – says the woman.

"He will not have the chance to see her for the last time!"

"Now, however, it would be better if you went back to your house!" – said the General.

"Constance will keep you company! The release of the skiff may take some time. I think you know how bureaucracy is like in this country!"

"Thank you very much, General, for your helpful assistance!" – exclaims Edith–Aurore.

Then, the two women take a hired carriage and head for Edith–Aurore's house. Long hours of intense suffering were to follow. Long hours of pain, cruel suffering, and atrocious despair, as only happens to those who lose their beloved children, so soon cut down by the claws of death...

Chapter 8

Goodbye to Sylvie

Colonel Hippolyte–Antoine Rousselet opened the telegram he had just received from the army courier with nervous hands. His eyes scan the laconic words written in large letters:

"*Retournez vite. Sylvie trop mal.*"[1]

Signing the telegram was General du Servey, who had chosen not to be so cruel by sending the other such terrible news so suddenly, even though he knew that the girl's father was a well–balanced man who was well used to the horrors of battle. However, as he was also a father, he knew how hard such a blow could hit his valiant companion...

Colonel Rousselet, despite his hardened and serious character, which had already been honed over many years on the harsh battlefields, nevertheless felt his eyes darken and his legs weaken when he learned of the terrible news he had just received. A sudden dizziness went through his head, and he had to lean on one of the stilts that made up the frame of his tent. Good heavens! If it was General du Servey and not his

---

[1] "Come back soon. Sylvie very bad.", in French.

wife, who had sent him the telegram, then surely something very serious that was afflicting his little girl!

With his mouth extremely parched from the heat of the desert and the shock of the news he had received, Hippolyte-Antoine Rousselet, tremendously embittered, picked up his canteen and took a long sip of water from it. Then, for a moment, he lost his sight of the vast expanse of scorching sand that opened up before him. He thought and sorted his thoughts.

He had to go to his superior without delay and hand over the post. What could be so serious about his daughter that he would be sent for with such urgency? It could not be a good thing! Then, determined, he called for the orderly who was a few steps from the hut, and gave him a quick order. Then, he went to his horse, which was saddled in the shade of the tent, and with a precise leap, he won the saddle and set off in search of the fort, which was just a few kilometers away, where the command of his regiment was based.

Sylvie's coffin had been laid to rest in the living room of the Rousselet mansion. Edith-Aurore, dressed in black, sat beside her and stroked her daughter's waxy hands. Often, she would get up and tenderly caress Sylvie's pale face, kissed her, bathing her in tears.

"Oh, *ma petite*! Oh, *ma petite*!" – exclaimed the long-suffering mother, as she stroked her daughter's silky honey-colored hair.

"Why are you leaving me so soon? What will become of us without you, without your joy, always spreading to everyone in this house?"

Her friends kept her company in a vain attempt to console her for what was notoriously inconsolable: she had lost her most precious treasure. What consolation could they give her?

Next to the front door of the hall, welcoming friends and acquaintances who were still arriving, Pierre stood mutely at his post. Although he was serious and doing his job, his eyes could not hide what was going on in his soul.

Extremely red from crying too much, they were swollen, and yet the boy was still crying when he saw his beloved's body in the white coffin. What would become of his life from now on? What reason would he have to keep living there? None... The sun of his days was going out forever. Even though he knew that she did not love him and that she turned, body and soul, only to the passion she devoted to... – he did not even like to say his name! – to the other... to the detestable Cadet Rounet, yet he had stayed there, serving her every day, simply for the pleasure of seeing her, of being in the same environment as her, of hearing her voice, which always sounded like delicious music to his ears! But what now? How dull his life would be from then on! Suddenly, even though he did not like the other man, Sylvie's boyfriend, he remembered him. What would become of the bastard when he heard about the tragedy?

"You and I have lost her, my dear!" – he thinks sadly, and yet truly, without any sense of euphoria, gloating or revenge for his rival's misfortune, he concludes:

"From now on, we will both be two slobs wandering around this wretched and cruel world!"

Pierre was still mortified that he had not been able to get the doctor there in time, on that stormy night when she had begun to show symptoms of the disease.

"It took me so long to get to Rheims in search of the doctor!" – he thought, full of regret.

"But what could I do in the middle of that deluge? I tried, but the horse's legs got bogged down in the mud..."

Pierre felt like running out of there, going in search of the silence and seclusion of his little room behind the cellar. He could not bear to stand there and look at her in that coffin! It was too much for him! He would rather not see her like that, so pale in the arms of death! Oh, how hopeless it all was! However, he contained himself. It was better to stay! He felt sorry for his mistress too. The poor thing was alone, enduring that terrible drama! Berthe was in the kitchen, making tea and cinnamon biscuits for the visitors... Poor Berthe... This time, her delicious cinnamon biscuits would turn out more salty than sweet, the more tears she shed over the dough! She, also, had grown very fond of Sylvie! She had seen her born, grow up... And the boss? Good heavens! When the Colonel found out! He certainly would not bet in time. Algeria must be so far from Paris!

In the living room, people sat on the large divans and straw chairs, talking quietly, respectfully, sympathetic to that mother's pain.

"Edith..." – Marie–Louise called out to her, coming closer and confiding:

"I was talking to Céleste–Marie. Tell me, did you also tell François–Armand?"

The other lifts her head and, with an infinite expression of pain, looks at her, her eyes deeply bruised from the excess of tears.

"*Oh, ma amie! Quelle distracción! J'ai m'oublié de ça complètement!*"[2] – she replies.

"And then I left such things to General du Servey! Even my husband, he was the one who told him!"

"We will take care of that, *ma chérie...*" – says Marie-Louise, kissing the other on the cheek.

"You have nothing else to worry about..."

Then Marie-Louise looked around the room and spotted the General talking in a very low voice to another gentleman.

"I certainly warned Lieutenant Berg!" – says the General.

"It is possible that, by now, her father, the Lieutenant and Cadet Rounet know everything and are on their way to Paris!"

Wilfred Berg read the telegram quickly and his eyes suddenly filled with infinite sadness. The General had not spared him the truth.

"*Sylvie est morte. Variole. Informez Rounet.*"[3]

"Good heavens! Poor François-Armand!" – he knew how much his cousin loved that woman!

"Poor Sylvie! Still so young!"

---

[2] "Oh, my friend... What a distraction! I forgot all about it...!", in French.

[3] "Sylvie is dead. Smallpox. Inform Rounet. ", in French.

Lieutenant Berg takes the paper out of his tunic pocket once more, unfolds it and re-reads it. What adisgrace, my God! It was already night, and the cold desert wind was starting to blow. Soon, the boy would be there chatting to him. They enjoyed talking. As well as being relatives, there was an enormous affinity between them. Berg had not yet had the courage to tell him the terrible news. It was up to him to give the poor boy that fatal stab, from which he would certainly never recover!

"Ah, François!" – mutters Lieutenant Berg softly, with the telegram between his fingers.

"This will finish you off for good!" – then, sighing deeply, he called out to the orderly who was standing by, a few paces from the hut, and ordered him in a firm voice:

"Boy, look for Cadet Rounet! I want him here immediately."

The soldier stands at attention and salutes. His voice sounds firm and strong.

"*Oui, Monsieur!*" – and leaves quickly.

While waiting for his cousin to arrive, Berg runs his eyes across the clear, starry desert sky. His thoughts searched the infinite distances. He was not very credulous about religious things. However, he believed that there was a Sovereign and Intelligent Force governing things and people's destiny. He was not used to praying, but at that moment, he remembered God. He needed help to strike the heart of that young man. He needed a lot of courage to strike him, albeit very unwilling, the fatal blow! He swallowed several times. He had already been through very difficult situations in his life; however, he could not remember any other that had displeased him so much!

"What a thing!" – he mutters.

"So, me? And then with François!"

Oh, wretched life!

"Berg!" – he hears his voice calling him from behind.

Wilfred Berg did not turn around immediately to face him. A sudden unease came over him. There was no way he was going to kill his friend like that. Good heavens! What kind of disgrace was that! Why did things always have to be like this? People were dying every day: old people, young people, adults; even countless children were dying all the time! You should be used to that, but you never are when wretched death blows its putrid breath in your face and robs our loved ones!

"Berg!" – insists the other.

"You sent for me! What do you want?" – and, finding his friend's attitude strange, he touched him lightly on the shoulder:

"Are you all right?

"I am!" – replies the Lieutenant, turning around and looking at him firmly in the face. And he continues, visibly nervous:

"I mean... no! I am not!"

The boy just gave him a puzzled look. He could not immediately understand his friend's strange behavior! Few times he had seen him so out of control! What could be going on to make him so unbalanced?

Finally, faced with the expression of obvious confusion on the young cadet's face, Wilfred Berg took extreme courage and handed him the telegram. Why prolong the agony any longer? He gave him the paper to read and said nothing. No preamble, no preparation, no words to alleviate the misery that that tiny piece of paper contained.. And what kind of words could he possibly say at that terrible moment? Would they stifle the explosion that would follow? Of course, nothing he could say to him, or anything else in this wretched world at that moment, could in any way alleviate that kind of pain...

François–Armand picks up the paper, unfolds it, and his eyes quickly wonder over the words scribbled in large letters. His lips tremble and he suddenly turns pale. Then, an rictus of intense pain congests his features, his legs lose their sustainability, and he falls to his knees on the soft desert sands. His eyes glaze over with tears and he screams. He screams so loudly, a cry of pain so poignant that very few people in this world have ever heard it like it!

Deeply moved by his friend's pain, Berg knelt down beside him and tried to hug him. The boy, however, maddened by the intense pain, shakes himself violently, freeing himself from the other man's arms and, out of his mind, gets up in a flash and, emitting piercing cries of pain and despair, starts running across the sands, already whitened by the moonlight.

"François! No!" – shouts Lieutenant Berg. He gets up and runs after him.

The boy was running madly, dangerously far from the camp. Berg knew that if he left him alone, he would be in serious danger. Without the protection of his companions, he would get lost in the treacherous dunes and it would be a very difficult mission to find him again, especially at night, in that vast expanse of sand that was already beginning to freeze from the cold wind that was blowing relentlessly. There was also the risk that he would come across an enemy patrol that would certainly imprison him, enslave him or, depending on the situation, mercilessly behead him with a scimitar, a practice that the native used to apply to enemy soldiers when they casually found them lost in the desert. So Berg had to to do his utmost to reach him and, managing to touch him with his hand, he jumped on top of him and knocked him face down onto the cold white sand. He then turned him over and sat on his abdomen, holding both fists tightly in his hands. This feat was only possible because the Lieutenant, being older and larger in body, was able to easily overpower the other, who was still just a boy of seventeen.

"Listen, François!" – says Berg, still wheezing heavily from the excessive efforts to capture the boy.

"I know it has broken your soul, but now you have to be strong, accept it! I understand your pain! I know that, for you, it is the greatest pain in the world and that you will hardly recover from this blow, but that is life! We have to accept it! Is not death part of our life? The loss of our loved ones is a very difficult ordeal for us, but what can we do but accept it?"

"Sylvie is dead, Berg!" – exclaims the boy, his voice full of pain and despair.

"Do you not understand? She is dead! Do you know what this is?"

"I know!" – replies the Lieutenant.

"And if you promise me that you will not run off like a madman in the desert, I will get off your back!"

The other does not respond. He only cries intensely. Berg then felt defeated. The crisis of the first impact had passed. Now, he felt the laxity of the muscles that always follows nervous tension. Tears of pain and despair came pouring out of him. The Lieutenant then let go of his arms and slowly got up and lay down, also on his back, next to his friend, on the icy sand.

"What will my life be like without her, Berg?" – says the boy, looking at him out of the corner of his eye.

"Difficult, François! Very difficult! – replies the Lieutenant.

"And you will have to get used to it and its horrors, which will be your companions from now o! You will have to get used to the horrible pain of loneliness; you will have to get used to an agonizing wait that will never end, and you will have to fight like a lion to find the consolation and courage to go on living! And a strong willpower, but very strong! So that you do not go mad with grief or allow yourself to be dragged into alcohol addiction and thus fall into a really unfortunate life! Look, before I am your cousin, I am much more than that, I am your friend, who you can always count on! You know that! If I say such things to you, it is because I like you and I do not want to see you lost, becoming a wreck and disgraced, aimlessly wandering around! Consider that you still have your career in the army! And that you have just begun to take the first steps towards your future! Now you need to have courage! A lot of courage, really, to understand, above all, that this dream that you cherished so much abot making a happy home with Sylvie has gone forever and that, even though it is full of pain, it is suffocating you, terrible, the soul, you must go on, until time, the only effective remedy for forgetting great pains, makes you forget, and everything you are now experiencing is nothing more than a deep scar reminding you of how mercilessly life once hurt you!

"No!" – exclaims the boy, abruptly sitting down on the sand and, staring at his friend with wildly open eyes, in which there were hints of madness, he continues:

"Never! You have my word that I refuse to live in this world without her! From now on, *mon ami*, I am already starting to die!"

"I understand your pain, François, but you are talking nonsense!" – rebuts Berg.

"I know you refuse to accept what I am saying, but you are quite young and you will still be able to rebuild your life! Time will bring you a new direction."

"You are the one who is talking nonsense!" retorts the boy, rudely.

"You definitely do not know what you have just said! How can anyone live without their own thoughts? Sylvie was all my thoughts, Berg! From now on, my head will be as hollow as an idiot's! My heart used to beat only and exclusively for her; now it beats empty, without any resonance! My words were almost entirely about her and, from now on, what will my lips talk about? It would be better if I were silent forever, because what is the point of words if I can no longer speak the name of my love?"

Berg looks at him, full of compassion. Poor boy! I wish he was strong enough not to lose his mind!

"Come on!" – says Berg, getting up. And holding out his hand, he invites him:

"Let's go back! It is very cold here!"

In the coziness of the tent, Lieutenant Berg picks up a bottle of wine and two glasses.

"Drink the wine!" – he says, handing François one of the glasses. And, with a slightly sad smile, he continues:

"It will warm you up, as well as temporarily and illusorily dulling the pain in your soul!"

The boy picked up the glass with both hands, as he was still very shaky from the high emotional charge he had been through.

"Do you think I should go to Paris?" – he asks, after taking a small sip of wine.

"If you like..." – replies Berg, taking a seat next to him in a camp chair.

"I can keep you company on the journey! But if you think you will find her corpse waiting for you..."

"I know I will never see her again, Berg!" – says the boy, his eyes welling up with tears of pain and feeling.

"I am leaving, and I will never return to Algeria..."

"We will deal with that later..." – says Berg, tapping him lightly on the shoulder.

"Look, do you not want to spend the night here? If you stay with the other soldiers, the pain will be crueler, do you not think? There are always bad jokes and mockery... You know how it is..."

"I would really like to be alone..." – says the boy, lowering his head, shaking with sobs.

"Alone, with my misfortune..."

"You will feel more alone here than there! I guarantee it!" – exclaims Lieutenant Berg.

"It will just be you and me... I will leave you alone, I promise! Now come, settle down on my bed, and I will make myself very comfortable in the sleeping bag!"

"When are we leaving, Berg?" – asks the boy, after they have both lain down, waiting for sleep.

"Tomorrow." – replied the other.

"Now, clear your head, if you can, and try to get some rest!" – and he lowers the light of the lamp, then blows out the deadly flame, which goes out without reluctance.

Lieutenant Wilfred Berg's tent is plunged into darkness. Outside, there is only the silence of the desert, often cut short by the gloomy howl of a jackal, which enchanted by the luminescence of the full moon, paid tribute to it with its mournful song...

When Colonel Hippolyte–Antoine Rousselet returned from Algeria, his daughter's body had already been buried for eight days.

"Oh, mon Dieu! Quelle tragédie!"[4] – exclaims the man, as he comes face to face with his grieving wife, crying and dressed in mourning.

"What happened to our little girl?"

"Smallpox, Hippolyte! The damn smallpox stole her from us!" – exclaims the woman, overcome with despair.

"How could you let this happen, woman?!" – cries the Colonel, driven to despair.

"I come back from the battlefield, apprehensive, yes, but thinking she was sick! But, how do I find her? Dead! My little girl is dead!"

"Oh, my darling!" – exclaims the woman, hugging her husband.

"You do not know how hard I fought to save her! But death proved stronger and took her! Oh, how unhappy and unfortunate I am! What will become of us now?"

"The main reason for my existence is gone..." – mumbles the Colonel, letting himself sit dejectedly on the divan.

"Now, nothing else matters... Nothing else..."

"Oh, I suffer as much as you do!" – exclaims the woman, full of pain.

"You do not know what it was like to carry everything alone, without you!"

"And I was so far away..." – says the Colonel, oblivious to what his wife was saying.

---

[4] "Oh, my God...! What a tragedy...", in French.

"Poor Sylvie! What did life have in store for you? Almost nothing! Almost nothing! What have you lived for? How long have you been here? A few years, only! Just a few years, nothing more!"

"What will we do, Hippolyte, without her?" – said the woman, hugging her husband tightly, who was already starting to weaken enormously, to the point of losing his mind.

"What will become of our lives from now on?"

"What will become of our lives?" – asks the Colonel, his eyes filling with tears. Even though he was used to the harshness of war, he felt weak in the face of the difficult ordeal of losing his daughter at such a young age.

"What life, Edith–Aurore? From now on, there will be no more life for us! Only pain..."

And, embracing each other, they let themselves to be overcome by convulsive weeping. There was no way of consoling each other, because they were both suffering the same pain, the same inconsolable pain...

The day after Colonel Rousselet's arrival, Lieutenant Berg also returned to Paris, accompanying the inconsolable François–Armand. The boy had visibly lost weight and was looking very down.

"Are you not going to stop by your house first?" – Berg asked, while they were still in the coach that was bringing them from the city station.

"If you want, I will go with you, and you will meet your mother; then we will go together to Sylvie's parents' house..."

"No!" – retorts the boy, without hesitation. And, full of anger, he continues:

"Maman, I will see her later! First, Sylvie!"

"But Sylvie is no longer there!"

"If you repeat such a blunder, I will forget you are my commander and slap your mouth!" retorts the boy, looking at him with fierce eyes.

The Lieutenant just looked at him for a long time. The boy stared straight ahead again, coldly and inexpressively, his lips pressed together, discolored, as if they were two oblique lines blurring his pale face.

"God in heaven!" – thought Berg, steering steadily at the profile of his friend's face. François's features feature looked like they were carved out from a block of ice.

"He will not last! He will not! He has been weak for a long time and shows no sign of recovering! He has lost in the maelstrom of pain and does not have enough strength to get out of it! I am afraid he is going mad!"

Shortly afterwards, they both jumped out in front of the old gray stone house belonging to the disgraced Rousselet family.

"*Eh, François, halte!*"[5] – Berg shouted, when the other man furiously opened the high iron gate and dashed forward, climbing in pairs up the steps of the small staircase that led to the entrance door of the vestibule.

"Wait for me, François!" – snapped the Lieutenant, struggling to follow him.

---

[5] "Hey, François, stop!", in French.

"Let us not go in like this without announcing ourselves!"

The other man, without listening to what his friend was saying, frantically pounded on the door like a madman.

"Open the door!" – he shouted, slamming it shut with his hands.

"Open this damn door!

Before long, the door opened and Pierre cocked his head, visibly annoyed by the boy's antics at the entrance to the house.

"*Pardon, Monsieur!*" – says the butler, ostentatiously standing in his way.

"There is no..."

"Get out!" – shouts the boy, to the point of fury, cutting off his words. And, staring at him with a fierce gaze, he threatens:

"Get out, you bastard, or I will smash your snout in!"

With a sharp jerk of his shoulders, François pushes the butler aside and abruptly enters. Pierre, overcome with astonishment at the boy's strange behavior, immediately pulls himself together and runs after him.

"Sylvie!" – screamed the boy, out of his mind.

"Sylvie, *ou est toi?*[6] Come, my love! Listen to me! It is me, your François, coming back from Algeria! Come quickly! I promise you: I will never go back to that hellhole! From now on, I will stay here with you, forever! Come..."

---

[6] "Sylvie, where are you?", in French.

Berg and Pierre now stood at a relative distance, while the boy, his eyes welling up with tears, pathetically with his arms open in the middle of the drawing room, looking at the white columns of the mezzanine balustrade at the top of the stairs.

"I think François is losing his mind, Pierre!" – Berg whispers in the butler's ear.

"I had a feeling this would happen, *Monsieur le comandante*..." – replies the other, in a very low voice.

"And where are your bosses?" – asked Lieutenant Berg.

"They left very early..." – replied the butler.

"Madame wanted to go to church to order a mass for Sylvie's soul!"

"Do you know which church?" – asks the Lieutenant.

"No, sir. But I think it is the Sacré–Cœur, because that is where Madam usually attends Sunday mass."

"So they should be back soon. I do not think they will be in the mood to wander around the Cité..."

"Certainly not, *Monsieur le comandante*..." – replies the butler.

"Feel free to wait for them if you wish..."

In the meantime, François starts to climb the gray granite steps and, running up the stairs, screaming, he goes in search of his beloved's room. The butler follows him, his eyes highly appalled.

"Come on, let us follow him!" – Berg suggests.

François, overcome with despair, was already searching Sylvie's old room, opening the wardrobe doors, looking under the bed, behind the curtains...

"Where have you been, *mon amour*? Are you hiding from me?" – he said, tears streaming down his cheeks, as he desperately searched for his beloved.

"Come on, stop playing games, I miss you so much! Come on, come out..."

Berg and Pierre only followed him with their eyes as he intensely scrutinized his dead girlfriend's old room. Finally defeated, he fell to his knees and burts into intense sobs of convulsive weeping.

"François!" – says Berg, approaching him.

"Come on! Let us go downstairs and sit and wait for Sylvie's parents! They are not at home! They have gone to church to order a... a..." – the Lieutenant did not want to finish his sentence, for fear of another hysterical attack from the other.

"Come, let us sit in the living room and wait for them..."

"So, Sylvie is with them!" – François's eyes suddenly light up, and he stood up quickly.

"So that is it!" – and pointing at the butler, he continues:

"Why did that creep not tell us right away that she was out walking with her parents?"

Berg and Pierre exchange a brief glance. The butler lowered his eyes. He began to feel very compassionate towards the boy. It was obvious that he was losing his mind...

"Drink, it will do you good!" – Berg said to François a short while later, when they were already sitting in the living room, offering the young man one of the two glasses of wine that Pierre had kindly brought them on a tray.

"Will they be long?" – asks François, barely touching his lips to the ruby–red liquid.

"What did you say they were doing? Oh, I know! They went for a walk in the Cité... Certainly, Sylvie went to eat *tarte à fromage* at the *pâtisserie* on *Boulevard Saint–Denis*..." – he says, his eyes lighting up with intense brightness.

"You know, Berg, she loves *tarte à fromage*, and then boating on the river! Sylvie is truly tireless! The last time we were there, she nearly killed me with exhaustion as she made me of row the boat up and down the river non–stop; she wouldn't stop, up and down the river non–stop! Ha! Ha! Ha! Ha! But I do not mind! Not a bit! It kills me to row the boat so much, but the pay I get makes up for it enormously: I keep seeing her face, her eyes, all the time! There is no better landscape for me!"

Berg looks at him with pity. Poor boy! Could he not bear the weight of this tragedy? What would life hold for him from now on? And his mother, who had only him for a son, how would she react? Poor aunt *Amandine*! François's mother was his aunt, his mother's younger sister. Both were war widows. Two lonely women, living in huge houses full of memories and ghosts!

"Poor Maman! Poor Amandine!" – thought Berg.

"You too are victims of this cruel and unfortunate life that we have all been living lately! We do everything for peace, equality, fraternity, freedom... But when has there ever really been peace? Never! We have definitely never lived in peace!"

"Berg..." – François's voice snapped him out of his thoughts.

"I am leaving the army! I am going to marry Sylvie. I definitely do not want to follow a military career! I will not follow in the footsteps of Papa and my ancestors! Look, I am going back to the *Lycée des Offices*! I want to get involved and maybe study medicine... I want to start a family with Sylvie, in peace! No battlefields, no medals on my chest!" – and, looking at the other man, his eyes red and badly affected by the intense crying, he continued:

"I want to be happy, Berg!"

Wilfred Berg swallowed. He lowered his eyes, deeply pitying his cousin. The situation was worse than he thought. He felt powerless in the face of it. It was new, unusual for him. Hewas used to living with misfortune, with extreme pain. He dealt with life and death on a daily basis. He thought he was strong enough; but his cousin's situation was making him weak. Good heavens! How to act in that situation? It was one thing to console strangers, to deal with other people's pain. However, now the pain was right next to him, in his family! In a way, he felt responsible for François! He had always protected him. He felt in him the brother he had not had and he knew this feeling was reciprocal. Even though he was much older than François, that was how François felt about him too, Berg.

"You will do what is best for you!" – replies Berg, holding his hand tightly.

"And I will always be ready to help you in whatever you need..."

"Thank you, Berg..." – says the other, opening a smile full of gratitude.

"Sylvie and I will be eternally grateful to you..."

In a corner, Pierre watched in silence. Poor boy! He did not like him. They had never really been nice to each other. They used to get jealous of each other; but now, what Pierre felt was intense pity for the wretch! He knew these things that attacked people's heads were usually very serious! Would to God that that poor devil could bear the terrible blow that fate had prepared for him! Was he, Pierre, not suffering too? Perhaps even more than the boy, since he was not there, day after day, by her side? It was hell for him too, living in that house without her, but he stood firm. Suffering hell, but standing firm! People were definitely not the same, they did not behave in the same way when faced with life's great trials! Some endured the hard knocks of life with a certain resignation; others, however, allowed themselves to become dementia!

"Do you not think Pierre is a jerk like that?" – François whispers in Berg's ear.

"I wonder why Colonel Rousselet keeps a vulgar fellow like that in his house?"

"Sssh!" – says Berg. And, with a slight smile, he continues:

"He is twice your size, isn't he? If he listens to what you are saying about him..."

The other also laughed amusedly. He loved to poke fun at his enemy. Poor guy! Temporarily, he forgot his pain and little did he know that it would return, very soon, more painful, more forceful, even more devastating...

Chapter 9

Faced with Extreme Pain

François and Berg had been waiting for the Rousselet couple for an hour and a half when they suddenly heard the sound of the vestibule door open, after a click of the doorknob.

"The bosses are back!" – Pierre exclaimed, coming out of the bovine muteness he had been keeping all this time, standing in a corner of the living room. And, ready as a cat, he went to greet the owners of the house, who, highly dejected, were returning from their morning foray.

"You have visitors, gentlemen!" – he said in a low voice, telling them that François and Berg were in the house.

"Who will be there at this hour?" – asked Edith-Aurore, visibly upset. She felt so discouraged to talk to anyone.

Pierre did not have to answer his mistress' question. François was right behind him and, rudely pushing the butler aside, he jumped on top of him and, without even greeting his beloved's astonished parents, asked them, bursting with anxiety:

"Where is she? Where is Sylvie? Did she not come with you to the Cité?"

Colonel Rousselet and his wife exchange astonished looks.

"François! Oh, François!" – exclaims Edith–Aurore, holding out her arms to the boy and, bursting into abundant tears, she continues:

"So have they not told you yet, dear?"

"They told me what?" – he replies, letting himself be hugged by his old girlfriend's mother.

"Why is not Sylvie with you? Where did you leave her? Do you not know that it is very dangerous to leave a maiden wandering around Cité alone? Oh, Edith..." – and, shaking his head in disapproval, turned to Sylvie's father:

"And you, Colonel, should know how dangerous Paris has been lately! Oh, tell me where you left her and I will go and get her right away!"

At this moment, Lieutenant Berg had already approached and exchanged a brief, meaningful glance with Sylvie's parents. Understanding the situation, Colonel Rousselet gently touches the boy's shoulder and invites him in:

"Oh, François, come with us! Let us sit down and we will explain! Pierre will pour us a glass of wine and then we will talk!"

Edith–Aurore embraced the boy and gently led him into the living room. Sitting next to his beloved's mother, who had taken his hands in hers and was caressing them, full of zeal, François was highly agitated. It was clear that his emotional state was altered; his hair was disheveled; his eyes restless, moved restlessly in their sockets, as if searching for something; the flaps of his nose, widely dilated, indicated that he was having difficulty breathing; his hands were always trembling, cold and sweaty. Even his uniform, which he had always worn impeccably, was battered, with streaks of dirt around the flaps of his trouser pockets, as well as unusual dirt on his coat. Poor François! He was a slob!

"You still have not told me where Sylvie is!" – he says, abruptly removing his hands from Edith–Aurore's.

"I am starting to lose patience!" – he exclaimed, with a terrible gleaming in his eyes. And, turning to Sylvie's father, he says ostentatiously:

"Colonel Rousselet, why are you lying to me? Come on, tell me once and for all: where is your daughter?"

Hippolyte–Antoine Rousselet looked, somewhat bewildered, at Wilfred Berg, who until then had remained silent, watching everything, and asked:

"Have you told him the truth, Lieutenant?"

"Yes, Colonel..." – replies the other.

"But he refuses to believe it..."

"Sylvie is dead, Cadet Rounet!" – says the Colonel, his voice strong, looking the boy in the eye.

"And I believe they have already told you! It is horrible, it is very sad to tell you this, but it is true! Smallpox killed our little girl!"

The boy began to tremble and his eyes filled with tears. A convulsive cry came over him, and he let himself fall to his knees, slowly, under the thick wool carpet. He wrings his hands in a fit of extreme nervous imbalance, and then he screams at the top of his lungs:

"No! It is not true! Colonel Rousselet, you are a liar! You and Berg are liars!" – and turning to Edith–Aurore, who was also bursting into tears, and he said to her, his words wet with tears:

"And you, Edith? Do you also confirm that she has gone?"

Colonel Rousselet's wife was unable to answer with words, as her throat was clogged with tears and an immense knot of pain and anguish. She merely shook her head, looking him in the eye, an eye that showed a mixture of despair, extreme pain and expectation, the ultimate expectation, a last, fleeting hope....

At Edith–Aurore's affirmative response, François let out a loud cry of pain and, getting up, ran wildly towards the door to the vestibule.

Astonished, the three men quickly ran after him too. The young Cadet, agile as a fox, reached the door to the vestibule and, jumping up and down, overcame the small staircase that led to the entrance door, and in a flash, opening the iron barred gate, he quickly gained the street.

"Do not let him get away!" – Berg shouted at Pierre, who, being the youngest of the three, managed to quickly catch up with François, who was already leading the way, running like a madman down the middle of the street.

"Grab him! If we lose him, he will be difficult to catch later!"

Pierre, in fact, being the biggest of the three, easily managed to jump on the runaway and overpowered him with relative ease, as the other was highly dejected from days of almost complete starvation he had been subjected to. Applying a strong tie, the butler managed to subdue him. In the meantime, the boy was kicking and screaming like an hallucinated man. With the help of Berg and Colonel Rousselet, they managed to bring François back home. Then, using strips of cloth, they manacled him tightly, tying his ankles together, and made him sit on the carpet in the living room.

"What do you think we should do now?" – Colonel Rousselet asks Lieutenant Berg. "Do you not think we should call a doctor?"

"Yes…" – replies Berg.

"However, before that, his mother needs to be notified. Leave that to me, because, as you know, she is my aunt."

An hour later, Wilfred Berg was leaving the rental car in front of the Rounet family's old gray granite house. He stopped for a moment in front of the high gate with its dark bars and surveyed the sober façade of the manor house where the Marquise of Montpelier lived.

"Poor aunt Amandine!" – thinks Berg.

"Another blow to her poor heart!" He looks at the house once more. The manor of the Marquises of Montpelier… And, very sadly, his Aunt's features flash through his mind. She was his mother's youngest sister. She had married Louis-Henri Rounet, the heir to the Marquises of Montpelier. Berg remembers his big uncle, in his imposing uniform, his chest covered in glittering medals. But, like his own father, his uncle had also died in the bloody war of conquest of Algeria!" For a few more moments, Berg stood in front of the gate, his thoughts lost in his reminiscences. Everything was running out... People nearby were dying, or went mad... François... Céleste–Marie... Good heavens! A shiver ran through him from top to bottom and he was suddenly afraid. He was getting lonely! Alone in this wretched world! Then, resolute, he opened the gate and went inside. Now was the time to kill Amandine, to stab her fatally.

"Oh, is it you?" – exclaimed the Marquise de Montpelier, smiling broadly when she saw that it was her nephew who had entered the room.

"*Ma tante...*"[1] – said the Lieutenant, kissing affectionately the perfumed cheek that his aunt, full of expectation, was presenting to him.

"So, are you back in Paris?" – exclaims the exquisite, exuberant–looking woman, despite being quite mature, alreadywell into her fifty years old. Amandine sits down on a chaise longue upholstered in sky–blue velvet and, indicating a large, comfortable divan to the young man, continues, now with an air of concern:

"You have recently been on leave, and now you are already back... Do not tell me something has happened?"

Berg looks her in the eye. She already sensed doom. Mothers have a special sense for such things...

"*Oui,*" – he replies laconic, lowering his eyes.

---

[1] "My aunt...", in French.

"You are not going to tell me that something happened to François, Armand?!" – exclaimed Amandine Rounet, suddenly turning pale and leaning back on her couch.

"Come on, Wilfred! Do not hide anything from me! Tell me: is François dead?"

"Oh, no! No..." – Berg hastened to reply, noticing that his aunt had gone very pale.

"I mean, not exactly... dead..."

"I do not understand what you are saying, my son!" – exclaims the Marquise, overcome with grief.

"If you say he is not dead, then what?"

"François is ill, Auntie!" – Berg replies.

"My cousin is ill and you need to see him!"

"But, do I have to go all the way to Algeria?" – the woman in amazed.

"No. François is right here in Paris" – the young man replies.

"So, is he in the army hospital?" – she asks.

"No, *ma tante*. He is at Colonel Rousselet's!"

Shortly afterwards, in the luxurious coach that was taking them to the Colonel Rousselet's residence, Wilfred Berg was telling his aunt in detail about the latest developments in François–Armand situation.

"I always thought that François would not be able to bear this setback that has befallen him!" – exclaimed Amandine, her eyes welling up with tears for the first time since she had learned what was happening to her son.

"He has always been weak in the heart! You know how he is! Not everyone has the same fortitude in the face of life's vicissitudes!" – and, shaking her head slightly, she continued, with a tone of intense bitterness in her voice:

"I do not know... I think I protected him too much! I saved him a lot of grief. I hid the true face of the world from him! I did not want him to suffer! And yet..."

"Oh, dear!" – says Berg, feeling sorry for her. He takes her hand and squeezes it tightly.

"You did what was best for François! You were his mother and his father too! And if you ask me, your son has become a great man! Contrary to what you might think, he is not a coward! He always showed courage and bravery in the face of danger! I am telling you because I am his superior, and I am watching him carefully! Rest assured: your son is a real man! It is just that he has come up against an enemy stronger than himself: his own heart! François was defeated by the wiles of passion! Are there any things more treacherous than that in this world? And who can do anything against such traps? No one, my dear, no one at all...

Amandine let out a deep sigh. That young man next to her had just temporarily eased the anguish in her chest. And, bringing his hand, which she held between hers, to her lips, she kissed it tenderly.

"*Merci beaucoup*, Wilfred!" – she exclaims, smiling slightly in gratitude.

"With your words, you have eased my pain a little. And what do you think we should do about your cousin?"

"I suggest that we first go to a specialist doctor." – the young man said seriously.

"I firmly believe that François will overcome this crisis! He is young, still very young! He will have enough time to restructure his life! With your unstinting help, I know he will be able to overcome this terrible struggle! Let us trust that everything will work out!"

"Oh, God be right, my dear!" – exclaims Amandine.

May God be right!"

The reunion with her son was touching. François was showing strong signs of madness. He was extremely agitated, talked loudly, became aggressive and violent. He hardly cared about his mother's presence. He just stared at her, without showing any sign of actually recognizing her. And when she, weeping and overcome, got down on her knees in front of him on the wool carpet in the Rousselet's living room and hugged him, sobbing, the young man became more agitated and tried to bite her, in a ferocious and highly hostile attitude.

"You're right!" – exclaims Amandine, her eyes streaming with tears, after realizing the seriousness of her son's case.

"A specialist doctor must be called in without further ado. My son has gone mad!"

A few hours later, an ambulance pulled up in front of the Rousselet manor. Restraining the maddened boy proved was no easy task for the pair of strong nurses who were there at the request of the doctor who had previously come to examine François. After a meticulous and preliminary clinical examination, Dr. Edouard Leforestier decided to have the boy admitted to the Charenton[2] clinic, located near Paris and famous for its research and treatment of mental illness in particular.

Berg and Amandine, along with Dr. Leforestier, followed the ambulance in the Marquise's large carriage. Amandine Rounet sobbed quietly, hugging her nephew, who tried to comfort the poor mother with tender words.

"He will be fine! He will be fine! It ifs just a nervous breakdown! You will see, he will be back with us soon!"

The Charenton Hospital had been founded in the 17th century and, after the monumental renovations it had received years earlier, it was an excellent center for medical treatment and a reference point for Europe at the time.

"In Charenton, François will be well looked after, *n'est-ce pas, Monsieur le docteur?*"[3]

"Perfectly, Lieutenant!" – replies the doctor solicitously.

---

[2] Charenton was founded in 1645 and was originally maintained by a religious brotherhood. After a brief period of closure during the French Revolution, the hospital was reopened and became a state institution.

Subsequently, a general restructuring work, based on a project begun in June 1838, resulted in the construction of a new, monumental building. Located six miles south-east of Paris, Charenton housed between 600 and 700 patients, as of 1870. Most of the patients admitted to the large institution belonged to the more favoured social classes. Charenton not only treated psychiatric patients; it also housed convalescent surgeries, as well as those affected by fevers and other illnesses. In 1973, this monumental institution was renamed the Hôpital Esquirol, in honour of its famous director of the late 19th century, Jean-Etienne-Dominique Esquirol.

[3] True, doctor? – in French.

"Without any shadow of a doubt, our clinic is currently the most qualified in the whole of Europe! You certainly will not find more modern care anywhere else than in Charenton!

Amandine felt a little more encouraged after hearing Dr. Leforestier's reassuring words.

"Please, do not mistreat *mon petit garcon, n'est-ce pas?*"[4] – asked Amandine, full of apprehension.

"We hear so many things about the treatment of the insane... A lot of abuse! Cold baths in the morning, snake pits, simulated falls and fires, as well as scorpions and spiders bites! Scares and more scares for the poor! I hear they are even using electricity! Just imagine! They shock their heads!"

"Oh, certainly not, Madam..." – replies the doctor, with a sardonic laugh.

"As I said, Charenton is a model of treatment for all illnesses, especially mental disorders. Rest assured that your son will be treated with the utmost respect and dignity by the entire team, which, it should be noted, is made up of people who are highly specialized in dealing with this kind of patient, something which, I confess to you that is not an easy task! In the meantime, rest assured, because I give you my word of honor that all these things you have heard are nothing more than people's wildest imaginations! They are just wild fantasies! In Charenton, only drugs are used! Medications and nothing else! There are already substances, extracted from herbs from the East and the New World, which have been attributed exceptional healing powers for a whole range of ailments! We have already widely tested the action of these

---

[4] (...) my little son...! – in French.

substances on our patients and have obtained a large number of cures. But you have to trust!"

An hour and a half later, having overcome the distance of almost ten kilometers between the clinic and the center of Paris, you can see the imposing building rising from the middle of the well-kept forest. And as the coach made its way the few remaining meters to the main entrance, Amandine studied, with highly oppressed eyes, the extensive and well-kept park that surrounded the lush clinic. And, under the shade of the verdant grove, a countless patients, clad in bright cotton nightgowns and accompanied by diligent nurses, rested at dusk, reclining placidly in lazy chairs or sitting in wheelchairs. The apparent tranquility of the place momentarily calmed the woman's desperate heart.

The ambulance had pulled ahead of the carriage in which the three of them were traveling. When the carriage parked in front of the imposing white marble staircase that led up to the main entrance of the building, François-Armand was already being taken out of the car with the help of two more nurses who, ready, rushed to help the two companions who were running themselves ragged in the face of the boy's reluctance to peacefully accept his admission to the clinic. François-Armand was extremely agitated. Even when he was restrained in a straitjacket, he was extremely vigorous, attempting to hit the nurses who were caring for him on the head, or biting their hands, or even kicking them violently. It was very difficult for the nurses to get the boy onto a stretcher and tie his feet and head firmly, as his arms were already restrained by the straitjacket.

"Let's take him to one of the padded cells…" – ordered the doctor who was supervising the patient's transportation.

"Carefully, so that he does not hurt himself!"

Amandine and Berg accompanied the transport of the boy to one of the wards of the very large clinic, which was intended for mentally ill people who were kept in seclusion. The poor mother was sobbing quietly as she followed the sad procession through the endless corridors of the hospital. François, his eyes wildly wide, did not seem to realize where he was. He emitted weak cries, as his voice had already gone weak, and his mouth was filled with viscous, abundant drool, which gathered at the corners of his lips and soaked his chin and chest. Poor François–Armand! How pathetic it was to see him like that, for someone who had known him as a dash and vain young man, so careful in his personal hygiene and in the neatness and refinement of the clothes he wore! What excessive pain does not cause. When there is too much suffering, it can lead to total insanity! Few are those who manage to endure the great trials that life invariably presents to everyone, without allowing themselves to be overcome by extreme despair and facing everything with resignation and patience!

"We need to leave him alone for a while…" – said the doctor, spying through the small screen of the locked cell door, the boy who was struggling furiously, throwing himself against the wall and rolling on the floor, overcome with extreme despair.

"Soon, his fury will cool down and he will be prostrated! Then, we will begin his treatment! Have confidence, madam! Your son is in the right place!"

Amandine sobbed intensely as the sight of her son's dementia. Faced with such an eloquent display of madness, it was hard for her to believe that the boy would one day come to his senses.

"God be right, *Monsieur le docteur*!" – she cried out.

"May God hear you!"

"Let's go, Auntie!" – invites Berg, taking her gently by the arm.

"What we have to do for him, we have already done! Now we just have to stay calm and wait!"

It was dark outside when they both took the carriage back home. The majestic woods that surrounded the imposing hospital were now deserted: no one was there but the gentle wind, the spring breeze, tenderly cradling the branches of the grove, which was peacefully allowing itself to be dyed black by the hands of the coming night...

Berg drives his aunt back home. The Marquise of Montpelier was still extremely upset and distraught.

"Do you not want me to take you home with me?" – asked the boy, deeply moved by the terrible situation in which his aunt found herself.

"You can stay with Mom! I am absolutely sure she will welcome you with open arms!"

"*Oh, non, mon chéri!*" – replies the matron.

"Better to mull over my pain alone!" – and with a bitter smile, she continued:

"I am used to solitude! Do not worry: life has just added a little more absinthe to my soul! Nothing more! Go in peace and do not forget to pass on my regards to Simone..."

Berg says goodbye to the suffering woman, hugging her tightly and kissing her tear-stained cheek. Then he hurries off. The carriage was waiting for him, parked in front of the mansion, and he decided to go to his mother's house. He had not been there since he arrived in Paris. His mother complained about him all the time: when he came back to the city first, he visited everyone: Céleste-Marie, his friends, the bars, Lulú Fontainebleau's house, the last was always her.

"Poor mother!" – he thought.

"You are always alone too, lost in your memories..."

"Oh, what happened to you to be back to Paris so quickly? It is not even a month since you returned to Algeria... You are not going to tell me that damn war is over?" – remarks his mother, highly intrigued, as she sees him entering the hall.

"No, Maman, the war is not over yet..." – he says, hugging her tightly and kissing her cheek.

"I had to accompany François-Armand back."

"François?!" – asks Simone-Francine d'Oubigny Berg, holding his hand tightly and finding it extremely strange.

"But, was he not recently on leave, just when you were here too?" – asks the woman, suddenly overcome with pallor. And she orders resolutely, looking him in the eye:

"Come on, Wilfred, tell me: what happened to him?"

"François is ill." – the boy replied, letting himsefl sit down heavily onto the sofa. And, realizing that his mother was deeply moved, he said to her:

"But, calm down! Come, sit here and I will tell you everything!"

"*Oh, mon Dieu!*" – exclaimed Simone–Francine, getting up, highly upset by the news her son had brought her.

"Oh, poor François! Poor Amandine! And how is my sister?"

"*Ma tante is*, of course, completely desperate." – the boy remarked.

"Oh, and why did you not bring her here with you? She needs to be looked after!"

"I invited her, but she did not accept…" – says the boy.

"No!" – says the woman.

"I will get the carriage ready right away and I will go there!"

"Are you going out at night, alone?" – the boy is astonished.

"I will!" – replies the woman resolutely.

"Besides, it is not that late, and Benoît, the coachman, will be with me driving the car! Besides, your aunt does not live far from here! It is only three kilometers! No! No! Absolutely not! I will not leave my sister alone at such a difficult time! I know that now, as tired as you are, you will sleep like a stone until tomorrow! Have you eaten? No? But you will manage with the servants, *n'est–ce pas?* Oh, poor

François! Did you know he is my godson? Your father and I baptized him! Oh, you poor thing!"

His mother left him, getting ready to leave, and Berg remained alone in the huge living room. How nicel it was to be there, surrounded by comfort! Mentally, he compared it to his little shack in the lodge. There, there was an excess of comfort. There, there was the complete absence of everything; only what is strictly necessary. His eyes scan the extensive gallery of portraits on the wall in front of him: his maternal grandfather, General Frédéric-Armand d'Oubigny, all decked out in his sumptuous uniform, with medals on his chest. Then his eyes stop on the portrait of his father. His father! So little had he lived with him! But he knew he had loved him very much! A knot of emotion fills his throat, and he gets up and stands in front of his father's imposing portrait. He scrutinized the smallest details of the physiognomy so skillfully reproduced on the canvas: the deep blue, sparkling eyes, the slightly bald forehead, the vast light mustache, the triangular goatee, the hair as yellow as ripe wheat... His father had been a handsome man! How many things had that brave German not had to give up in order to keep his love? He had giving up his promising military career and his German citizenship to be with his beloved! How many prejudices did he have to overcome to fulfill his dream of love! As a soldier, he had to end his carrier early in his country, but as a man, he had become great in the forge of suffering...

"*Monsieur le commandant!*" – he hears the butler's voice calling him from behind him.

"What is it, Sébastien?" – asks Berg, without turning around.

"Your mother sent me to prepare dinner for you..."

Later, back in his room and lying on his large bed, Berg would go over the recent events in his mind. The pathetic image of his cousin, all disheveled, came to his mind.

"Poor boy!" – he thought.

"What will become of you from now on? I will miss our conversations at dusk in front of my tent..." Then his thoughts flew to Céleste–Marie. She certainly did not dream he would be back in such a short time. Céleste–Marie... His fiancée's situation worried him enormously. He knew that the girl had weak nerves, that she would not be able to withstand the strongest clash than life might throw at her and that, inevitably, as had happened to his cousin, it would end up happening to her too. He had to be very careful with this kind of creature, so sensitive, so fragile in the face of a setback! They lost their senses so easily!

When dawn breaks, Berg wakes up and realizes that daylight is streaming through the gaps in the window. He decided to leave his bed, as the morning should be well advanced. He needed to make good use of the time; his leave would not last more than a week and there was so much to do in Paris!

While getting dressed and looking at himself in the large crystal mirror, Berg listed the day's task. First, he was going to Montmartre. He wanted to surprise Céleste–Marie! He would invite her to lunch at a boulangerie in the Cité, and then he would go to meet General du Servey. He would like to talk to the old military man. He was always up to date with the main events in the city, and was a man of firm character and confident propositions, always ready to assert and make thoughtful judgments about the most varied events and also about the new discoveries in science that were being presented to the public every day.

An hour and a half later, Lieutenant Berg jumped out of the rental car in front of the old mansion that Céleste–Marie and her mother occupied in Montmartre.

"*Toi?!*"[5] – Céleste–Marie was enormously surprised to see that it was he who was waiting for her, anxiously in the living room.

"But you came back so quickly!"

"I had to accompany François–Armand, my cousin..."

"François!" – wonders the girl.

"But what is wrong with him that he could not return alone?"

"François is ill, Céleste–Marie..."

"Oh, was he wounded in battle?"

"Not exactly..."

"What is wrong with him?"

"You know that Sylvie left recently, *n'est–ce pas?*" – says Berg.

"Oh, yes!" replies the girl.

"We were at her wake, Maman and me."

"And you knew they were both boyfriend and girlfriend, right? François could not bear the pain of losing Sylvie, and..."

5

"I see..." Céleste–Marie put up with it, lowering her eyes sadly.

"And where is he now?"

"We sent him to Charenton..."

"Did it have to come to that?" – she wonders.

"You have no idea how much..." – he explains.

"He was furious! He had to be locked up in a padded cell!"

"Oh, poor François!"

A heavy silence then fell between them, during which Berg began to study Céleste–Marie's features in detail: her long hair falling over her shoulders in a wavy cascade of mistletoe and contrasting expressively with her white, soft complexion; the dark, frightened, eyes, slightly sunken and surrounded by almost imperceptible but stubborn dark circles under her eyes; her lips slightly arched downwards, indicating her usual absence of laughter... Céleste–Marie hardly laughed at all. She remained silent and sullen the whole time, in her usual endless bad mood.

"I think I will end up in Charenton too..." – she says quietly, almost in a whisper.

"Why do you say that?" – asks Berg, getting extremely upset.

"You have no reason to say such nonsense!"

"That's what you think, Wilfred!" – she says, abruptly getting up, from the sofa. And, being highly agitated, she taps her chest with her fingertips and continues, looking at him with eyes full of despair.

"You have no idea what I am carrying around inside me, trapped like an abject monster gnawing at my soul, relentlessly and mercilessly! You and Mom think I invent such things, don't you? Well, you are both completely wrong... That, or whatever it is, will eventually drive me mad... If it does not kill me first!"

Berg looks at her, very worried. Until now, he had not taken what he thought were simple chirps from Céleste–Marie seriously enough. However, after seeing his cousin literally collapse after Sylvie's death, he became seriously worried. What if she really was ill? What if she suddenly started behaving like his cousin, becoming so enraged that he had to keep her in custody, also in a padded cell?

"Come, sit here and tell me everything that is on your mind!" – he says, his voice full of tenderness.

"Do you not trust me?"

"That is not it!" – she retorted, extremely agitated.

"It's not a question of trust, Berg!" – and nervously wringing her hands and reluctant to sit down again next to him on the sofa, she continued:

"You and Mom have shown very simplistic attitudes towards what I am feeling! You think that doctors and medicines will solve these things for me! But I do not feel that way!"

"Come! Sit here!" – he repeats. "Let's talk!"

"Oh, Berg! Berg!" – she bursts into tears as she hugs him back on the sofa.

"Sometimes I feel so far way from you and it is so hard for me to open my heart to you! I am afraid you will think I am crazy and leave me forever!"

"Oh, silly you!" – he says, tenderly stroking her back with his hands.

"How can you think such things about me? How long have you and I been together? Long enough, I think, for you to know me well enough to deduce that I would never leave you for the world! Never! You know how much I love you!"

"Oh, how it is to hear that from you!" – she says, calming down a little more.

"But I want you to know that things are getting harder and harder for me every day! I do not know if I can hold on!"

"If you tell me everything that is on your mind, who knows, if I will be able to help you more than those know–it–all doctors?" – he jokes, giving her a mischievous smile. It was an attempt to make her laugh, to forget her suffering...

"You know how doctors think they know everything..."

"Only you can make me laugh, Berg!" – she says, cracking a smile.

"Look, why do we not have lunch in the Cité?" – he invites her, taking advantage of the gap she has opened up for him.

"Then we will go to the barracks to visit General du Servey... What do you think?"

"I think I would like to go out for a while!" – she says, after a moment's thought.

"I am alone. Maman went to church."

"Then go!" – he says, pushing her gently.

"Hurry up and get ready!"

Céleste–Marie kisses him unexpectedly and effusively on the mouth and, like a little girl, almost runs away.

"Do not leave, huh?" – she shouts from the middle of the stairs.

"If I am late, it is because I am doing my makeup!"

Berg laughs at her spontaneous manner. He liked the way Céleste–Marie acted: always surprising him with her unexpected behavior! And he wondered if it was not just a lack of affection that she felt... was it not a lack of love? Once again, Lieutenant Berg is mortified. If he chose to live only next to his love, would life perhaps not be smoother, more fulfilling? Why did he have to devote himself so much to patriotic duties? Had he already not done enough? Had his family not devoted themselves almost exclusively to France, for generations, tirelessly fighting for the ideals of liberty, equality, and fraternity among peoples? Was it not time to think about himself, about his own well–being, to start his own family, and alongside Céleste–Marie, to see his children born?"

"What would family and children be worth without freedom?" – he mutters softly, bitterly, with a huge knot forming in his throat.

Then he gets up and slowly walks over the window. He pulled aside the white lace curtain and looked outside: few passers–by were walking along the street, despite the sun flooding everything with its brilliant light. "Why look for non-existent happiness amid this chaos? First, we need to re-establish hierarchy and order and strengthen the foundations of the Republic..." he thinks, gazing at the piece of blue sky visible from the window.

"Then we need to build a society based on the principles of liberty, equality, and fraternity... And I sense that this will not happen just yet! It will be a long time and a lot of blood before these things are actually established among us..."

Wilfred, visibly bitter, reaches into the pockets of his dark blue tunic and pulls out his cigarette packet. Then he sat back down on the divan and gazed inexpressively at the column of blue gray smoke that was forming above his head. Céleste-Marie was lingering... And she was going to take a long time yet. He knew her well enough: she used to spend forever on her make-up... and, sighing deeply, Lieutenant Berg looked down at the burning cigarette clutched between his fingers and then took a long drag. He knew he had to be patient, very patient...

Chapter 10

In Charenton

The nurse slowly opens the peephole in the padded cell and peeks inside. Huddled in a corner, François–Armand was hugging his knees and resting his chin on them. Dressed in a white cotton sweater and visibly slim and very unkempt, the boy was apparently calmer; all that intense agitation had given way to an aloof passivity. Not even the slightest movement was noticeable, not even in his eyes, which were fixed, stopped in a void and filles with an almost frightening inexpressiveness.

"He has calmed down..." – whispers the nurse to the doctor accompanying her. The doctor went ahead and spies on him tool.

"I think I can go in now..." – says the doctor. And turning to the nurse, he orders:

"Open the door!"

The doctor crouches down in front of the boy and studies him meticulously. François–Armand does not react in the slightest.

"Are you going to start the therapy today, doctor?" – asks the nurse in a low voice.

"I don't think so..." – replies the doctor.

"He is still in a deep state of apathy. Let's wait a little longer. By the way, has he been eating? Has he been drinking water?"

"Very little, doctor..." – replied the nurse, as they both left François's cell and walk side by side down the hospital long corridor.

"Let's take a close look at this..." – recommends the doctor.

"And continue the administering camphor[1] every two hours. Has he experiencing seizures symptoms?"

---

[1] The first descriptions of the use of camphor in the treatment of people with mental disorders date back to the 16th century, when Paracelsus used it to cure "lunatics". The resumption of this procedure is attributed to the Austrian doctor Leopold Von Avenbrugger who, from 1764, treated *mania vivorum* with camphor, administered every two hours, until the convulsions appeared. At first, camphor was used for this procedure and then, with the development of pharmaceutical chemistry, cardiazole or metrazol (pentylenetetrazol) was used. Thus, convulsive therapy was widely used in the treatment of some psychopathy's, since psychiatric treatment options until the third decade of the 20th century were quite limited. Until then, for outpatients, treatment was almost entirely restricted to psychotherapy and, for inpatients, practically nothing could be done except provide social support, sedation and vigilance so that they didn't harm themselves or others. It wasn't until the second decade of the 20th century that psychiatry showed its first advances, and the main existing treatments consisted of Wagner-Jauregg's malarial fever therapy (1917), Klaesi's prolonged sleeping therapy (1922) and convulsive therapy, recovered by Ladislas Joseph von Meduna (1930), who resumed camphor injections at first and then Pentylenetetrazol. However, the first major treatment uncontested by science and widely used by psychiatry was electroconvulsive therapy (electroshock), used from 1937 onwards following research by Italian doctors Ugo Cerletti and Lucio Bini, as well as Sakel's insulin coma (1933) and Moniz's psychosurgery (1935).

"No, sir..." – replied the nurse.

"After applying the medicine, he has not shown any significant reaction: just tremors and spasms, nothing more."

"Continue with the camphor. If he does not react, we will move on to the eel shock[2]. We have to make him convulse or he will not get out of this crisis..."

Alone in his cell, François did not react in the slightest. He had already been in Charenton for five days. For the first few days, in a rage of insanity, he had systematically thrown himself headlong against the walls of the cell in an attempt to destroy himself. At first, he still had a glimmer of reason. However, as the days went by, the loss of Sylvie seemed insurmountable. He could not accept such a blow from fate. Good heavens! How cruel it seemed! He screamed with all his might at the revolt that was eating away at his soul! No, he would never accept that! To live without her love? Never! Death is a thousand times preferable! And, with extreme despair overpowering his reason, he threw himself screaming, against the padded walls of the cell in which they had locked him up!

How many times had he tried? He had tried so hard, until he got tired, until he collapsed from intense fatigue. And, after a short rest, when he had regained a little strength, he would try again and again, but to no avail... Poor François! How long had he stood there like a puppet, manipulated by demonic and invisible hands, performing such degrading jumps against the mattress–covered wall! Then he would run

---

[2] In Ancient Rome, doctors used electroshock treatment with electric eels. It is also recorded in the papyri that Ramses II, king of Ancient Egypt, was treated with electroshock by a doctor of that time.

out of steam and gone to sleep! He slept so much, he slept for many hours, for more than a whole day and night... and when he finally opened his eyes, he no longer recognized anything about the place or himself: it was total alienation! His eyes saw nothing but emptiness; his head buzzed, just emptiness, total nullity... Nothing or no one else came to mind... Only thirst... He registered his thirst, his dry mouth and, next to him, water in a small waxed cardboard container, but he did not relate it with the sensation of thirst. His muscles were tight from the syncope of the previous days. He wanted to get up, but his legs would not let him. The hours drained away slowly, interminably, horribly slowly. Was it night or day?

At some point, the peephole in the cell door opens and a pair of scrutinizing eyes appear. But François did not even know what they were. Then there was the sound of a key in the lock, the door opened and two nurses came in and squatted down in front of him.

"He must be given the medicine!" – exclaims one of the men and orders his companion:

"Get the water."

The other man reaches out and picks up the paper cup that was lying on the floor close to the wall and then, from the tray he had brought with him, picks up a small bottle and lets a few drops of the clear liquid pour into the water.

"He must be dying of thirst!" – said the nurse smiling slightly.

"He will not give us any trouble! He will drink water!"

François remained impassive in front of the two men. His eyes remained still, staring into the void, without showing any expressiveness.

After waiting for a few moments for the medicine to mix completely with the water, one of the men presented the glass in front of the patient's eyes. François did not react. Slowly, then, the nurse brought the glass to his lips and, upon contact with the water, the boy began to sip slowly, with difficulty, as his mouth and tongue were still numb from the excessive screaming and gnashing of teeth over the previous few days. Little by little, he sipped all the liquid.

"We will not be giving him more water for a while" – says one of the nurses.

"Let's keep him thirsty all the time, to make it easier for us to give him the medicine!"

"Yes!" – agrees the other.

"And we are not going to leave any more water here! Since we have to come back in two hours..."

"I do not think he will have a seizure yet..."

"This is unlikely to happen at the beginning of the treatment, but we will have to keep an eye on things..."

The nurses squatted in front of the boy, testing his reactions. Apart from a series of strong tremors, François showed nothing different; he remained apathetic. After twenty minutes, the nurses got up and prepared to leave the cell.

"Let's go!" – exclaims one of them.

"He is not going to wake up very easily!"

"I do not think so either..." – agrees the other.

The two men left, locking the cell door with the key, and François remained silent, still huddled on the padded floor. His stomach begins to feel extremely sick; his mouth fills with thick drool, and he vomits, soiling himself! And a succession of painful spasms hit his belly in a vain attempt to expel what was not there...The complete absence of food for many days had disordered his stomach enormously, causing him intense nausea. The medicine, whose active ingredient was camphor[3], caused him enormous discomfort.

Extremely dejected and softened by the effects of the medicine, François falls asleep. That is exactly what the treatment was designed to do: relax his muscles, so that he would sleep a lot, after the endless attempts, every two hours, to provoke convulsions, as it was believed at the time, that the strong neuro–muscular spasms could eventually bring psychotics back to their senses. However, this clinical procedure did not often produce the expected result, and the patient suffered more than he was cured and ended up dying as a result of the inoperability of the treatment methods employed. François would be no exception to that rule: if he was lucky, he would come to his senses with the medicated shocks or the other procedures that were used at that time. If not, he would end up starving and dying of progressive starvation and the accumulation of aggressions he would

---

[3] Camphor is a white, crystalline substance with a strong characteristic odor, obtained from the sap and oxidation of pinene (the main part of turpentine), taken from the camphor tree (*Cinnamomum camphora*), a tree belonging to the Lauraceae family and the *Cinnamomum* genus, the same as the tree that produces cinnamon. This tree is native to some regions of the Far East, particularly Taiwan, Japan and China.

suffer as the ludicrous and almost ineffective treatment unfolded. The poor boy's ordeal, however, had only just begun....

The late spring morning was already tinged with the sultry haze of approaching summer. The blossoms on the lush almond trees on Boulevard Saint–Denis were beginning to wilt and droop languidly from their branches, swirling down to the cobblestones below, forming an ephemeral pale yellow carpet, on which passers–by hastened by the need to get on with their lives, walked with light steps.

"What do you want to eat?" – Berg asks his girlfriend.

"Anything..." – she replies.

"I will let you choose today..."

Sitting in the bustling boulangerie, while they waited for the food they had ordered, Berg took Céleste-Marie's hand and kissed it tenderly. The girl smiles at him. A beautiful smile, with ruby–red lipstick.

"You look beautiful!" – drawing her to him, he whispers close to her ear.

"Oh, you always look so handsome and elegant too..." – she remarks, kissing him affectionately on the cheek. She continues, looking him in the eye:

"I am very proud to be with you! Look at how the little girls who swarm around you look at you with lustful eyes!

"Oh, as always you exaggerate, *ma belle*!" – he retorts, laughing.

"You are the one who attracts the attention of half the men on the street when you walk past in your exquisite clothes!"

"Oh, you are jealous, aren't you?" – she jokes.

"You are the one who is overdoing it! Most of the time I live locked in my room... When you are not in Paris, I hardly leave the house!"

"You should leave!" – he remarks, becoming serious.

"This is bad for you, this voluntary confinement you have got yourself into! In fact, I am bursting with pride when I see that you are wanted! You know perfectly well how beautiful you are, Céleste–Marie! And why are you hiding from the world like this? You and your mother should go out, go to the theater, go to restaurants! Paris is full of great places offering entertainment like no other city in the world, and yet...."

"When you are with me, I feel a little safer, Berg..." – she says bitterly. And, trying her best not to cry, she continues:

"But when you are away, I do not feel like going out at all! Maman keeps saying the same thing you said, but I have it inside me... a monster gnawing at my insides!" – she says, showing annoyance.

"I know! You have repeated it so much that I have memorized it."

"Oh, Berg!" – she says, annoyed.

"Definitely, you and Maman cannot understand what is going on in my soul... But I will tell you once again: it is going to kill me!"

"Why do you not react, why do you not fight it, my dear?" – he said, holding her hands as he realized that he had hurt her enormously.

"You know you can count on me for anything!"

"I do not know, Wilfred..." – she says, in a low, highly sentimental voice.

"I do not think I can count on anyone... not even you."

"Oh, you hurt me like that!" – he says, squeezing her hand tightly.

"If you do not trust me anymore..."

"You are making me lose faith in yourself, Berg..." – she says, looking at him with sad eyes.

"I know that, deep down, you think I am unbalanced too..."

"Oh, why are you saying such things to me?" – he asks, very shocked.

"I definitely never thought you were..."

"Crazy? Insane?" – she said, her voice wet with tears. And, beginning to change, she continued:

"You do not need to lie anymore! And do you know why you have not married me yet, Wilfred? Because you think I am crazy! And you do not want to get hitched to a madwoman, do you?!"

"Sssh!" – he says, putting the tip of his index finger to his lips. And, looking around, he continues:

"You are starting to attract attention! Look! They are all looking at us!"

"What do I care about those people?" – she exclaims. And, standing up abruptly, she continues, almost shouting:

"What do they have to do with my life? Nothing!" – and leaves, roughly pushing those who were in her way.

Berg gets up, stunned, and follows her, almost running. All heads were automatically turned toward him.

"Céleste–Marie! *Eh, halte!*" – shouts Lieutenant Berg, running after his girlfriend who, already on the sidewalk, and highly determined, was walking at a very fast pace, among the passers–by.

"Wait for me!" – he shouts, afraid of losing her in the crowd.

With a tremendous effort, the boy manages to reach her and holds her tightly by the arm.

"Let me go, Berg!" – she says, with a strong tug, trying to get loose.

"I would better go home! And you do not need to accompany me. I know very well which way to go!"

"Oh, forgive me!" – he says, standing in front of her, blocking her way.

"Forgive me, my dear, please! I am an idiot! You are really ill and you need to be looked after!" – and, trying to hold her, he continued:

"Come on! Let me stay with you!"

"No!" – she exclaims, her eyes fill with a strange glow.

"You do not like me anymore! You have been pretending that you still love me, but it is not true... I am sure you have someone else and you do not have the guts to say it, do you? Look, Berg, you do not have to! I already know: you have someone else and that you do not care about me anymore!"

"Oh, how you deceive yourself!" – he says, holding her hand. And realizing that people were looking at them arguing in the street, he invited her:

"Come on, let's sit in the park and let's talk!"

"All right!" – she agrees, letting herself be won over.

"But nothing you say to me will convince me otherwise: you have already found someone else and now you are trying to get rid of me!"

"I have no one but you!" – exclaims the boy, lovingly holding Céleste–Marie's hands.

"You are getting things into your head. If you have any doubts about me, why do you not ask around? The gossips would not spare me…"

Céleste–Marie just looked at him with tearful eyes. How handsome her love was! If she lost him to some other little girl, she would kill herself... He insisted with his eyes. Could someone so handsome be lying so shamelessly? It did not fit... Ah, it definitely did not suit Berg.

"Oh, Berg! Berg!" – she exclaimed, sinking her face into his chest and giving vent to the flood that were drowning her breasts.

"You really are my undoing... Why cannot I rid myself from you?"

"I think it is because, deep down in your heart, you do not want to, my dear..." – he exclaims, gently pulling her by the scruff of the neck and looking deep into her eyes.

"It is true! It is true!" – she explains, offering him her mouth.

"I do not want to... I do not want to be away from you!"

And he kisses her, full of passion. How delicious Céleste–Marie's kiss was! A crimson–red kiss, a kiss of passion...

"We will never go back to that boulangerie, will we?" – she says, a little embarrassed.

"And why should we go back there one day?" – he replies. And with a sly smile, he continues:

"There are at least twenty in the Cité..."

As the afternoon began to fall, Berg and Céleste–Marie left the rental car in front of the barracks gates.

"Does the General know you are in Paris?"

"Yes. It was he who telegraphed me about Sylvie's death." Soon they were in the office of the old military man, who welcomed them with a warm smile.

"Lieutenant Berg! Céleste–Marie!" – exclaims General du Servey, getting up from his desk and coming around it to welcome his friends with open arms.

"What a joy to see you again!"

"General!" – says the boy and, bowing to his superior, salutes him.

"Oh, sit down here!" – invites du Servey.

"How about a glass of wine?" – and, going over to the familiar cupboard, he takes out a bottle and the glasses. Then, handing the drink to the couple, he takes a drink from his glass and sits down on the divan next to them.

"And young Rounet, how is he...?"

"Badly, General!" – replies the boy.

"Very badly! He could not bear the difficult ordeal and is currently in Charenton!"

"So serious?" – astonished the General.

"I understand it is very serious, sir!" – explains the Lieutenant seriously.

"I accompanied him to hospital, along with his mother, who, as you know, is my aunt, and his condition was one of total alienation!"

"Poor boy!" – exclaims the General, visibly moved.

"And how is he now?"

"I do not know yet, General..." – replied the young man.

"I am thinking of visiting him tomorrow..."

"I would also like to see him too, Lieutenant..." – says the soldier. "If you do not mind, we could go together..."

"It would be a great pleasure for me, sir..." – replied the boy, pleased with his superior's request. Berg was very fond of General du Servey: he was a very intelligent man with a vast culture.

"I will stop by your house at nine."

"Perfect!" – says the General and, turning to the young woman who was following the conversation in respectful silence, asks her:

"And your mother, Céleste–Marie, how is she?"

"Maman is fine, General!" – the girl replies gently.

"I mean, after all this time, she is finally getting over the loss of Papa. She is busy with the housework; she goes to church a lot..."

"And you?" – continues the man, looking her firmly in the eye.

"It seems to me that you do not think you are doing very well..."

"Ah, sir..." – she said, blushing slightly.

"You know how it is! Strange things are happening to me... I hear voices, I see figures that sneak up on me... I have a lot of insomnia and when I fall asleep, I have terrible nightmares..."

"You have already been to the doctors, of course..." – observes the General, rather thoughtfully.

"Oh, yes!" – says the girl, giving a nervous smile.

"Of course, I have been seeing the doctors!"

"And what do the doctors say?"

"Oh, General, they say very little... In fact, they say almost nothing, they just pump me full of medicine! And I sleep all the time or, if not, I walk around the house half-stoned by the excess of sedatives they prescribe me!"

"I, in particular, believe that such illnesses have their origin in the soul!" – observes the General, getting up and walking in circles with his hands behind his back.

"And I believe that many things will yet to be discovered about the soul! I do not know if you are aware of it, but about two years ago, I think it was around 1848, a strange case that took place in America, in a small town called Hydesville[4]. The fact was so extraordinary and unusual that it caught the attention of the whole world!"

"I think I remember such things, yes!" – exclaims Lieutenant Berg.

"Are you not referring to the case involving two sisters who claimed to talk to spirits?"

"Exactly!" – says the General, with a gleam of enthusiasm in his eyes.

"And I think their names were Fox! Yes, the Fox sisters, Kate and Margaret!"

"And it seems to me that there was a murder case that took place years before in the house the Fox family moved into!" – adds Berg.

"Yes!" – continues the General.

"It was the ghost of a Charles B. Rosma, a traveling salesman, who had been murdered by the Bell couple, former residents of the house. They killed the poor peddler who had

---

[4] These events have gone down in the annals of Spiritism as the Hydesville "raps", perhaps the initial milestone of the ostensible manifestation of spirits and which, followed later by the phenomena of the spinning tables, led to the research carried out by Allan Kardec, the insignificant Codifier of Spiritism, years later, with the launch of "The Spirits' Book" on April 18, 1857.

asked them to stay that night and stole five hundred dollars from him, according to the spirit himself."

"But the corpse of the alleged Mr. Rosma has still not been found!"[5] – remarks Céleste–Marie, joining in the conversation.

"I remember very well that my mother was following the story in the newspapers and that she once commented that the whole thing was turning out to be a well-woven fraud! Do such things not seem strange to you?"

"I remember that too, Céleste–Marie!" – says the General.

"Only the numerous excavations carried out in the basement of the Fox house did not turn out so disastrously! Evidence was found that a body had been buried there! There were traces of bones, hair... Do you not think the body was then moved to an unknown location? You know, there was so much interest in the spirit not really communicating! Proving this fact would certainly put an end to a lot of people's livelihoods, do you not think?"

"Possibly..." – says the girl.

---

[5] Immediately after the revelations made by the murdered spirit in the house, it was decided that the solution would be to look for the corpse in the cellar, where it was buried. The excavations, however, did not lead to definitive results, as they ended in water, without any evidence being found, and for this reason they were suspended. However, in the summer of 1848, Mr. David Fox himself, with the help of some interested parties, resumed the project. At a depth of one and a half meters, they found a plank. Once they had dug deeper, they found charcoal, lime, hair and some bone fragments that a doctor recognized as belonging to a human skeleton; nothing else. The evidence of the crime was precarious and insufficient, which is perhaps why Mr. Bell was not denounced as the perpetrator.

"So, what do you think, General, about all this?" – asks the boy.

"I understand that you are very interested in these matters!"

"We will have news for me!" – observes the soldier.

"Of course, you remember the spinning tables we saw at Marquise Adèle de Souvigny's, *n'est–ce pas?* And no matter how much we speculate about it, no one has yet been able to unmask the fraud! Journalists are always on the lookout for someone to give them such pleasure; but, so far no one has managed to unravel the mystery!"

"You are right, General..." – said Céleste–Marie.

"I was very impressed by the phenomenon! By the way, you and Constance still attend the séances held at the Marquise de Souvigny's house?"

"Oh, yes!" – replies the General.

"My wife and I have not missed a single session! You know, my part is not just limited to the fun side of the question. I am very interested in the scientific, phenomenal aspect of it. I believe there are facts behind this extraordinary occurrence that will decisively change the course of humanity... Do you not realize how fast things have been moving from time to time?! I was born in the last century, I am a witness to how the world used to be restricted, small, limited to a few miles around! Today, however, a large part of humanity travels everywhere, in the comfort and safety of very fast, modern trains going almost fifty kilometers an hour! Amazing, isn't it? And the telegraph shortening communication time? I think heaven is beginning to reveal itself to us, my dears! And, if you really want to know, I think that those who have gone before us are as alive as you and I and are itching to telegraph us!

Have you not noticed how similar the tables are to the telegraph? What is more, I am convinced that nobody dies! I still do not know what actually happens to us after we die, but reason tells us that we will not end up simply plunging into a sea of oblivion or annulment! Consciousness, thought or whatever, must remain... I still do not know how this happens, but death is not the end, is it?

"I think you are right, General..." – says Lieutenant Berg, exchanging a slight, meaningful glance with his girlfriend, in the face of the firm convictions presented by the old soldier. And, taking advantage of the opportunity, he asks:

"Do you then believe, then, that spirits could interact and influence us?"

"Why not?" – said the General.

"I still do not know how they do it, but as scientific experiments and discoveries are accelerating in this century, I believe that in a very short time, we will know everything! Everything will be made clear! There is strong evidence that spirits do act on us! And what about cases of possession? The Church and Protestants attribute this phenomenon to the devil, but I know better! The Bible is full of accounts on this subject! Did Jesus himself not cast out spirits?"

"And demons too!" – says Céleste–Marie.

"Do not forget that Jesus refers to the devil in the Gospels!"

"You are right, my dear!" – agrees the old soldier.

"I will not discuss whether or not you believe there are demons, but I must warn you that this word comes from the Greek language, and we will find it widely used by the famous philosopher Plato, when referring to the excellent teachings of his master Socrates, about the *daimori*[6] which illustrates the origin of the term "demon", which at first had a very different meaning from the one it has now!"

"So, the term has been mischaracterized over time, sir!" – observes Lieutenant Berg.

"If it did not actually mean demon…"

"Yes…" – continued the General.

"But the translators of the Bible, allied to interests whose sole purpose was to establish Christianity of their own devising, tried to distort the meaning of things which, in their origin, differed greatly from what they now have!"

"But messing with holy things is sacrilege!" –said the girl.

"And what you say is very serious indeed, General!"

"Oh, Céleste–Marie…" – says the soldier.

---

[6] Plato, writing about Socrates, says that he communicated with an invisible spirit called *Daimon* (also spelled Daymon). In this context, another definition of a "demon" would be "full of knowledge", since its supernatural offspring is attributed with the ability to retain vast knowledge for an entire lifetime. In Eastern cultures, demons are all creatures considered to be mystical or spiritual. But not necessarily of an evil nature, as in the case of fairies, angels, gnomes… All of the above and more would be classified as demons in their generic term because they are either supernatural or possess vast magical knowledge or power. The only Eastern equivalent for an evil demon as seen in the West would be *Oni*, a type of spectral being whose nature was to torment other beings.

"I know that you and your mother maintain your belief in Catholicism, and my intention was not and is not to create schisms in your head! However, most people are unaware of the true content of the history of Christianity! Many facts had been deliberately concealed in order to protect big interests!

And what is more, most people do not tend to question anything, even the smallest things, let alone the very complex issues surrounding faith, *n'est–ce pas*? However, everyone is taught not to question the dogmas of faith! I, on the other hand, I think that all things should be questioned!

Is it not through questioning that people, dissatisfied with what has already been established, end up discovering things? There are two categories of men in the world, Céleste–Marie: those who are conformist and passive, and those who are non–conformist and active! I belong to the second category!"

"Exactly!" – remarks Lieutenant Berg.

"You are absolutely right, General! The great thinkers have always been men unconvinced by the situation of their time!"

"And if it were not for questioning, the world would not evolve!" – continues the General.

"I even think that progress would never come, and it would all be stagnation! The *"cogito ergo sun"*[7] – the maxim representing Descartes' methodical doubt[8] – was a very

---

[7] "I think, therefore I am", in Latin. A maxim of the French philosopher René Descartes.

[8] René Descartes (March 31, 1596, La Haye en Touraine, France – February 11, 1650, Stockholm, Sweden), also known as Renatus Cartesius, was a French philosopher, physicist and mathematician.

important step for science. Philosophically and metaphysically, it established a set of certainties for scientists to pursue their work, in the conviction that it was man's task to understand the world around him. This mental relaxation came from the awareness of one's own existence, through the *cogito* (I think, therefore I am) and the acceptance of the idea of God as an innate certainty arising from Cartesian doubt itself, in accordance with the Augustinian cogito itself, according to which God is the source of knowledge, existence and doubt itself. I consider the thought of René Descartes[9] to be the first great step away from brutal medieval dogmatism!"

"It gave the man the courage he lacked; you mean!" – remarks Lieutenant Berg.

"Yes!" – exclaims the General.

"Then there were others who complete his thought... Do not forget *Monsieur* Voltaire![9] Ah, Voltaire, Voltaire! He was not a democrat in the right sense, and believed that the common people were bowed down to fanaticism and superstition. For him, society had to be reformed by advancing reason and encouraging science and technology. Thus, Voltaire became an acid persecutor of dogma, especially that of the Catholic Church.

"But it is said that Mr. Voltaire converted back to Catholicism at the end of his life, when he was over eighty!" – remarks Lieutenant Berg.

"They say so..." – agreed the General.

---

[9] François-Marie Arouet (November 21, 1694, Paris – May 30, 1778, Paris), better known by his pseudonym Voltaire, was a French Enlightenment poet, essayist, playwright, philosopher and historian.

"It is even said that he left a document written in his own hand[10], declaring that he regretted having persecuted the Church so much! However, he had already done the greatest good: he had sown the seeds of doubt, and doubt does enormous good for reason! Loosen it up! And, if you really want to know, if it had not been for *Monsieur* Voltaire's famous letters, which sowed the seeds of dissent, especially his ferocious attacks on the established orders, the Revolution would never have happened, and we would still be living in the medieval times! If we are now reaping the benefits of science, we owe them to these audacious men..."

Berg and Céleste–Marie remained silent. The General really knew his stuff. The afternoon progressed and the couple decided to leave.

"We are really with your lesson, General!" – exclaims the boy, shaking his superior's hand.

"It did me a great deal of good to hear your words, General!" – says the girl, while the old soldier respectfully kisses her hand!

---

[10] The following excerpt is taken from volume XII of the famous French magazine Correpondance Litléraire, Philosophique et Critique (1753–1793), in the April 1778 issue, pages 87–88, confirming what Voltaire said, written in his own handwriting:

"I, the writer, declare that having suffered vomiting of blood four days ago, at the age of 84, and not being able to go to church, the parish priest of St. Sulpice willingly sent me to M. Gautier, a priest. I went to confession with him, and if God would forgive me, I will die in the holy Catholic religion in which I was born, hoping that divine mercy will deign to forgive all my faults, and that if I have scandalized the Church, I ask God and the Church for forgiveness. Signed: Voltaire, March 2, 1778 at the house of the Marquis de Villete, in the presence of Monsieur le Abbé Mignot, my nephew, and Monsieur le Marquis de Villevielle, my friend."

"I hope you will invite us to Madame de Souvigny's sessions."

"I am sure we will invite you, Mademoiselle!" – he says, pleased.

"You and your mother, you will soon receive our invitation!"

Outside, in the coach that was taking them home, Céleste–Marie felt more serene, more at ease. A warm breeze was playing with her black, wavy hair and she broke out into a wide, ruby–red smile. "A beautiful smile..." – thought Berg, looking at her, full of tenderness. "Too bad you change your mood so much... Too bad, really..."

Chapter 11

In the Darkness of Madness

Time passed slowly for François–Amand, who was still hospitalized in Charenton. Six months had passed since Sylvie's tragic and unexpected death. The young man now had a few glimmers of lucidity; however, when memories came back to him, he would fall into a new state of despair and let himself be seized by intense fury. He was then locked up again in the padded cell and given intensive treatment. Once the crisis was over, he closed himself off again in mutism, in almost total alienation. And this had been repeated systematically until then. The doctors had managed to open little of the young cadet's mind. He had been given the latest that the incipient psychiatry of the mid–19th century could offer to those suffering from mental illness: a series of convulsions caused by camphor; shocks to the head with electric eels; terrifying scares, being lowered, bound by the wrists, into horrifying snake pits (despite the fact that this treatment, at the time, was already widely condemned by most doctors, however, in difficult cases such as François's, they still resorted to this expedient, for lack of better options), as well as excessively cold baths and simulations of intense fear, generated by supposed fires, as well as simulated falls from high places. New drugs that emerged from exotic plants from the most distant parts of the world were also tested, however, the vast majority of them were nothing more than the folklore of indigenous peoples and had little or no effect on the patients. Around this time, François gradually stopped being violent. The excessive shock treatments literally turned him into a rag. The restlessness and exuberance that had once been so peculiar to him were no longer there. He had become quite thin; his eyes were sad and framed by dark, eternal circles; his skin was emaciated and pale, and his lips, greatly discolored, were more like two simple oblique scratches indicating that they had forgotten how to laugh...

It was late fall and winter was already setting in, with icy winds blowing insistently from the north. At that time, François, when he was not suffering from intense seizures, used to be placed in the large garden that surrounded the imposing hospital, along with the hundreds of patients, to soak up the sun and fresh air, since one of the precepts of the new directions that medicine was beginning to take was precisely that patients should no longer be confined to the wards all the time, but should be put in contact with the open air. Thus, the immense park, carpeted with well-kept lawns and shaded by magnificent trees, was filled, especially on the clearest days, with hundreds of patients from all the wards: the convalescents, who were already able to move around on their own; others, who were still incapacitated, were gently wheeled around by kind nurses in wheelchairs.

However, the mentally ill occupied a reserved part of the park and were subject to closer surveillance, both by the friendly nurses and the diligent orderlies who kept a close eye on everything to avoid any unwanted incidents. François, who was a little weak, strolled through the park's lush lawns, gently guided in a wheelchair by a helpful nurse.

"*Oh, mon chéri...! Il vas très bien le soleil aujourd'hui, n'est-ce pas?*"[1] – says the nurse, as she pushes the wheelchair François is in with extreme care.

Unusually, the boy raises his head and, with extremely scrutinizing eyes, looks at the nurse.

"Oh, you looked at me!" – exclaims the girl, overjoyed.

"We need to tell Dr. de la Roche!"

And, full of joy, the girl took off, almost running, pushing the wheelchair into the building.

"Oh, the doctor will be pleased to hear that!" – she exclaims, almost flying down the corridors of the huge hospital.

After a long search for the doctor, the young nurse finds him examining an elderly woman, lying on one of the beds in a huge ward.

"*Monsieur le docteur...! J'ai des nouvelles...! François m' a regardé!*"[2]

"What are you talking about, Marie-Victoire?!" – exclaims the doctor, highly interested.

"So, he looked at you? How did he do it? Tell me how it happened!"

"I was walking with him, pushing his wheelchair through the park, when I made a comment about the day,

---

[1] "Oh, my dear... The sun is beautiful today, isn't it?", in French.
[2] "Doctor...! I have news! François looked at me...", in French.

about the sun, and he raised his head and looked at me! I got the impression that he understood what I had said..."

"Really?" – says the doctor, sleaving his examination of the frail old woman and turning to the boy who was sitting in his wheelchair.

"Look! He seems to be interested in our conversation!" – and, kneeling down in front of the boy, says to him:

"*Eh, François! Comment ça va?*"[3]

The boy stares at him with a certain expressiveness and cracks a smile.

"Oh, you are right, Marie–Victoire!" – exclaims the doctor, full of joy.

"You did it! Perhaps your voice reminded him of something! We have made a start! And I think that, from now on, I will leave him exclusively in your care! You were the only one to open his mind!"

"Do you think I remind him of someone, doctor?"

"Possibly, Marie–Victoire!" – continues the doctor, very excited.

"And talk to him a lot! Even if he does not answer you at first; talk to him! I think you will succeed! Take him for a walk whenever possible and try to make him talk!"

Marie–Victoire left the doctor and started to drive François back to the park. The boy's eyes brightened slightly. He began to pay attention to his surroundings.

---

[3] "Hey, François...! How are you?", in French.

"I think the doctor is right, François!" – says the nurse, sitting down in front of the boy on a bench in the park, under a leafy tree.

"You are beginning to open up to the world! It's a bit cold in here, but it is better than that horrible cell, isn't it?" – and she gives a wink to the boy who was looking at her with a pair of attentive eyes.

François then opens a slight smile that shows the tips of his incisor's teeth.

"Ah, you get my drift, don't you, naughty boy?" – she jokes.

"I think you were just pretending, *n'est–ce pas?* Just to get some love!"

"No..." – mutters the boy, his voice very weak.

"Oh, you spoke! – she exclaims, enthusiastically.

"You spoke! The doctor is going to be thrilled!" – and, winking at her, she continues:

"But look, we are not going to tell him this news just yet? It will be our secret! *D'accord?*"

"*Oui...*" – replied François, smiling.

"So, it is a deal! From now on, you will only talk to me!"

Marie–Victoire took both of François's hands and held them lovingly between her own. Then, in silence, she began to look insistently into his eyes. She did not know why, but that boy filled her with strange feelings. She was absolutely certain that she had never seen him before, yet she felt as if she had known him for so long!

"Where can I know you from, François?" – she murmured, caressing his thin face with her fingertips.

"I am not from Paris... I was born and raised in Marseille. I have only been here for two years..."

And he looked at her insistently, opening a succession of slight smiles, apparently of great joy.

"Sylvie..." – he murmurs, his voice still extremely weak, but full of tenderness.

"What did you say?!" – she exclaims, laughing.

"Sylvie? *Mais, non! Je suis Marie–Victoire, l'infirmière! Tu te trompes...*"⁴

"Sylvie! Sylvie!" – he repeats, caressing and kissing the young nurse's hands. Two tears sprang to his eyes and start rolling down his cheeks.

"Oh, you are wrong!" – she repeats, amused.

"You are taking me for someone else!" – and, noticing his tears, hurries to wipe them away with her fingertips.

"But you are crying! No, do not cry, darling!"

"*Oh, ma Sylvie!*" – he exclaims, holding her hands tightly.

"*C'est toi, mon amour!*"⁵

Marie–Victoire looked at him in pity. The boy was mistaking her for someone else. Such things used to happen there! Patients came out of one crisis and often entered

---

⁴ "Sylvie?... But no! I'm Marie-Victoire, the nurse...! You're wrong...", in French.
⁵ "Oh, my Sylvie...! (...) – It's you, my love...!", in French.

another, perhaps more difficult and more dangerous than the previous one.

"Oh, you have come out from the darkness of alienation and you are in another mess!" – she murmurs, almost imperceptibly. And with a deep sigh, she continues:

"And the worst thing is that you include me in your madness..."

"Sylvie..." – he continued, his eyes welling with tears.

"*Ne me quitte jamais!*"[6]

"Oh, nI certainly will not leave you, my dear!" – she says, comforting him.

"Calm down, I will never leave you..."

Marie–Victoire looked him in the eyes once more.

"What a thing!" – she thought, very intrigued.

"Not only do I think I have met him before, but he is confusing me with someone else... I wonder who Sylvie is!"

"Now, come in, François!" – she says in a firm voice. And she gets up and starts pushing his wheelchair.

"It is already quite cold in here and the way you are feeling, you might catch a cold or something worse! Then, we will have serious trouble, you and I..."

And while she was taking the sick man back to his room, Marie–Victoire was thinking intimately: she needed to find out more about François's story. What would that woman represent in the boy's life?

---

[6] "Sylvie... (...) – Do not ever leave me...!", in French.

Shortly afterwards, the nurse approached Dr. Marcel-Édouard de la Roche, who was dealing with François-Armand's case, and gave him a detailed account about what had happened between her and the boy a short time before.

"Did she show such behavior then?" – asked the doctor, highly interested.

"*Oui, Monsieur le docteur...*" – the girl replies.

"But he called me Sylvie..."

"Oh, I will tell you, my dear!" – says the doctor.

"I will tell you everything..."

"Poor François!" – Marie-Victoire thought to herself a short while later, as she walked through the long corridors of the hospital, back to her post after her conversation with the doctor.

"So young, and tragedy has already dismantled his life!"

That night, Marie-Victoire, lying in her bed, in her humble little room in a boarding house, because she was alone in the world, could not get the image of François out of her head.

"What a thing!" – she thought, highly aggravated.

"We must not get involved with patients, at least not so emotionally to the point of taking away our peace of mind!"

It was almost dawn when Marie-Victoire finally managed to fall asleep. She dreamt systematically about François, but in the dream, the young man did not look like he did no: he was a little more muscular, with a larger physique. But she knew it was François, and she hugged him, full of voluptuousness, but the boy rejected her. Then she got angry and threw herself at him, clawing at him and trying to bite him. Then the dream shows them transported to a room, along with other people, while François and another boy were engaged in a fierce fight. Then another scene, and a corpse was lying on the floor, in the middle of a pool of blood, and she, Marie–Victoire, huddled by the wall, was screaming like a possessed person, while François, desperate, run out the door.[7]

When Marie–Victoire woke up in the morning, she was bathed in sweat, despite the intense cold. Shivering profusely, she wiped her hands across her face and recalled the terrible nightmare. Good heavens! What a thing! Even in my dreams now? She was beginning to worry. Still dizzy from her bad night's sleep, she got up and, picking up the ice–cold water contained in a brass vase, badly dented by the many knocks it had already suffered in its long existence, she poured it into a white agate basin, largely peeled by years of intense use, and washed her face repeatedly to expel sleep.

Then she sat down on the edge of her bed, with no desire to get ready for the hospital. By her calculations, it must have been four o'clock in the morning, because her landlady was also up, making intense and purposeful noises in the kitchen. So, she had to get dressed quickly and catch a ride to the hospital. What a life! Without much desire, she got dressed. Before long, she looked at herself in a small mirror,

---

[7] Such scenes are recounted in the novel "*The Stone's Smile*", by the same authors as this one, when the character above, in a previous incarnation, lived as Marguerite, lover of the then François–Armand, who at the time was the coudel Tonton (Antoine Jouvenchy). This dream is actually a memory from the past.

the steel of which was badly corroded around the edges and, without much encouragement, she closed the door of the little room and, after eating a light and frugal breakfast, went out into the darkness of the street. The cold chills her to the core, and she pulls the collar of her coat to her ears. Why are coats never enough for the poor? There are always a piece missing. In a hurry, she walked about three hundred meters and stood on the side of the road that led to the outskirts of the city. She was alone in the darkness. Afraid? She had always been afraid, but the need was greater! After being orphaned at the age of seventeen, she had come from Marseille on the south coast of the country, in search of a job. And, given her good looks, cleverness and spontaneous way of laughing and talking, she was given the job of nursing assistant at the imposing Charenton Clinic. She was now in her twenties: she had not married yet, because she did not want to give herself to just anyone, since the vast majority of the proletariat at that time were rude, ill-educated men who invariably filled their wives with children and often became alcoholics, providing their families with more distress and abandonment than actual support and protection. Marie-Victoire was terrified of such things, which is why she remained single, despite the fact that she had dozens of suitors because she had good manners and was also very pretty.

"Oh, François-Armand..." – she thought swaying in the small bus that, along with about twenty sleepy companions, was heading to the Charenton Clinic.

"You were so in love with your Sylvie then, and she has gone..."

About two hours later, it was still dark when Marie-Victoire jumped out the car outside the clinic. In the mist of the group of gloomy co-workers, she hurriedly began the short walk of three hundred meters to the hospital entrance, crossing the park which, at that hour, was completely taken over by the frigid, dense fog. Shortly afterwards, warmed by the internal heating of the room, she returned to her post, attending to the infinite number of inmates, in her daily eagerness to make the first of countless visits to them, to attend to the minimum needs that the patients presented, as well as accompanying the doctors during routine clinical examinations. It was an arduous task, lasting sixteen hours and invariably on her feet, hurrying through the long corridors of the imposing hospital.

On that day in particular, Marie-Victoire was a little down because of the bad night's sleep, but that was not the main reason for the lack of her usual vivacity and loquacity; her thoughts were constantly filled with the memory of François-Armand.

"What a thing!" – she thought with irritation.

"That boy is a patient of the clinic! And what is more, he is crazy!"

"What is on your mind today, Marie-Victoire?" – asks a co-worker, noticing her unusual behavior, as they walk side by side down a long corridor towards one of the many wards crammed with patients.

"Oh, nothing, Yvette!" – she replies, slightly harshly.

"I just did not sleep well! That is all!"

"I know..." – observes the other, looking unconvinced by her friend's answer. She continued, with a hint of irony in her voice:

"You tend to lose sleep when your heart is not in the right place..."

"I see..." the other woman remarks, looking at her unconvinced about the response her friend had given. She continues, with a hint of irony in her voice: "It's normal to lose sleep when things aren't going well with the heart..."

"Come on, Yvette!" – exclaims Marie–Victoire, annoyed by the other woman's ironic remark.

"When my shift is over, I am so tired that I do not even have time to think about such things. You are the only one who could say such nonsense!"

"Come on!" – continues the other.

"I get tired as much as you do around here, but in the evenings, I have not been short of breath to curl up with Jean–Baptiste..."

"That you have a fire like that consuming you, outside and inside, the whole clinic already know, *ma chérie!*" – exclaims Marie–Victoire, full of sarcasm.

"However, that is not the case with me! Do not worry!"

"That is exactly what I think you are missing, ma amie!" – continues the other, insisting.

"Do you not know that men are a delight, a holy remedy to take away this weight, this disdain that we feel around here? Try it and you will see!" – and burst out laughing:

"Ha! Ha! Ha! Ha!"

"I do not know!" – says Marie–Victoire.

"Sometimes, I think that if I do that, I will just be making more trouble for myself!"

"For me, men have always been the solution to my problems, my dear..." – says the other, amused.

"And if you really want to know, from the way you look, I think you are really in love! Ha! Ha! Ha! Ha! And you do not want to admit it!"

"You are crazy!" – Marie–Victoire exclaimed, becoming extremely serious and angry at the other woman's words.

"In love, me?! And who do you think I would be in love with?"

"I do not know!" – replied the other, laughing.

"It must be one of the patients! Ha! Ha! Ha! Ha! Which one of the madmen is he? Delieux? Matriot? Benoit? Ha! Ha! Ha! Ha! Or is it Louis Danterre? Ha! Ha! Ha! Ha!"

"François–Armand Rounet!" – comes abruptly to her mind.

"Oh, what am I thinking?" – she mortifies herself in thought. And she continues:

"It is the fault of this shameless pest who is spurring me on with malicious insinuations, but she is wrong: I am not in love with anyone!"

"Your face does not deceive me, *ma amie*!" – continues the other.

"Your behavior is betraying you! Come on, confess: who did you fall in love with? Let me guess once and for all: Cadet Rounet!"

Marie–Victoire almost collapsed. She had to hold on tight with both hands to the little tray of medicines she was holding. Good heavens! She had blushed up to her ears! The wretched woman would get suspicious! She had betrayed herself!

"Did I not say so?" – exclaims the other, triumphantly.

"You're as red as a cherry! Your face is on fire! See how I got it right?"

"Y... hit... hit, nothing, you fool!" – she shouts back, trying to regain her cool.

"You are playing a game!"

"Do you think I have not noticed how passionately you have been carrying him up and down in that wheelchair, all full of happiness in your eyes? Only a woman in love acts like that! You cannot hide a strong passion, *ma belle*! No one can, least of all you! Passion betrays us, impudently, without pity! You would be no exception to the rule! Have it stamped on your face!" – and, pretending to be intrigued, she continued:

"But tell me: why did you fall in love with a scarecrow like that? He is so finished, so ugly, do you not think? You could have found something better! Hercule Tissot, for example! Oh, yes, he would make you reach for the stars with just one hug! And would he not be running after you like a hound, sniffing out every step you take down in hospital corridors?"

"Oh, you are the only one who thought I would connect with a bastard like that!" – exclaims Marie-Victoire, full of indignation.

"Come on, Yvette, honestly, who do you take me for?"

"But you are in love with the young cadet Rounet, aren't you?" – continues the other.

"Nothing will get it out of my head! You can deny it all you like, but it is true!"

Marie-Victoire gave the other woman a look full of disdain and, just then, the two girls arrived at the infirmary door. Before they entered, Yvette looked at her, full of malice, and whispered to her:

"After that, I will go with you to François Rounet's infirmary!" – and flashes a mischievous smile.

Marie-Victoire simply gave her a hateful look and walked decisively into the infirmary.

"*Bonjour, Messieurs!*" – she shouts, giving forced a smile. That day, the beautiful young nurse had smiled forcedly, very forcedly...

In the meantime, still lying in his bed lined with white sheets, François-Armand stared insistently at the infirmary door. He was anxiously awaiting someone's arrival. Then, tired of waiting, he got up with some difficulty, went to the large window and, pulling aside part of the curtain, looked outside. It was a horrible day! The thick fog reduced everything to grotesque ghostly shapes. Low clouds were speeding across the plumy sky, heading south, carrying the terrible cold of another harsh winter that was arriving with all its impetuosity. Soon, everything would be covered in frost and, eventually, a thin layer of snow! François looks at the faded landscape and thinks back. The anachronism boggles his mind. What was that place? What was he doing there, among those depleted, squalid, emaciated-skinned people who coughed and spitting non-stop? He looks closely at the faint image of his face reflected in the glass. His eyes insistently follow the features of his own physiognomy, searching for an identity and, naturally, forcing the memory. A sudden, intense headache makes him groan and withdraw. For a moment, he squeezes his eyes shut tightly and tries to calm down. The pain subsides and he opens his eyes again.

"*Por quoi?*" – he murmurs in a breath. And a discreet tear runs down his face.

"*Pour quoi... moi?*"[8] – he continues, quietly, as he looks at his own features reflected in the glass.

At that very moment, Marie-Victoire entered the infirmary door. She had escaped by taking advantage of Yvette's slight distraction and had gone ahead of her snooping companion when they were changing wards. She did not want the other woman to come after her when she saw François. She could betray herself by becoming even more entangled in her clever colleague's web. As she walked down the corridor, the young nurse had fought hard to ensure that the person her eyes were intently searching for was not François, but there was no way: involuntarily, her gaze sought out the boy's bed. It was empty. Then, in a flash and full of despair, her eyes searched here and there, scanning the entire room, full of bright beds occupied by about thirty patients,

---

[8] "Why... me?"

and finally stopped on the only one standing in front of the window, peering out at the landscape outside.

"Oh, there he is!" – Marie–Victoire murmured with a sigh of relief.

And before she could even start to administer the medication to the large number of patients, she approached François from behind, slowly and imperceptibly. The boy instinctively senses her presence and turns around.

"Sylvie!" – he exclaims, giving a satisfied smile.

"*C'est toi!*"[9]

Marie–Victoire just smiled at him, a little disappointed. It was extremely unpleasant for her to hear him call her by the other woman's name; however, she knew very well how to disguise the annoyance it caused her.

"*Oui, c'est moi!*"[10] – she replied at last, thinking that, for the moment, she should pass herself off as the other.

"For your sake, for the moment, I will let you confuse me with your Sylvie..." – she thought, gently pulling him by the hand. She continues, making him lie down on the bed.

"It is cold, and it is good that you are keeping warm!" – and, giving him one of her trademark smiles, she said:

"Open your mouth wide for your medicine! Look at that! Well done!"

"Sylvie... Uh... You are still beautiful..."

"Oh, you are a first–rate flatterer, Mr. Rounet!" – she exclaims, laughing.

---

[9] "It's you!", in French.
[10] "Yes, it's me...!", in French.

"Where were you, Sylvie?" – he asks, now holding Marie–Victoire's hand.

"You did not live here in this place before..."

"Oh, yes..." – she says, continuing the farce.

"I have just moved here..."

"I thought you lived in another house..."

Marie–Victoire looked at him in pity. She felt like to run. It was not her nature to lie, even if it was to help the boy.

"*Excuse–moi...*" – she says, withdrawing the hand he was holding so passionately.

"*Je quitte...*[11]

"No, Sylvie!" – he exclaims, trying to hold her back.

"No, please do not leave me!"

Just then, Yvette, the other nurse, entered the ward and surprised them both in this conversation.

"Ah!" – she exclaims, approaching them both. And, with a mischievous smile, she continues:

" See how I was not wrong?"

"It is not like what you imagined!" – replies the other, retracting and, leaving the boy highly disconsolate, goes off to visit the other patients.

"You are seeing things where there are not any!"

"Oh, I know!" – continues the other, following her and now opening up broadly sarcastic.

---

[11] "I'm sorry... (...) – I'm going...", in French.

"Come on, Sylvie! Why do you not confess that you are in love with him?"

"My name is not Sylvie!" – mutters the other, getting very angry.

"You know that very well!" – and then, dragging the other girl away, she continued, in open defiance:

"You want a fight, don't you?"

"Oh, why would I fight with you?" – said Yvette, trying to restrain herself from mocking her companion. As she was clever, she realized she was touching a very painful wound that her poor companion kept hidden deep in her chest.

"How are you today, *Monsieur* Girardi?" – Marie-Victoire asks a middle-aged man, who stared at her with a pair of highly alienated eyes.

"Open your mouth for the medicine! Uh–lá–lá! Well done!" – and she gently strokes the poor man's unruly hair, who gives her a childish smile back.

The other nurse followed her, helping her to medicate the patients, only now unusually silent.

"It is not really my intention to fight with you, Yvette!" – says Marie-Victoire, turning to the next patient.

"*Comment ça va, Monsieur* Patrick?"

"Bad, mademoiselle…" – replies the old man, his eyes filling with tears.

"And where is Antoinette, who never comes to see me? You told me she was coming yesterday…"

"Oh, did the evil one not come to see you?" – exclaims the young nurse, pouring a spoonful of a colorless liquid into the old man's throat that her companion had previously resumed from a small bottle, counting the drops carefully, one by one, against the light, so as not to get confused.

"But do not worry, she will be here today... Look, your wife did not come, but she sent a message for you: tell my beloved Patrick that I cannot come to see him today because I have many things to do, but tomorrow, I will definitely be there to see him!"

The old man cracked a toothless smile and seemed to reassure himself.

"*Merci beaucoup, Mademoiselle!*" – he exclaims, highly appreciative.

"And what would be wrong with falling in love with François–Armand?" – continues Yvette, as they both head towards the next patient's bed.

"I do not think there would be any harm..."

"You know that is forbidden..." – says the other.

"If they find out, they will throw me out!"

"Oh, I assure you, no one will know!" – says Yvette, while dosing the medication for the patient.

"If it is up to me, no one in this world will know! I swear it!"

"How are you, *Monsieur* Oubignon?" – Marie–Victoire asks the next patient and, before the man can answer anything, she pours the medicine down his throat.

"Did you know that François is very rich?" – remarks Yvette, following her to the next patient.

"I have heard that he is a nobleman, and that he is an only child! If you want, we can investigate, you and I, if that is really true!"

Marie– Victoire simply gave the other a reproachful look and took the sick man's hand.

"How are you, Monsieur de Montaigne?"

"Are you going to miss such an opportunity like this, you fool?" – continues Yvette, insisting.

"Look, if you marry François, you could become a baroness or a countess or whatever... Have you thought about it? Oh, if it were up to me..."

"I do not worry about such things!" – exclaimed the other, shoving a spoonful medicine into the man's mouth, who burts into a violent coughing fit.

"Oh, did you choke, sir? Come on, sit back and breath deeply, like this! Like this! Now, open your arms! Breathe! Like this! Are you better? Stay with God, then!"

"Well, I think you should seriously think about it!" – exclaims Yvette.

"Or do you intend to spend the rest of your days working here, like an underpaid mule, and still living in that damp, cold, dreadful mansion, eating nothing but boiled potatoes with salt and moldy bread every day? Oh, no! I think you need to think a little more, before you throw the chance of your life down the drain!" – and, taking the other by the arm as they headed to the next bed, she continued, highly aroused:

"Have you ever imagined living in one of those mansions on the Champs–Élysées? Did you know that is where he lives? What a luxury! What about the clothes, the jewelry, the shoes you would get if you married him? Oh, Marie–Victoire! Think about it seriously! What a great deal would you not be doing?"

"You said it very well, *ma amie*: a great deal!" – replied the other, ironically.

"And do you think his family would let him marry a poor girl like me, just like that?" – and shaking her head, she laughs sarcastically and continues:

"Only you could dream up such a crazy idea!"

"Oh, surely you do not know what his relatives would do just to see him cured!" – Yvette continues.

"They would even marry him off to a chimney sweeper!"

"Oh, you are an exaggerator..." – says the other, laughing at her colleague's remark. Then, becoming serious, she continues:

"Surely, you have no idea what aristocrats are like, my dear! How proud they are! They simply abhor the poor!"

"I see you are as hard as a rock!" – exclaims Yvette, with a sigh of impatience.

"But I am not going to give up until I see you married to François..." – and, running her eye over to where the boy's bed was, she nudged her companion and said slyly.

"Look how he follows you around! He has not left your side for a single moment you have been here! He is madly in love! You have got him, my dear! He is yours! All you have to do is to reach out and pluck him from the branch!"

"Oh, how can you say such nonsense? He thinks I am Sylvie, his dead fiancée! Have you forgotten that detail?" – retorts the other, highly sulky.

"How can you think that he really likes me? Do you not realize that François is very ill, Yvette? Only you could come up with such ideas!"

"But, with patience and dedication, you will have cured him for yourself!" – insists the other.

"The dead are forgotten; did you not know? Time does that for us! Widowers or bachelors forget those who are gone! The living finds themselves! Do you not know what a beautiful plague the human heart is! You cannot live without getting caught up in one passion or another!" – and, speaking over Marie–Victoire's shoulder, almost whispering in her ear:

"And when you become Baroness–what's–her–name, you will take me with you as your secretary, *d'accord?*" – and she finishes with a smile full of complicity:

"We will be like flesh and blood…"

Marie–Victoire could not help but laugh. She concluded that Yvette must have been a little crazier than those poor bastards who stayed there…

Chapter 12
Spirituality Reveals Itself

It was 1857. It was already seven years since Sylvie had died. François had spent a long time in Charenton, almost five years, and now, apparently, for the last two years, he had been improving clinically, after a long succession of alternating improvements with relapses into crises that invariably forced him to return to hospital until he was well again. By that time, he had been relatively discharged. He was allowed to stay at home with his mother, but always accompanied by someone from the hospital, especially Marie–Victoire, because she was the one the boy always vehemently insisted should be the nurse to accompany him home. He peremptorily refused to allow himself to be care for anyone other than herself. François's mother, Amandine, at first did not notice the boy's excessive attachment to the young and beautiful nurse, but then, as time went by, she found her son's behavior towards the girl strange.

"You know that my son keeps calling you by the other girl's name, don't you?" – Amandine Rounet asked the nurse one fall afternoon, while the boy was asleep after receiving a dose of calming medication.

"And why do you agree to such a thing?"

"I want you to know, madam, that I had no other choice: your son has mistaken me for his dead fiancée and, the medical advice, that was the only way he could get him out of the crisis he was in..." – the young woman replies. She continued firmly, without showing any sign of being intimidated by the other woman's words.

"However, do not think I am taking advantage of that. On the contrary: I am only collaborating at the request of Dr. de la Roche, as you well know, the doctor who has been treating François for some time and who, seeing the possibility of curing your son, asked me to cooperate. There is nothing else! I can assure you, madam."

"I hope so!" – replied Amandine Rounet dryly.

"And you do not ever take advantage of my son's madness in order to profit from the mess the poor boy has gotten himself into."

"You did not even need to say such things to me, madam..." – replies the nurse, highly hurt.

"I know very well where I belong."

"I really wish that Dr. de la Roche would use more academic methods with his patients instead of using such empirical processes!" – François's mother remarked, without hiding her annoyance.

"He has been like this for so long... Almost seven years! Today I know that François will never be cured. For many years, I have harbored the illusion that he would one day come to his senses and return to what he once was. But now I realize I have been deluding myself all this time! My son's madness is irreversible. It pains me to admit this, but I know it is true!" – and thick tears rolled down her cheeks.

"Oh, Madam…" – exclaims the young nurse, trying to console the other.

"Have faith in God. Trust in Divine Providence!"

"Faith!" Faith! – explodes Amandine, full of boredom.

"I do not think God even heard my prayers! He was deaf to my pleas the whole time! But I got tired! I got tired of everything; you know? I am tired of this horrible situation, of having a madman in my house, of having to measure the words I say so as not to make him fall into crisis, of knowing how to look at him with a certain way or he will fall into crisis! Oh, it is all nonsense. Nonsense from the doctors at Charenton, who I think are just as crazy as their patients!"

"Oh, madam, surely you do not know what you are talking about!" – exclaims the young lady, verly offended.

"At Charenton, everyone does everything possible and even the impossible for the patients!"

"I know!" – exclaims Amandine, full of irony.

"For what they are charging for admitting patients, I would do it…"

"Oh, madam, you may not understand this, but your son has made a lot of progress with the treatment he received there!"

Amandine only stared at the young woman with a strong expression of annoyance. She was getting bored of everything! What is more, she had to tolerate the constant presence of that pretentious little girl in her house, dictating to her what to do and what the right thing to do with her son was. Deep down, she was disgusted with her. Even her pedantic voice, with her strong *Marseillaise* accent, made her nauseous! Above all, she could not tolerate her son's behavior towards this stupid little provincial.

"I think I will change the way I treat François'!" – exclaims Amandine at last. And she continues, bluntly, bluntly:

"And I would also like you to stay away from him! Come to think of it, I think I will be able to look after my boy myself from now on, here in our home, giving him more affection, more attention and more comfort! I will hire a trained nurse and I am sure we will be able to treat him much better than you did back in Charenton! What is more, Dr. de la Roche will be able to come and see him every week!"

"As you wish, madam!" – replies the girl, highly aggrieved.

"However, I must warn you that François is only apparently in relative equilibrium! If you do that, he may enter a new and deep crisis, which will be difficult to him to get out of! That has happened so many times before!"

"Oh, who are you to think what I should or should not do with my little boy?" – replies the Marquise de Montpelier harshly.

"It certainly will not be you who decides, but Dr. de la Roche! And I am absolutely certain that he will not deny me such a request! I am going to Charenton to meet him tomorrow! And the sooner you leave my house, the better it will be for everyone!"

"As you wish, madam..." – replies the young nurse, deeply moved. She stood up, bowed slightly to the matron and headed for the little room she had been occupying in the servants' wing.

"Pretentious!" – muttered Amandine, full of spite, as the girl left the room.

"Foolish! If you think you are going to grab my boy's possessions, you are sorely mistaken..."

Marie–Victoire arrived at her simple little room and therw herself on the bed. Tears streamed down her face, soaking the coarse cotton fabric of the pillowcase.

"*Oh, mon Dieu!*" – she exclaims softly.

"I have never been so humiliated in all my life! Just because I am poor, you are so dismissive of me! Oh, disgrace! How I hate poverty! – and, for a moment, her thoughts were flooded with a whirlwind of disparate and conflicting ideas. She had to get out of there! She had to get away from François–Armand! The old Marquise, proud and overbearing, did not like her. She saw her as a threat to her son's sentimental life! Sentimental life? What sentiment was left in that poor wretch's heart? Nothing! Only the rubble of a monstrous tragedy! The rubble of a passion so great and which had collapsed with such force, clogging up his heart and reason with a mountain of debris that it would be difficult for anyone to clear away completely in order to rebuild a new passion! Poor François! She had given him a reason, God knows what it was, to regain a little of his lost reason, which his mother was now foolishly beginning to curtail out of sheer jealousy and prejudice! And if she, Marie–Victoire, dared to stand up to that tyrant, surely the damned woman could use her influence and perfidiously urge the hospital board to theow her out! Good Heavens! What would she do? She liked François–Armand! She had gotten used to him, to his daily presence! And now? She would have to pray to God that, at best, the overbearing Amandine Rounet would not ask for her head! If she lost this job, it would be chaos!

In the middle of her musings, the young nurse, tremendously exhausted by the emotional burden she had suffered, ended up falling asleep. After a while, she was awoken by gentle knocks on her bedroom door.

"Marie–Victoire! Marie–Victoire!" – she hears the voice of one of the maids calling her.

"*Madame la Marquise t'apelle! Vite! Viens!*"[1]

Before long, the nurse found herself in front of Amandine, who was reading a book, reclining on a sumptuous chaise longue in the comfort of a large and cozy boudoir.

"Did you send for me, madam?"

"Yes." – replied the other, coldly, without taking her eyes off the book.

"I have thought it over and decided that you should leave today, before my son wakes up from his afternoon rest..."

"But, madam..." – says the young nurse.

---

[1] "Marie-Victoire...! Marie-Victoire...! (...) –The Marquise is calling you...! Hurry! Come...!", in French.

"Do not argue with me, young lady!" – says the matron, now taking her eyes off the book and staring at her with a pair of terrible cold eyes. And she continues, her voice as sharp as a razor:

"And I suggest you leave now, before it gets dark! My car will drop you off safely wherever you want to go! Come on... Pack your belongings! I do not want you here for another hour!"

"And your son's medicine, madam? And what will I tell Dr. de la Roche?" – the young woman still insists.

"As for the medicine, do not worry!" – replies the Marquise de Montpelier, directly.

"All you have to do is instruct Annette, one of my maids, because if you do that, she will be able to do it too! And as for Dr. de la Roche, I will take care of him tomorrow! Now, get out of my house immediately!"

Marie–Victoire turned towards the door and went out. She was melted, her shoulders were slumped and her soul carried the greatest sadness in the world.

"Go away, you, clever girl!" – murmured Amandine as she followed the girl with her eyes as she left the room in great sorrow.

An hour later, François–Armand woke up and, as he always liked to be by his nurse's side, the first thing he did was ask his mother about the girl, who was still reading her book in the tranquility of the luxurious boudoir.

"Maman, do you know where Marie–Victoire is?"

"Your nurse is gone, *mon petit!*" – Amandine lies.

"The hospital sent for her. In fact, while you were sleeping, Dr. de la Roche was here in person to pick her up."

"But, why is that?" – asks the boy, filled with disenchantment.

"And why did you allow the doctor to take her?"

"Oh, my love!" – exclaims the matron, leaving the book and opening her arms, drawing her son to her.

"Sit down next to me! I have good news for you! Do you know what Dr. de la Roche said? He told me that you are cured! That you will never have to go back to that horrible hospital again and that you do not need another nurse!" – and, pretending to be overjoyed, she continued:

"Is that not wonderful? From now on, you will always be here with me! The doctor personally instructed Annette to give you the medicine! You are free forever from the illness that afflicts you! Is that not good news?"

The boy lowers his eyes, full of hurt and disenchantment. Two tears suddenly spring to his eyes and run down his face.

"*Eh, mon bebé!*"[2] – exclaimed Amandine, noticing that he had not looked at her and had not replied.

"Are you not happy with the news?"

"*Non, Maman!*" – he says softly.

"Sylvie left me again and you did nothing to stop her!"

"Oh, François!" – says the Marquise de Montpelier, getting up, highly upset by her son's words and, moving towards the window and, with a quick and precise gesture,

---

[2] "Hey, my baby...!", in French.

she pulls aside the heavy gray velvet curtains and peeks outside for a few moments. Then she turned around and, full of grief, looked at her son, who was huddled in a corner of the chaise longue, and continued:

"Why do you not face reality once and for all, *mon chéri?* Look, I raised you to be strong, virile and determined, but what are you revealing yourself to be? A half–man, overly sentimental, romantic and given to fantasizing about everything around you! Oh, how different you are from me and your father! I wanted you to be stronger, bolder! Do you not realize that Sylvie no longer exists? That she is dead?" – and, returning to sit beside his son, she took his cold and trembling hands and continued:

"Look, you think that because you have not seen Sylvie dead, have you? But I saw her! She was dead, yes, in a coffin! Smallpox killed her, do you understand? That girl you think is your girlfriend is nothing but an impostor, a clever girl, deceiving you! Understand this once and for all! Be a man, François!"

"You are a liar, Maman..." – exclaims the boy, staring at her with horror in his eyes, which are too wide and filled with a strange glow.

"You're a big liar too! Sylvie did not die!" – and, with a smile full of a mixture of anger and disdain, he continued:

"You sent her away, *n'est–ce pas?* I know! You never liked Sylvie! You hate her, Maman!" – and, getting up, he abruptly left the room.

"François! Come back!" – exclaims Amandine, running after him.

"Come back, please!" – and, already feeling premature remorse for the harsh words she had spoken to her son, runs after him. She found him curled up on the bed, his gaze inexpressibly lost in nothingness. *"Oh, mon petit..."* – exclaimed Amandine, her eyes welling up with tears.

"Oh, forgive me, forgive me! I'm so stupid!" – and taking her son by the chin, she gently forced him to look at her. The boy's jaw was hard and clenched.

"Oh, what have I done to you, *Mon Dieu!*" – she continues, overcome with despair. This time, she violently pulls her son's face, with the intention of making him look at her.

"Look at me, François!" – she moans, full of regret.

"Look at me, my dear!"

The boy, however, seemed to be made of stone. Amandine then knelt down beside her son's bed and tried to draw him to her, but found to her amazement that he was completely rigid, all the muscles in his body were locked. No movement was noticeable apart from his panting and difficult breathing.

"Annette! Annette!" – the Marquise de Montpelier cries out for her maid, falling into extreme despair.

Before long, the maid appeared to answer her mistress's cries.

"François' medicine!" – snapped Amandine.

"Hurry! The medicine!"

"*Qual? Qual..., Madame la Marquise!*" – the poor maid shouts, highly embarrassed.

And then, standing in front of the sideboard, the bewildered Annette ran her nervous eyes over the array of transparent bottles displaying their contents, in a labyrinth of liquids of the most varied colors, and indicated on the labels by strange names. Completely lost, the maid alternately wanders her distressed eyes between the infinity of colored glasses and the face of her mistress, who was anxiously waiting for her.

"Did the other one not instruct you properly, you fool?" – Amandine scolds, finally letting her impatience take over.

"Yes... I mean... No! I do not know, *Madame Marquise*!" – replies the poor maid, wringing her hands nervously, allowing herself to be overwhelmed by despair.

"Oh, you are such an incompetent!" – exclaims Amandine Rounet, snorting with impatience.

"And now, how do we act, you slug? The other cretin has gone! Call an apothecary! Quickly! The man should understand these things..."

Half an hour later, poor Annette returned, accompanied by a distinguished gentleman sporting a long gray moustache and sideburns.

"I do not know about these medicines, Madam..." – says the man, after carefully examining the bottles one by one.

"These medicines are for the exclusive use of the Charenton Hospital and we, the apothecaries of the city, have no access to them. Most of them are distilled in the hospital's own laboratory and I do not even know what they contain! It would be foolhardy and a great responsibility for me to give the boy drugs like this, because I do not know their description and prescribed dosages! Only the staff of the hospital could give him these drugs in completely safety! I'm sorry!" – and, bowing slightly, he turns around and leaves.

Amandine is overcome with despair. And now? She has overdone it, she recognized. She had overdone it by overzealously dismissing that little brat!

"Tell me, Annette…" – she asked, turning to the maid in the corner, who was fidgeting nervously, pinching the back of her heand with her nails.

"Did that unfortunate girl tell you where she lived?"

"*Oui, Madame la Marquise!*"[3] – replies the servant.

"Get the car ready!" – orders Amandine with a firm voice.

"You and I will go there!"

An hour and a half later, the luxury car of the Marquise de Montpelier parked in front of a decrepit stone building in a poor suburb of the city. It was already dusk, and darkness was beginning mercilessly invade the bumpy, filthy street. Amandine left the car, following the maid who had preceded her and, highly frightened by the extreme ugliness of the place, instinctively put her hand to her nose.

"What a stench, my God!" – she thought. And she runs her eyes over the uneven ground so as not to be betrayed by one of those holes full of stinking mud. Indeed, the stench was intense. Fillets of dark, smelly water, open sewage streams, flowed through, carrying the waste from the miserable

---

[3] "Yes, Madame Marquise…!", in French.

neighborhood, where hundreds of poor families huddled in shantytowns that had been badly damaged by the weather. Amandine shuddered slightly.

"So, this was where the clever girl lived, wasn't it?" – she thinks.

"Now I understand why you were so keen to be by my son's side! But it was a good thing to come here, you naughty girl! Now, I know you a little bit more!"

"Marie–Victoire, *s'il vous plaît, Madame!*"[4] – said Annette to the scowling woman who had come to open the door.

"Whom should I announce it to?" – asks the woman sullenly.

Then, curious, she squinted and, squeezing her eyes shut to accommodate the dim light, she could see Amandine standing a little further away and, beyond that, the sumptuous car that had brought them. Realizing that these were big people, the old lady broke into a broad smile and, being extremely kind, invited them in:

"Oh, Excellencies, please come in! Please stay in my humble home while I see if the lady can receive you!"

The old woman disappeared through the door, and Annette and Amandine exchange a meaningful look.

"We would better go inside..." – said the Marquise de Montpelier.

"The stench out here is unbearable!"

---

[4] "Marie–Victoire, please, Madame...!, in French.

The inside of the house was desolate! The walls were made of rustic stone, covered in the slime of time, the windows and doors were made of roughly hewn wood, the roof was made of black thatch and smelled of mildew, and the beams that supported it were covered in dark soot that poured incessantly from the smoke that scaped from the precarious stone stove in the kitchen next to the only room in the house. The furnishings in the impoverished room consisted of a heavy carved wooden table and a half a dozen crumbling, old and grimy chairs.

"It is foolhardy to sit there, Madam!" – remarks the maid, after carefully examining one of the chairs with her fingertips.

"They are sticky with dirt!"

"How disgusting!" – exclaims the other, with a grimace of disgust.

"We would better wait standing up!"

Marie–Victoire soon emerged from the top of a stone staircase with steps worn by the passage of time. Beforehand she already knew who the beautiful and elegant people were that her landlady had told her about a short while before.

"Beautiful, elegant, and extremely cruel!" – she answered the old lady.

"You do not know, Henriette, what these aristocrats are capable of!" – and she added, after she had left herself down a little, combing her hair and running her palms repeatedly over her dress.

"These people simply abhor the poor!"

"*Madame la Marquise!*" – says Marie–Victoire, bowing slightly before Amandine. She continued, with a tinge of irony in her voice:

"To what do I owe such an honor?"

"Marie–Victoire..." – says Amandine Rounet, looking firmly into the young nurse's eyes. I know I was harsh with you this afternoon! But François is ill! Annette was not able to give him the medicine properly!"

"I do not know why!" – exclaims the nurse. And, turning to the maid who was breaking down in distress, she continues:

"I taught you until you memorize everything, Annette! How could you not?"

"Oh, Marie–Victoire!" – says Annette, approaching the other.

"I had understood everything, yes, but when the boss had his crisis, I was so terrified that I could not remember anything else you had taught me!"

"So, he has had a crisis, hasn't he?" – says the nurse, looking at Amandine.

"And why did he have such a crisis, *Madame*! When I left, François was fine, resting peacefully!"

"I do not know!" – replied the Marquise de Montpelier abruptly, lowering he eyes.

"It is just that he woke up in a crisis and is mute, closed in himself, and I cannot get him to talk!"

"No, Madam!" – said the other, firmly.

"Your son's crisis was certainly triggered for a reason! You would better tell the truth!"

"Nothing happened, miss!" – shouts Amandine becomes. And she continues, fiercely attacking the young nurse.

"Are you doubting me, young lady?"

"*Oui, Madame la Marquise!*" – replies the young woman firmly.

"I know François–Armand well enough to know that something caused him to relapse!"

"Well, I am telling you that nothing unusual has happened, and I think you would better act quickly and give him his medicine again, properly! I fear for my son's life!"

"I will not go back there, Madame, without telling Dr. de la Roche first! The doctor needs to be informed of everything that happens!"

"So, what are you waiting for? Call Dr. de la Roche immediately!"

"I will not call Dr. de la Roche until you tell me the truth, Madam!" – persists the nurse, reluctantly.

"*Il va bien! Il va bien!*"[5] – exclaims Amandine, highly irritated.

"I am to blame for everything. Satisfied? Look, I have humiliated myself to this point... When François woke up, he looked for you and I lied to him! I told him you had left on Dr. de la Roche's orders!"

---

[5] "All right...! Okay...!", in French.

"Frankly, *Madame la Marquise*!" – says Marie–Victoire, looking the other in the eye.

"All out of jealous for your son! I repeat, Madam, there is nothing between François and me, and there never will be! Do not worry, I am not attracted by your money! I am poor, yes, very poor, as you can well see! In the meantime, I have my dignity! Keep your gold, because I am definitely not interested in it!"

Before long, the three women were in the luxurious coach back to Amandine Rounet's house.

"François!" – Marie–Victoire called out to the boy a short while later, back at Amandine's mansion.

"François! It's me!" – she continued, sitting down beside him on the bed and drawing him to her, hugging him tenderly.

"Sylvie…" – he murmured, his eyes welling up with teras.

"*C'est toi que retournes!*" [6]

"Yes, it is me!"

"Oh, Sylvie! Sylvie!" – said the boy, lighting up.

"I'm so glad you are back!"

From the door, Amandine followed everything with a highly oppressed chest. A knot tightened in her throat. She knew she had a huge problem to solve from now on. A problem the size of the world…

General Emmanuel–Théophile du Servey placed the book he had been reading in his personal office on the white

---

[6] "You are the one coming back…!", in French.

marble–topped desk. It was late at night and the house was completely plunged into silence. Everyone had probably been asleep for some time. The old soldier closes his eyes, half–burned by hours of uninterrupted reading, and squeezed them tightly shut to rest them. Then he opens them and looks at the brochure highly excited.

"God in heaven! God in heaven!" – he murmured, running his fingertips along the spine of the book.

"That was! That is it!" – and laughs, highly satisfied.

Then he stood up. His legs were numb. He had been sitting there, reading, since the beginning of the afternoon. He took his watch out of his jacket pocket and looked at the time: it was just after one o'clock. His eyes once again sought out the book resting on the gleaming marble top of his desk: *Le Livre des Esprits*.[7]

---

[7] *The Spirits' Book*, in French. The first edition of Le Livre des Esprits was launched on April 18, 1857, at the Galerie d'Orléans in the Palais Royai in Paris, edited by E. Dentu. However, the initial text is not the same as the one published to this day. The second edition, considered definitive, only appeared in 1860. The first edition was more compact, printed in two columns and contained 501 questions, distributed in three parts: 1st – "Spiritist Doctrine", with ten chapters; 2nd – "Moral Laws", with eleven chapters, and 3rd – "Hopes and Consolations", with three. To achieve this monumental work, the tireless Allan Kardec made use of communications from spirits, through various mediums, and annotated in fifty notebooks, gathered by the famous playwright Victorien Sardou, his father, the professor and lexicologist Antoine-Léandre Sardou, the bookseller and publisher of the French Academy Pierre-Paul Didier, the Dutch philosopher Tiederman-Marthèse, as well as a number of other intellectuals of the time. By classifying, compiling, comparing and ordering the abundant material he had at hand, the remarkable Lyon master brought to light the work that would establish the first foundations of nascent Spiritism. Later, under the coordination of the Spirituality, Allan Kardec extended the initial 501 questions to 1018, which in reality

"*Mon Dieu!*" – exclaims the old soldier, now holding the book in his hands and gently stroking its cover.

"This is what I have been looking for all my life! All the answers! Everything so clearly laid out!" – and two tears roll down his venerable cheeks.

His eyes follow the large letters: *Le Livre des Esprits*... Allan Kardec... And his thoughts went back to the day before. It was a beautiful spring afternoon, and he had met Colonel Léonard–André Bettencourt near the Palais Royal.

"Where are you going so boldly, dear Léonard?" – he asked the other.

"The *Galerie d'Orléans!*" – he replied.

"Well, do you not know, General? Mr. Kardec has just launched a treatise on spirits at the Dentu bookshop..."

"Really?" he marveled.

"Well, I am going with you there! You know how much this subject interests me!"

And they were both so lucky! As they entered the Dentu bookshop, they asked for the book from the helpful Mrs. Mélanie Dentu, the owner of the store, who had come to see them herself, and they heard from her:

"Monsieur Kardec is in the store! He is currently with my manager. If you would like to meet him, I will take you to him. Maybe he will give you his autograph..."

General Emmanuel–Théophile du Servey then remembered Allan Kardec's face: he was pale, thin, with

---

are 1019, since there is an error in the numerical sequence of question 1011, a fact that certainly went unnoticed by the distinguished Codifier.

prominent zygomas and freckled skin, largely interspersed with wrinkles and a few warts. His forehead was vertical, long and wide, rounded at the top and raised on prominent orbital arches, with abundant brown eyebrows. His eyes were small and deep-set, with dark circles and papules. His nose was large, protruding above a sparse moustache, almost entirely white and trimmed close to the edge of his lip.

The General remembers the author's kind question when he signed the book:

"*À qui, Monsieur?*"

"*Général du Servey, s'il vous plaît!*"[8] – he replied.

Allan Kardec's deep-set eyes, filled with a mixture of almost rigidity and paradoxically gentle affability, caught the General's attention. His serene, yet firm and measured voice, together with his precise and sure gestures, gave him ana air of extreme seriousness to the whole.

General du Servey followed him with his eyes as he wrote the dedication. He knew him only by name. He had discovered that he now used a pseudonym; his real name was another, well-known throughout France.[9] He knew that he had already published other works, which were very popular in the educational circles, and that he was regarded as a renowned teacher. However, he had never thought that he was also an researcher into the things of spirits.

"Where could I meet you on another occasion, *Monsieur Kardec*?" – he had asked him out of the blue, without thinking

---

[8] "For whom, sir...?" "General Du Servey, please...!", in French.
[9] Allan Kardec's real name: Hippolyte-Léon Denizard Rivail.

much, when he had handed him back the autographed book with a smile on his lips.

"I will write to you at the appointed time to arrange a meeting, *Monsieur le general!*" – kindly replied the Codifier of Spiritism.

"For the moment, I find myself too overwhelmed by my tasks, but I promise you, on my word of honor, that I will meet you. Please wait!"

Extremely touched by the memories of that meeting the day before, General du Servey put the book away in one of his desk drawers and blew out the candles in the small candlestick. The hours went by. It was late, he needed to rest. He wore a smile of complete satisfaction on his lips. He was happy. He knew that things in the world would not be the same from now on...No, they would not...

Chapter 13

Spiritism

General du Servey never tired of talking about the extraordinary book that had appeared, enlightening minds about the world in which spirits lived. He had already bought a number of copies and distributed them to his closest friends, recommending that they read this magnificent work which, according to him, had the capacity to transform the world. He had thus become a staunch promoter of Allan Kardec's extraordinary work.

On that pleasant spring afternoon in 1857, Captain Wilfred Berg, on leave from his campaign in Algeria, was passing by the barracks on a visit General du Servey.

"Read it carefully, Berg!" – says the old soldier to his friend, handing him the book.

"There you have what I believe is something that is already starting to shake the whole of France! I will tell you something else: it will go further; it will spill over our borders and flood the entire world! You should see the headlines! The book was born strong, mercilessly beating the abject face of hypocrisy, confronting lies and besieging from all sides..." – and, breaking into a smile of complete satisfaction, he continues:

"This time, there is no escape! The strong content of these pages gives rise to controversy, my dear... A lot of controversy! The book is generating controversy in all circles, academic or otherwise. It is messing with people's heads, from the most enlightened to the most stubborn... But that is a good thing! We need to shake things up, make the foundations of the institutions tremble... I know that these ideas will shake all the structures that have been built up until now! Everything that has existed up to now will become old and obsolete and will crumble! If you can imagine what these pages contain, my dear. The greatest treatise on life beyond the grave that anyone has ever written. The enigmatic veil is finally torn!"

"Really?" – marveled Wilfred Berg at the effusive and encomiastic words with which the General praised the contents of that book.

Berg takes the volume from his friend's hands and reads the title:

"*Le Livre des Esprits*... Allan Kardec..." – and, jogging his memory:

"I do not know the author."

"I am sure you know him!" – says the General.

"He used a pseudonym... Do you remember Professor Rivail?"

"Of course!" – replies the other.

"Everyone knows him! Are you going to tell me it is him?"

"Yes!" – continues the General.

"Last week, I went to the Dentu bookshop in the Galerie d'Orléans with Colonel Bettencourt to buy the much-vaunted book that was being launched. He and I were so lucky that the author of the book was there at the time. Then i met Professor Rivail! And he promised me, with the greatest deference you can imagine, to see me in private one of these days. Oh, Berg, you do not know how much the discovery of such things excites me, even in the twilight of my existence. Oh, if only these things had fallen into my hands sooner, my life would certainly have been different. I cannot tell you what wonderful revelations are revealed in these pages! No more slavery to the dogmas that, for millennia, they have tried to shove down our throats, often to our exclusion! God reveals Himself to be wiser, fairer and more equitable! No longer crime and the consequent punishment, with eternal damnation, but the blessing of redemption, through palingenesis!"

"But such ideas are not new, General!" – Berg observes.

"Metaphysics and even reincarnation have already been thoroughly explored and discussed in this century by eminent thinkers!" And it should be noted that ancient religions such as Hinduism and some factions of Buddhism have it as a article of faith. What could possibly be new on this subject?"

"Yes, I know!" – said the General.

"You are absolutely right on that point, Berg. We know how much Schopenhauer[1] recently discussed this. This is not

---

[1] Arthur Schopenhauer (Danzig, February 22, 1788 – Frankfurt, September 21, 1860) was a 19th century German philosopher of the irrationalist current. His main work is The World as Will and

about metaphysics, pure and simple, or palingenesis based on metempsychosis², as the Hinduists believe! What Allan Kardec brings us is something unusual. He reveals God, Nature and the origin of things with unparalleled precision, all based on systematic observation and the most rational analysis I have ever seen on matters of faith!"

"So, is Mr. Kardec founding a new religion?" – Berg asked. And smiling slightly, he continued:

"Here comes a new reformer!"

"I can assure you that this is a new and extraordinary reformer, my dear!" – says the General seriously. And, his voice filled with intense emotion, he continued:

"He brings us the foundations of a new and different religion: the Spiritist Doctrine!"

"If you say so, General..." – Berg says.

"But I promise you, I will read the book, and we will talk about it in due course."

"And you? – continued the General, changing the subject.

"How is married life? Is Celeste–Marie improving or is she still the same?"

Representation, although his book Parerga and Paraliponema (1851) is the best known. Schopenhauer was the philosopher who introduced Buddhism and Indian thought into German metaphysics. He was known for his pessimism and saw Buddhism as a confirmation of this view. Schopenhauer also fought fiercely against Hegelian philosophy and strongly influenced the thinking of Friedrich Nietzsche, the creator and propagator of complete nihilism, in his youth.

² Doctrine according to which the same soul can animate, successively, different bodies, men, animals or plants: transmigration.

"My wife has always behaved strangely, General..." – Berg replied.

"Even before I took her to be my wife, she had an unhealthily behavior. I always knew she was weak in the head. My mother–in–law, Marie–Louise, and I came to the conclusion that perhaps marriage could bring her some peace, but the opposite has happened: Celeste–Marie is getting worse every day! She is aggressive and moody all the time; she hardly sleeps and cries all the time!"

"It is a good thing you did not have children!" – says the General.

"I do not think she would make a good mother!"

"I think you are right, sir..." – agrees Berg.

"On the other hand, Celeste-Marie's maternal instinct is getting the better of her. She is insisting that we have a baby. But it would be a big risk. She is already thirty–two. Marie–Louise also considers pregnancy to be dangerous at this time in our lives. Not that the child would be helpless! Not at all... The grandmother herself would take care of her grandchild with the greatest goodwill. However, we do not know what my wife's reaction would be!"

"Who knows, maybe Mr. Kardec will have the answer you are looking for to Céleste–Marie's illness?" – said the General, pointing to the book that Wilfred Berg was holding.

"Since the doctors and medicines have not helped her at all!"

"You may be right, General!" – says Captain Berg. In reality, the soldier was not very hopeful. He was not very unhappy in his marriage and, with great difficulty, he realized that he had done everything wrong! Deep down, he loved Céleste–Marie and married her with the intention of making her happy, but the result was different: they were both unhappy!

A little later, in the street, Captain Berg was thinking. It was still early and he had no desire to return home. There, he would have to be with Céleste–Marie, to listen to her crying, and he was already getting tired of it. The spring afternoon was beautiful, and the soldier really had no desire to go home. The fragrance of the city rekindled in his heart the old taste for bachelor freedom. Suddenly, intense anxiety seized him. Céleste–Marie was proving to be too boring! He did not feel the same emotion with her as before. All he got from his wife was whining and aggression. She complained about supposed ghosts chasing her; she complained that she could not be happy; she wanted to get pregnant. She wanted him to give up his military career forever, so that he could stay by her side all the time. It was all jealousy and demands! Demands and more demands, without giving anything in return! She insisted that he abandon everything, leave the world behind, and hide in the house with her! Good Heavens! If that happened, he would certainly go mad!

A long time ago, returning to the campaign was difficult for him because he had to leave her, but now, however, he felt relieved when his leave was over and he had to return to Algeria! Sometimes he felt sorry for Céleste–Marie! Pity! The love he felt for her had, over the time, turned into pity... Suddenly, Berg felt a nostalgic for his old days. And Lulú Fontainebleau! He smiles mischievously. How long had it been since he had visited Madame Fontainebleau's house?

Since he had married Céleste–Marie... Four years. He lights up, and then an enormous desire comes over him to rekindle the embers of the playful past from the ashes.

"I could do with some time off with Lulú's girls..." – he murmurs softly and smiles.

"I think I could do with a rest in the arms of a real woman."

Disguisedly, he looks in all directions. Apparently, no acquaintances in sight. He hesitates for a moment, then makes up his mind. He studies his footsteps and headed towards the Rue de Saint–Sulpice. The afternoon was beginning to fall when he spied the street in both directions before entering the door. He hurried up the white marble staircase of the luxurious townhouse, skipping the steps two by two. His heart was pounding when he got upstairs and, for a few moments, he stood in front of the door to the luxurious cabaret, shaking his head. From inside, there was the muffled sound of a clarinet singing a mournful melody, which was accompanied in the background by veiled voices and measured laughter.

Lulú Fontainebleau's house was known for its discretion and refinement: no excesses or scandals were allowed under any pretext! A pair of gigantic Africans guarded the place, and anyone who gagged them down was fatally kicked out of the place, literally and banished forever. The entrance door was constantly kept under lock and permanently guarded by a pair of faithful black giants.

Berg wipes his sweaty forehead with his handkerchief, then runs his hand through his hair and pulls himself together. Then, closing his hand, he knocks on the door lightly with his knuckles.

"*Monsieur le lieutenant!*" – says one of the Nubians as he opens the door. Respectfully, when he recognized Berg, he bowed slightly and invited him in.

"*Entrez, s'il vous,*" *plait, Monsieur le lieutenant Berg!*[3]

"Captain, N'dingo!" – Berg corrects him, smiles slightly and enters. When they heard the door opening, all the heads in the small, luxurious salon, seated around mahogany tables covered in exquisite linen tablecloths and on which rested long, fine Bohemian crystal glasses filled with bubbly, golden champagne, turned tautly towards the entrance.

"Berg!" – exclaims Lulu Fontainebleau, getting up from the divan where she was sitting sipping a glass of champagne. And, approaching the boy, she kissed him on his cheek, playfully exclaiming:

"Is it really you or your spirit that is returning?"

"Oh, Lulú..." – replies Berg, laughing.

"Have you even let yourself be contaminated by the wave of ghosts that is sweeping through the city? I was just talking to General du Servey and look what he gave me as a present! " – and showed her the copy of the book he was holding.

"Oh, I have read it too!" – exclaims the old pimp.

"And if you want my honest opinion, I will tell you that what is in it is the absolute truth. You know, Berg..." – she

---

[3] " Lieutenant...! (...) – Please come in, Lieutenant Berg...!", in French.

continues, gently pulling him by the hand and making him sit down next to her on a red velvet divan.

"I have never mentioned it to anyone, but I see my mother, who passed away over forty years now, constantly by my side, especially at night when I go to sleep!"

"Really?" – observes Berg, showing great interest. Lulú was seen as a firm and austere woman. She was not known for lying on her lips; on the contrary, she was known for her direct way of speaking and the frankness of her words.

"Yes..." – she continued:

"So, this fever that has suddenly gripped Paris about the things beyond is nothing new to me! I have always had it in the back of my mind that if my mother comes to visit me all the time, it is because she lives somewhere out of this world, *n'est–ce pas?*"

"Yes..." – replies the boy, deep in thought.

"And you?" – she continues, changing the subject and taking his hands maternally between hers.

"I heard you got married..."

"Yes..."

"With her, Céleste–Marie?" – and, when asked, she smiles, full of self–confidence, and continues.

"And let me guess: you are more unhappy and disconsolate than a monk in a cloister! You have regretted it, haven't you?" – she asks, looking him firmly in the eye.

"*Oui...*"

"And here you came to seek comfort in the arms of one of my girls, *n'est–ce pas?*"

Berg simply nods and lowers his eyes, a little embarrassed.

"I am telling you to leave, Berg!" – said Lulú Fontainebleau, staring at him. "You will be wrong again! And then, you will suffer more, with remorse gnawing at your soul! Go away! I do not want you here! If you stay, not only will you not forget your frustrations, you will add more to your already troubled heart! I know you, my friend! You will not be able to betray your love for long! You will be betrayed by your heart instead! You love Céleste–Marie! Stay with her!"

"But, Lulú, Céleste–Marie is going mad! You do not know what it is like to live with a madwoman!"

"I know..." – she replies, without being convinced otherwise.

"Not exactly living with a demented person, but I am old enough to understand how difficult this task must be! But I tell you, Berg, things in life do not usually come easy to us, do they? Not for me, not for anyone! You know how much I know people in Paris, especially men, and men of high standing like you! I live among them! You do not know that they often come here, not so much for my maidens as to listen to me! Do not think I do not know what an excellent advisor and highly experienced woman I am. Even the Emperor[4] has been here!" – and winking mischievously, she adds, laughing.

---

[4] Reference to Napoleon Bonaparte, in French Napoléon Bonaparte, born Napoleone di Buonaparte, (Ajaccio, Corsica, August 15, 1769 – Saint Helena, May 5, 1821) was the effective ruler of France from 1799, and adopting the name Napoleon I was Emperor of France from May 18, 1804 to April 6, 1814, a position he briefly retook from March 20 to June 22, 1815.

"Not for advice, of course. He did not need anyone's advice." – and becoming serious again, she continues:

As you can well see, from a very young age, I have been surrounded by eminent men of the world, my dear."

"But I am extremely unhappy, Lulú..." – he moans.

"And you will be much more if you leave your wife!" – she says firmly.

"You do not want to deceive me and say that, when you arrived here, your head was not full of the desire to do that!"

"Yes..." – he says, very disconsolate.

"As I passed *Place Pigalle* just now, the desires of the past were rekindled in me, and then I remembered you! You do not know what a man's needs are, Lulú!"

"Oh, how do I not know?!" – exclaims Lulú, reproaching him firmly.

"Do you not know my profession? And I also think that men are all the soft–headed! They are exchanging what is certain for what is doubtful. They think that what is on the streets is always better than what they have at home! Oh, how wrong they are! Dirty pleasures are always fleeting, dear Berg! And they usually leave a bitter taste in the mouth! It is like getting drunk on water hyacinth: you regret it tremendously afterwards! You should know better! You are no longer that fifteen or sixteen–year–old boy who escaped your mother's surveillance and used to come to my house every day! First thing in the morning, you were already at the door! Remember how I always had to throw you out when it got dark, so as not to get into trouble with Commissioner

Lefèvre!" – and, laughing at those memories of the past, she continues:

"You were so honest and straightforward that you could not even lie about your own age! Remember when the commissioner caught you fooling around and you revealed your true age? Not only did you get a scolding like that, but you were also brought before your mother by the commissioner himself. After that, you disappeared from here for a long time. Ha! Ha! Ha! Ha! Your mother grounded you, huh?" – and, getting serious again, she continues:

"Even though you are now a grown man, full of experiences and tired of all the adventures you have had all over the world, you have not changed a bit! You could not lie to your wife! You would let yourself be betrayed sooner than you think! You are too honest! Love affairs and mistresses are for the worldly, for the crazy, Wilfred! Not for you! It does not suit you! You have always been right all your life! You are different from the others who are worthless, who live by stealing from the poor, who lie, who plunder and who are even capable of murder, without moving a single muscle in their face, so cold and insensitive are they! I know you are upset, unhappy, but this is your life. Do you want pleasure and fun? Here is sell you. Just choose the product! But did you hear what I said? Selling you! You will get mechanical, mercantile pleasure, without a hint of passion or tenderness! And if it seems to you, in your thirst for pleasure, that one of these girls is interested in you, I will tell you in advance that it is a lie! These creatures are trained to pretend! Pretend, do you understand? They love nothing but gold! I know them very well!"

Berg looked at the woman who, despite being seventy years old, still bore indelible traces of the splendor she had once possessed, capable of enchanting kings and emperors! As well as being extremely beautiful, she had a unique intelligence, everyone loved talking to her and respected her advice.

Lulú Fontainebleau reaches into the pocket of her rich white silk dress with her hand, and pulls out a packet of cigarettes, tying one of them to the end of a long, shiny golden cigarette holder. A short silence falls between her and Berg.

"Now, go home, Wilfred!" – she orders, her voice firm, breaking the short silence. And, after taking a long puff of blue–gray smoke from the cigarette she was smoking, she added:

"Your wife must be worried about your delay!"

Stepping out onto the sidewalk, Berg no longer bothered to look in all directions before leaving Lulú Fontainebleau's door. It was dusk, and the streets were dimly lit by the faint, yellowish light of the gas lamps which, as they burned their fuel, buzzed like a swarm of excited bees. Suddenly, the rumble of thunder rumbled through the air, and a light shower of spring rain fell, its thick, cool drops drumming on the cobbled floor. Berg fixes his hat on his head and pulls up the collar of his jacket. He was going to get soaked if he did not go into a café. That is what he did. He went to the door, along with a small crowd of passers–by, squeezing under the threshold of a nice patisserie on Rue du Commerce. Berg sighed in annoyance, looking out at the rain, which was now coming down harder. He was going to be even later!

The rain lasted for almost half an hour and then subsided. Berg went out into the street and, with long strides, headed towards *Place Pigalle*. Soon after, he took a rental car. During the journey, he would have plenty of time to think of a plausible excuse to present to Céleste–Marie.

A week later, General du Servey and his wife Constance received a visit: Berg and Céleste–Marie.

"Oh, what a surprise, my friends!" – exclaims the general, overjoyed.

"I want you to know, sir..." – Berg continued, after they had settled comfortably on the sofas in the living room of the General's mansion:

"That when I read the book you gave me, I was taken aback by the ideas it contained! They are truly unprecedented!"

"Did I not tell you, Captain?" – exclaims the General enthusiastically.

"Did it not go beyond your expectations...?"

"Yes!" – replies the boy.

"Céleste–Marie has also read it and has a similar opinion, hasn't you, my dear?"

"Yes..." – agrees the girl.

"The book reveals very important things about the existence of extracorporeal life!"

"From now on, new expectations are opening up for humanity!" – exclaims the General's wife.

"No more of the enigmatic silence of the tombs!"

"I agree with you, my dear..." – adds the General.

"And I have something new! Mr. Kardec wrote to me!!"

"Really?" – observes Berg.

"Yes..." – continued the General.

"And he agreed to receive me at his own house in the *Rue des Martyrs*. However, as it was a small space, a small apartment I believe, he politely asked me to go alone..."

"Oh, what a shame!" – exclaims Constance.

"I would love to meet Professor Rivail in person! Did you know that he and his wife have always been involved in the fight to extend higher education to women as well?"

"No..." – replies Céleste-Marie.

"Who is his wife?"

"She is also a teacher!" – explains Constance.

"I know her by sight from the Lycée des Arts. She is Amélie Boudet![5] A very distinguished and cultured person. I understand she is already the author of three books!"

"And did Mr. Kardec not tell you anything about what you could discuss at this meeting?" – asks Berg.

"No, but if I have the chance, I am thinking of bringing him a series of questions that are still gnawing at my soul, concerning, of course, the world in which spirits live! Surely

---

[5] Amélie-Grabrielle Boudet was born in Thiais, a small town in the French department of the Seine, on Department, on November 23, 1795. As well as teaching first letters in elementary school, Amélie was also a teacher of Literature and Fine Arts, as she had an innate ability for poetry and drawing. A cultured and intelligent woman, she published three works: "Spring Tales", 1825; "Notions of Drawing", 1826; "The Essentials of Fine Art", 1828. She was married to Allan Kardec for 37 years, until his death on March 31, 1869. Madame Allan Kardec, as she became known, died in Paris on January 21, 1883, at the age of 87.

Mr. Kardec have the answers to all of them!" – replies the General. And, looking at Céleste–Marie, he continued:

"And one of these questions is about these strange ailments that afflicts some people who claim to be persecuted by hidden enemies and who are still hearing voices! This has always bothered me!"

"The case of Céleste–Marie, for example..." – observes Berg.

"Who has always lived in disturbed state, seeing figures and claiming to be tortured by a strange man who constantly appears to her in her dreams, demanding things from her that she knows she owes no one! Does it not sound like a typical case?"

"Yes..." – agrees the old soldier.

"The case of our dear Céleste–Marie has always intrigued me! Who knows, maybe he will get the answer? And I have something new to tell you: the other day I met Mr. René de Montségur, who assured me that Mr. Allan Kardec was holding *séances* at his home! And that he himself, Montségur, had already been admitted to some of these sessions and assured me that they were very serious! He told me that Mr. Kardec uses sensitives[6], highly sensitive people who allow themselves to be influenced by spirits! And yet, through these people, some of the greatest figures in history, the Church, the Arts, Sciences, and Philosophy have already manifested themselves! They write messages in which they address topics

---

[6] The term medium was not yet commonly used at that time; it was becoming commonplace. After the publication of The Spirits' Book, in April 1857, and the consequent dissemination of the thought contained therein.

of the highest philosophical, scientific, or religious content, the content of which, prepared in highly cultured language and always based on foundations and theses aimed at good conduct and superior morality, has amazed people! And, invariably, they are subjects that stand out because they are far above the level and knowledge of the sensitives and even Professor Rivail himself!"

"If this is really happening, things will soon be on fire!" – exclaims Constance.

"And what I am afraid of are the consequences of all this! Do you realize how these revelations are shaking up the structures of society? Do you think the Church will let everything go unnoticed? Do not forget that the new Doctrine totally contests all Catholic dogmas and even Protestant ones! Do you not think there will be reprisals?"

"Oh, my dear..." – exclaims the General.

"You can be absolutely sure that we will have the natural reaction of those who feel aggrieved by the revelation of the Truth! Especially the peddlers of the temple, whom Jesus vehemently fought! Or do you think the Catholic hierarchy is not already scratching its head, highly annoyed by such a publication, which is completely full of crystal-clear truths about the true faith, without the hypocritical mask of mysteries and miracles, as well as explaining, on a highly scientific basis, the origin of things, as well as the future that lies in store for the soul after death, without any allegory or threat of punishment by eternal damnation? They certainly will not forgive you for how lying and deceitful they are! We can all stand by now, because Mr. Kardec will not go through this unscathed! He has been whipping the beast with a very short stick!"

"You are right, General!" – remarks Berg.

"Imagine if the bonfires of the Inquisition still existed!"

"Oh, Mr. Kardec would inevitably be burned alive for such heresy!" – exclaims Constance.

"Do not forget that the Inquisition has not been completely abolished yet, *ma chérie*!" – continues the General.

"It still works! Thank God, not in the way it once was, but unfortunately, it still has strong arms to persecute and punish! There are other ways of roasting someone at the stake! Of course, not by annihilating their body, as they used to, but by killing their morals through slander! There are creatures who specialize in spreading false rumors, created on purpose of with the sole aim of morally murdering a person! Rumors spread like feathers in the wind! Once they are released, it is impossible to slow them down or even stop them from advancing!

And despite being false, there will always be those who believe in them, and their spread will be inevitable! That is what I am afraid of, and Mr. Kardec may not be able to escape their fury!"

For a moment, the small group of friends remained silent, deep in thoughts.

"You pay the price!" – Céleste–Marie finally breaks the silence.

"You always have to pay the price for what you do! Everything has a price..."

"You are right, my dear!" – says the General.

"And a higher price is paid by those who wish to shine a little lighter in this world! Just look at the example of Jesus! Has anyone ever brought lighter to the world than Him? And yet, what have we paid Him?"

"Death..." – says Constance, thoughtfully.

"The price was the cross..."

"And I fear that Mr. Kardec will suffer a similar fate..." – continued the General.

"He will soon be asked for his head! You can be sure of that!"

After General du Servey's speech, everyone remained silent, absorbed in their thoughts. Why did things always have to be like this? Was history not full of examples? Would humanity never learn? Why do we always remain so reluctant to accept the truth? Did Jesus not say that one day the truth would be restored?[7] And how many, like Jesus, had not given their lives in exchange for the truth? Jan Huss, Johannes Kepler, Jeanne d'Arc... Martyrs who did not hesitate to immolate themselves in the flames of the Inquisition, so that the light of truth would shine down on this world still so clouded by the darkness of ignorance...

"We are really ungrateful to those who bring us freedom!" – exclaims Captain Berg.

"All you have to do is leaf through the history books and we will find records of the holocausts of the past!"

"Yes!" – agreed the General.

---

[7] Gospel of Saint John, 14:16–17

"The list of those who have sacrificed themselves for the sake of the truth is already quite long! And here I add not only those who were literally immolated in the flames of inquisitorial bonfires, but also those who were burned in the fire of persecution, slander, the seizure of property, arbitrary segregation in infectious and inhuman prisons..."

"You are right, sir!" – agrees Berg.

"As you have already said, there are many ways to burn a person! Not necessarily by tying them to a post surrounded by sticks of wood..."

"Preferably by using green, wet wood, so there is more smoke and slower "cooking"!" – adds the old soldier.

The pleasant spring afternoon continued, while the friends were now chatting animatedly about the news that the city invariably had to present every day. They lived in the heart of the civilized world of the time and were the first to drink from the fountain of all the events that emerged as fads to be copied by the rest of the world.

When night fell, Berg and Céleste–Marie left the du Servey couple. They felt a little more cheerful, as it was always good to be in the company of highly pleasant and cultured people like Constance and the old military man. That time, Wilfred Berg left the General's house with a glimmer of hope in his eyes. Would Céleste–Marie finally be able to rid herself of her ailments?

Chapter 14

Monsieur Allan Kardec

When General du Servey stopped in front of number 8 Rue des Martyrs, it was exactly eight o'clock and fifteen minutes in the evening.

"I only insist on punctuality, Monieur le General…" – recalled the old soldier of the letter he had received from Professor Rivail a few days before, arranging that meeting.

"From the street, you must go up the stairs to the first floor, take the corridor to the back apartment…"

In front of the black varnished door, Emmanuel–Théophile du Servey stopped for a few moments to pull himself together. Then, he knocked slowly with the knuckles of his closed hands.

"*Bonsoir, Madame!*" – he exclaims, in front of the kind, distinguished face that had opened the door for him.

"I am General du Servey… *Monsieur* Kardec is waiting for me!"

"*Parfaitement, Monsieur le général!*"[1] – exclaims the lovely little woman with the clear, radiant eyes.

---

[1] "Perfectly, sir general…! (…) – Please come in!", in French.

"*Entrez, s'il vous plaît!*"[2]

The General walks in and is confronted by a crowd of people squeezed into a small but comfortable apartment.

"Oh, welcome, Excellency General!" – Professor Rivail stood up and kindly welcomed the visitor, indicating a chair for him to sit on. Then, he introduced the others one by one:

"*Madame* Plainemaison... *Monsieur*, *Madame*, and Mademoiselle Dufaux... *Monsieur* Levin..."

With brief, meaningful nods, one by one, those present greeted the newcomer.

"You said, *Madame* Plainemaison?" – continues Professor Rivail, after the appropriate introductions.

"I was telling you, sir, that Mademoiselle Dufaux is sensitive and has been in contact with spirits since 1853. And that she had published, in a book published in 1854, a series of writings received from King Louis IX."

"That is true! I remember that!" – exclaimed Professor Rivail, highly interested.

"However, I still have not been able to get my hands on that publication! Is it out of print?"

"No, *Monsieur* Kardec..." – replies Mr. Dufaux, the young medium's father.

"In reality, these writings contain the autobiography of King Saint Louis, a fact that greatly disturbed high Church dignitaries, who felt threatened by the revelations contained therein, aa well as understanding that the book contained

---

[2] "Come in, please!", in French.

offenses against the person of His Majesty![3] It was then decided to add the work in the *Index Librorum Prohibitorum*[4] and consequently to seize the copies that were on display in bookstores for sale."

"Oh, what a shame!" – exclaims the Codifier of Spiritism, highly indignant.

"And what is the title of this work? Did you keep any of the copies?"

"The book is called *"The History of Luis IX, Dictated by Himself!" – says* Mr. Dufaux.

"However, it has caused us such a headache that you cannot imagine, sir! If you wish, at a suitable time, I will bring you a copy of the remnants that we have stored in our chateau in Fontainebleau. And besides that, there is another work, sir..." – continued the father of the remarkable medium, who at that time was still a young girl of sixteen. *"Spiritualiste"*, which also greatly displeased the authorities! And, in addition to these two books, we published another which is still in

---

[3] Reference to Napoleon III of France, born Charles Louis Napoleon Bonaparte (Charles-Louis-Napoléon Bonaparte) (Paris, April 20, 1808 – Chislehurst, Kent, England, January 9, 1873), nephew of the great Napoleon and who was President and later Emperor of France from 1852 to 1870.

[4] This was the Index *Librorum Prohibitorum* (index of forbidden books), a list that the Roman Catholic Church began in 1559 and which lasted until 1966, listing books that were "more harmful to the ignorant than useful to the learned" and which automatically excommunicated those who were caught reading such works. In the more than four hundred years of its existence, more than thirty editions of the Index have been published, condemning one hundred and nine writers for their total work and approximately more than four thousand books. It ended in self-deterioration, because by 1966 nobody cared about excommunication any more.

circulation in the spiritualist circle,[5] *The Life of Joana d'Arc, dictated by Herself...*"

"I would like to analyze all these writings, *Monsieur* Dufaux!" – added Professor Rivail, highly interested. And, taking his watch out of his vest pocket, he checked the time.

"We can start our session now!"

Mrs. Allan Kardec, holding a small ream of paper and half a dozen pre-pointed pencils, approached and placed them on the table. Professor Rivail appointed people to sit around the table, especially those with mediumistic sensitivity, and he finally sat down at the head of the table.

The rest of the small audience, approximately twenty people, remained seated around the room, in straw chairs and on a small moss-green velvet divan.

"*Mes amis!*" – you hear the firm, but at the same time soft and gentle voice of the illustrious Codifier of Spiritism:

"*Faisons maintenant du silence!*"[6] – and he goes on to ask the classic question:

"Is anyone there?"

Not immediately, but after a few minutes of silent and expectant waiting, the young Dufaux picked up one of the pencils and, visibly taken over by a spiritual entity, hinted that

---

[5] It is worth mentioning that around April 1857, the time of the publication of The Spirits' Book, some terms relevant to Spiritist terminology, such as "medium", "Spiritism", "psychography" and others, were not yet known or used; the vocabulary most used until now was limited to terms imported from the works of "Mode Spiritualism", a spiritualist sect created at the time of the Fox Sisters, in the United States, and existing to this day.

[6] "My friends... (...) – Let's be quiet now...!", in French.

she wanted to write. Rivail then greeted the spirit briefly and gave her some sheets of paper. Ermance Dufaux then began to write slowly, but firmly and decisive, under the command of the spirit entity. Complete silence ensues, broken only by the characteristic sound of graphite rubbing against the paper. And while he was waiting to hear what that spirit had to say, Professor Rivail's thoughts went back in time. He remembers his first contact with Zéphyr, his guiding spirit. It had happened at a séance he had been invited to, along with his wife Amélie–Gabrielle, at the Boudin family's house. The couple's girls, Caroline and Julie, were mediums.

And, as it had happened at that very moment, he remembers perfectly the *roc*[7] in the hand of the young Caroline Baudin, lightly scratching the slate:

"I am the Zéphyr[8] of truth. Call me by this name."

Through this absolutely rudimentary means came the first psychographic writings with which the spirit Zéphyr and others began to dictate the inaugural work of the Codification, *The Spirits' Book*. And the mediumistic characters chosen for psychography would be precisely the young and childish girls, daughters of the Baudin couple, Caroline and Julie, the former eighteen and the latter just fifteen. It had to be that way! Those two girls, with no intellectual preparation whatsoever, were certainly chosen for this important task.

---

[7] Stone pencil tied to a tupia, i.e. a wicker basket in which chocolates or other sweets used to be packed at the time.

[8] Zéphyr is the name of the westerly wind on the European seaboard and is also known as a gentle breeze. In Greek mythology, he is the son of Eos (goddess of the dawn) and Astreu (one of the Titans, father of the winds and the stars). Zephyrus married Iris and his brothers were Boreas, Noto and Euro.

Rivail gets emotional. His eyes tear up.

"Hail, dear Pontiff, three times hail!" – these were the first words hastily scribbled on the slate by the hand of young Caroline Baudin. He did not immediately understand the meaning of this strange greeting, which, at first glance, seemed strange to him. Those present at the session burst into gales of laughter.

"Pon... Pontiff?!" – he shouted, highly vexed. Monsieur Baudin had felt embarrassed, because he could not understand what had happened and had tried, breaking down into profuse apologies, to attribute the probable joke to Zéphyr's witty nature.

However, Professor Rivail ended up accepting the joke and, relaxed, said:

"My apostolic blessing, my son..." – and the small audience burst into effusive laughter again. However, Zéphyr hurried to put an end to the mockery and embarrassment, explaining that Rivail had been a Druid high priest by the name of Allan Kardec at the time of the Roman Emperor Julius Caesar, in ancient Gaul, now France, in the 50s BC. And that he, Zéphyr, was a contemporary of Rivail, an incarnation of those distant times. The Druids were philosophers, judges, teachers, in short, highly respected personalities occupying prominent positions among the Celts, a was like people who were eventually dominated by Julius Caesar after a terrible and barbaric invasion of Gallic territory. The Druids held a lot of knowledge that was considered "occult", passed down orally from one to another, without leaving any written records. For this reason, very little is known about them. In the relaxation of that Baudin family gathering, a new time of knowledge was dawning for humanity.

"A new dawn..." – thinks Rivail, at the exact moment when Ermance Dufaux put down the pencil, after psychographing a series of pages, that were collected and sorted, one by one, by *Madame* Plainemaison.

After rearranging the sheets of paper, Madame Plainemaison politely passed them on to the Codifier of Spiritism, who read them a priori and silently, attentively and meticulously.

"This is a message from King Louis..." – remarked Allan Kardec, his voice filled with emotion after reading those memorable pages. And with his voice still filled with emotion, the illustrious Codifier of Spiritism set about reading:

"*Beloved Brethren,*

The time has come for the new advent of Christ! The angelic trumpets are blowing, the drums of Eternal Glory are beating and behold, the sublime figure of the lovable Comforter appears again in the opening heavens, softening the yoke of the afflicted and fulfilling the promise made two millennia ago![9] *The first big step has already been taken*[10]*, and we need, more than ever, to be firm in our struggle to prepare the table for the new Lord's Supper! Let's cover it with the white tablecloth of purity of our hearts, which we must always keep immaculate and clean from the toils and passions of the world, so that the Sublime Lamb may can dispose of them, since the Truth will need to be founded on faith that is an unshakable as rock!*

---

[9] The Gospel of Saint John, 14:16

[10] Reference to the publication of the first edition of *"The Spirits' Book."*

And, in particular, I salute you, my good friend, for the heritage of wisdom and faith that you acquired in the distant plains of Gaul, in front of the Druidic bonfires where you officiated as a distinguished priest and when, as a holocaust, you offered to Belenus[11]: the Great Father–Light, the most subtle perfumes that can be enjoyed from nature! And you too, beautiful child, who once welcomed the Sublime Master, my praise and gratitude for now once again joining you to carry out such a splendid task under the command of Christ!"[12]

After reading Saint Louis' succinct but highly expressive message, no more communications took place. The intention of the meeting that evening at the end of April was more to celebrate the good sale of the book. In such a short space of time, the book had already been such a success and was spreading like wildfire!

Shortly afterwards, when the meeting was over and everyone had left the house, Professor Rivail found himself alone in his small office. His wife, Amélie–Gabrielle, had already retired to the bedroom and was probably asleep. *Monsieur* Kardec had that message from Saint Louis in his

---

[11] Belenus or Bel was the Celtic god of light who, at the time, was worshipped by setting fire to gigantic representations of forest animals, such as fallow deer and elk, in elaborate wooden frames filled with dry straw and moss, which were then transformed into huge bonfires in the center of large clearings in the forest. This was Beltane, a festival held in honor of this god and celebrated on May 1, at the height of the European spring, with dances around these huge bonfires.

[12] Reference to the young Ermance de la Jonchére Dufaux, who would become the main medium to assist Allan Kardec during the revision of The Spirits' Book in its second edition, that of 1860, which was broader and more complete.

hands and was re-reading it once again. Again, the allusion to the Druid priest...

The first time, it had happened during his first contact with the Boudin family, when Zéphyr, his guiding spirit, had joked with him, calling him a Pontiff... Now, Miss Dufaux, who would certainly have been completely unaware of that fact, brought up these words from Saint Louis... "Distinguished priest of Bel..." He had even adopted the name he had at the time and which had been revealed to him by Zéphyr: Allan Kardec... He had molded himself to him so much that people hardly called him by his baptismal name anymore... The press, his friends... And now he received the revelation that young Dufaux had lived contemporaneously and very close to him, in ancient Gaul as a Druidess... They were meting again as their mission unfolded... Things were falling into place and, in order to carry out his task in full compliance with the expectations of the Spiritual Team assisting him, he would need collaborators of Miss Dufaux's importance.

"The work....it was not us who wrote the *Book*, but the Guides, Professor Rivail, and *roc*..." – said Miss Caroline Baudin in her innocence, answering the young Ermance Dufaux who, had asked how the *Book* had been composed.

At the memory of what had just happened that night in his house, Rivail smiled and shook his head.

"The book, dear Caroline, is actually the fruit of the tireless work of us..." he thought deeply moved. He then took a notebook from a drawer in his desk, opened it and checked the data. It contained a detailed day-by-day account of the *Book*'s sales. Of the twelve hundred volumes of the initial edition, in just over a fortnight, more than half had already been sold!

Rivail closes the small notebook and puts it back in the drawer. He sighs deeply. In the semi-darkness of the small room, his face looked like polished bronze, reflecting the flickering light of a candle burning in an iron candlestick in the corner of the desk.

"The fight has just begun..." – he thought, suddenly filled with intense bitterness.

"The attacks are already starting... Ignominy is being hurled at my name... I know it will not be an easy task!" – and a huge knot arose in his throat. He felt the weight of age on his shoulders... Life had not been easy for him. He had to fight like a Moor to keep his house. And, at his own expense, he had the *Book* printed. Penny by penny, saved at great sacrifice by him and his wife. Gabi[13], the loving figure of his companion comes to mind.

"If it had not been for your help..." – he murmurs, with emotion clogging his throat.

"Always tireless, by my side, supporting me in everything!" – and thick tears ran down his face.

Then, resolute, he got up from his desk and blew out the candle. He was going to sleep. It was past midnight and he was exhausted. He needed rest, because the next day he had a multitude of things to deal with...

François-Armand, after Marie-Victoire's return, had found relative equilibrium again. His mother, Amandine, was

---

[13] This is how Amélie-Gabrielle Boudet was intimately known.

worried about her son's excessive attachment to that poor, pedantic little nurse. It was a burden for her to have to put up with that young woman in her house, and what was worse: having to witness the boy's unbridled affection for the girl. And the girl, on the other hand, was vehement in her displays of care and attention for the boy.

One day, on her way out of the Opera, Amandine meets General du Servey and his nice wife, Constance. François-Armand's mother had left house that night more to clear her head of the constant nagging she was getting from her son's intense interest in his nurse.

"Amandine!" – exclaims Constance du Servey when she sees the other woman.

"You are so gone, darling! Where have you been hiding?"

"Oh, home!" – replied the other, after greeting the couple.

"Where else could I go with my son in such a deplorable state?"

"Has your boy not improved yet?" – asks General du Servey, highly interested.

"Unfortunately, almost none, General!" – replied Amandine Rounet, rather dejected.

"Oh, what a pity, *ma chérie*!" – exclaims Constance.

"So, you are saying that all that time he spent in Charenton was of little use to him?"

"Not only has it hardly done him any good, but it has brought me an even bigger problem!" – says the other, very disconsolate.

"Really?" – the General is interested.

"Yes, dear General…" – Amandine continues.

"My son has fallen in love with his nurse!"

"Oh, and what could be wrong with that?" – asked Constance.

"You are not having fits of prejudice, are you?"

"No, it is not prejudice, Constance!" – replies the other.

"Far be it from me to do such things! You know me very well! The thing is, my son is confusing the young girl with Sylvie!"

"No!" – exclaim the du Servey couple in chorus.

"Yes!"

"And how does that happen, Amandine?" – asks the General.

"Simple, *mon ami*: my son thinks that one is the other, understand?"

"Oh, things in the head!" – remarks Constance du Servey, highly astonished.

"Poor François–Armand…"

There was a brief lapse of silence between the three of them. Amandine lets discreet tears escape, which she quickly tries to wipe away with the white linen handkerchief she had at hand.

"I think we can try something with your son, Amandine..." – said the General, breaking the respectful silence that had formed.

"Would you allow us to visit you sometime?"

"Oh, of course..." – says Amandine, giving a nervous smile. She had a hard time summoning up the strength to conceal what had just crossed her mind. In fact, she was very disbelieving of anything anyone said to her or recommended regarding treatment for her son. She was already disillusioned with everything, however, she tried to smile and carried on:

"It is always good to have someone who cares about us and our pain! You can come to my house whenever you want!"

Three days later, Amandine receives a visit from Emmanuel–Théophile du Servey and his wife.

"Where is your son?" – asks the General, after the three of them have settled down on comfortable divans in the large living room.

"François is resting, General!" – replied the Marquise de Montpelier.

"He has to do that every afternoon. It is the doctor's recommendation, because the poor boy cannot stand the terrible drowsiness caused by the tranquilizers he takes in huge doses every day!"

"Oh, what a pity!" – exclaims Constance.

"I wanted to see him very much!"

"Dear Amandine..." – began the General.

"I do not know if you are aware about the launch of Professor Rivail's book on Spiritism...."

"Oh, my nephew Wilfred told me about that!" – says Amandine.

"And if I am not mistaken, you, General, gave him a copy of the book!"

"Correct!" – said the old soldier.

"And at the time, did he tell you anything more about the contents of the book?"

"He has told me a lot, General..." – the woman replied.

"But I have not read it yet, despite all the controversy it is already causing in all the newspapers!"

"Exactly!" – remarks Constance, entering the conversation.

"Ther is no other talk in town! Paris has taken on a wave of Spiritism like never before!"

"I have been studying this book with attention and interest and I can assure you that it is a serious and reliable work! And I have even been in touch with Mr. Kardec, the author of the work!" – said the General emphatically.

"But you did not say that Professor Rivail was the author of the book!" – Amandine said.

"I know him by sight!"

"Oh, you are right to confuse everything!" – explains the General.

"Professor Rivail launched the book using a pseudonym: Allan Kardec." – and tells her about the whole process.

"However, how can such a book be of any help to François?" – asks Amandine, overcome with anxiety.

"Not exactly the book, Marquise..." – explains du Servey.

"But Mr. Kardec, who has been conducting serious experiments with sensitives for some time now. And who, with the cooperation of these people, has been systematically studying the influence of spirits on people living on earth and the harm they can cause! I have been attending, at the invitation of Mr. Kardec himself, the sessions that take place every Tuesday at his house in the Rue des Martyrs, a newly founded meeting of a few adepts. The main medium is Miss Dufaux, although there are others. However, the venue can only hold between fifteen and twenty people, and sometimes as many as thirty. Every day, these meetings become very popular because they are of great interest due to their serious nature and the high importance given to the issues dealt with there. Aristocrats, high–ranking government dignitaries, even foreign princes and other highly distinguished figures are often present. The venue, which is not very comfortable due to its layout, is obviously becoming very cramped. Some of the regulars proposed that Mr. Allan Kardec join forces to rent a larger space in a more convenient location. He is still thinking about it. In addition, permission must be obtained from the authorities for the Society to operate[14]. And, as you well know, after the attack[15], such things usually take months!

"I see..." – says Amandine, after the General has explained it to her in detail. And after a moment's thought, she asked:

"And what does this influence of... of spirits consists of?"

"I am still not particularly familiar with these processes, but I am absolutely certain that Mr. Allan Kardec will already have many of the answers to so many questions that, to date, no one has been able to give us to our satisfaction! And with each session, I have seen incontrovertible evidence that we do survive after the phenomenon known as "death"!

---

[14] Once legal authorization had been obtained from the authorities, through the influence of Mr. Dufaux, who knew the Prefect of Police personally, the Société Parisienne des Études Spirites began to operate every Tuesday from April 1, 1858 to April 1, 1859, at the Palais Royal, Galerie de Valois. However, it moved from there and, from April 1, 1859 until April 1, 1860, it operated on Wednesdays in one of the rooms of the Douix restaurant in the Palais Royal, Galerie Monlpensier. On April 1, 1860, it moved to its permanent headquarters at 59 Rue de Sainte-Anne.

[15] A reference to the attempt made by Felice Orsini, an Italian patriot and member of the Rome Constituent Assembly in 1849 who, when the Republic fell in his country, took refuge in Paris and, in 1858, threw a bomb at the carriage in which Napoleon III was traveling because he had re-established the Pope's authority in the Papal States. For this deed, Orsini was guillotined on March 13, 1858, almost twenty days before the founding of the Société Parisienne des Études Spirites. It is important to note that, having come out of this attack unscathed, the French emperor sought to take greater care and sanctioned the General Security Law, which gave the Minister of the Interior the power to transfer or exile any French citizen found guilty of conspiring against the security of the state. It was a strict law, which was not derogated from until 1870, with the fall of the monarchy, a fact that contributed to Mr. Dufaux having to present assurances to the Prefect of Police that the Paris Spiritist Society was fully apolitical in character.

There is so much proof that I personally no longer have any doubts about it! And I will tell you something else: you do not even know how much a spirit can influence someone! I have witnessed so many phenomena that you cannot imagine.

"Do you think that my son's madness could be rooted in one of these influences?" – Amandine asks.

"From whom, for example?"

"Sylvie herself, who left so young and so abruptly and unexpectedly!" – replies the General.

"But I warn you: these are my thoughts! Mr. Kardec is the one who really knows about such things! I am still just an observer! However, I repeat: your son's cure may be involved in this process!"

"If you say so, General..." – says Amandine.

"Look, why not give it a try, darling?" – observes Constance, entering the conversation.

"I think any attempt will be worthwhile, don't you?"

"Yes..." – agrees the other, still slightly reluctant.

"But how to proceed?"

"The first step you should take, in my opinion, is to attend one of those sessions held at the *Société*..." – says the General.

"And I am thinking of introducing you to Mr. Kardec, so we can hear his impressions! What do you think?"

"I think we should try..." – replies Amandine, gaining a little courage.

"I will do anything to restore my son's health!"

"Yes!" – says Constance.

"And did you know that Captain Berg has also agreed to take the case of Céleste–Marie to the *Société*? I think you know how complicated she has always been!"

"That is right!" – agrees Amandine.

"My nephew's wife has always behaved strangely, ever since I met her! Marie–Louise was always trying everything she could to find a cure for her daughter, but so far, she has been unsuccessful!"

"And she has already taken her to see specialists in Germany and Switzerland, but it has all been in vain" – adds Constance.

"I think she is giving up trying, poor thing, because she has never gotten anything concrete!"

"Do you think that Céleste– Marie is also the case for Mr. Allan Kardec, General?" –Amandine asks.

"Perfectly, Marquise…" – replied the military officer.

"The case of Céleste–Marie seems to me even more typical than François'!"

"And how do you plan to get them both to the *Société*, General?" – Amandine asks.

"Oh, we do not usually take the sick there, Marquise!" – replied the old soldier.

"And it is not even necessary! Cures are attempted from a distance!"

"From a distance?!" – the woman is amazed.

"But how is that possible? And has it had any positive results?"

"Oh, you cannot imagine, dear Amandine!" – hasten to reply Constance.

"The times I have been there with Emmanuel-Théophile, I have witnessed extraordinary things! And Mr. Allan Kardec knows how to conduct his work at the Société so well! You would not believe the spirits who come there!"

"Really?" – Amandine is interested.

"Yes! In addition to Saint Louis, who is the guide-mentor of the Société, Saint Vincent of Paula, the Emperor[16], Santa Joana d' Arc, Platão, Aristóteles, Fénelon, São Paulo, Santo Agostinho. The list is enormous!"

"All those famous people?!" – astonished the Marquise de Montpelier, turning her eyes to the General, slightly suspicious, waiting for the acquiescence of the most honorable military man.

"The group of renowned spirits there, Madam, is very large indeed!" – said the General, confirming his wife's words.

"And the teachings they have brought us, through pneumatography[17], carried out by various sensitives who welcome *Monsieur* Allan Kardec, are truly expressive and

---

[16] Reference to the French emperor, Napoleon Bonaparte.
[17] Or psychography.

unprecedented! Never in the world have we seen philosophical thoughts that contain such a high sense of depth and rationality as those received from these spiritual personalities who bear the most famous names of the past! These lessons are sure to contain the deepest and most touching things that can touch hearts that are pure and devoid of prejudice or conceit! I can assure you, Madam, that there have never been more loving lessons about the Gospel of Our Lord Jesus Christ, in all these centuries of Christianity's existence, than those received at the *Société Spirite*! And before you ask, Amandine, I will tell you: there is not the slightest possibility of fraud, since the subjects dealt with therein amount to unheard-of revelations, unknown not only to *Monsieur* Allan Kardec, but also to all the sensitives, or to anyone in any corner of this old world! You have my word of honor! There is only one person more rational than me: Professor Rivail himself!"

"If you say so, General..." – says Amandine, deep in thoughts.

Later, at dinner table, while she was having her evening meal with her son and the nurse, François made sure that the girl was at the table with them, Amandine was quieter than usual.

She had not always made much of a point of hiding her displeasure at having to share the table with that coarse girl. She was more subjected to that humiliating situation in consideration of her son's demands! To see him well, she would do anything, even that!

"I would thank God so much if all this were over!" – thought the Marquise de Montpelier, with a deep sigh of despondency, as she followed the passionate glances that the boy and the young woman undisguisedly exchanged. Then she shook her head, almost imperceptibly, to get rid of that bad feeling. She needed to replace that tremendous grief with a little hope. The hope that General and Constance had just brought her... Who knows, maybe Mr. Kardec and the spirits would be able to help François! It was, therefore necessary to start trusting again, to regain a little hope...

Chapter 15

The Société

On that Tuesday in July 1858, almost a hundred people sat in the rooms of the *Société Parisienne des Études Spirites*, now in its new headquarters in the Galerie de Valois, in the Palais Royal. From the rostrum, *Monsieur* Allan Kardec opened the evening's studies by saying a short, simple prayer, a habit he had developed at the beginning and end of the sessions held there, under the guidance of the house's patron, the spirit of Saint Louis. The full members of the Society sat around a long table, covered with a bright linen tablecloth.[1] In front of the table, there were almost a hundred chairs, completely taken up by the audience who, in respectful silence, attended another of the famous and crowded sessions of *Monsieur* Allan Kardec, as the first Spiritist meetings held in Paris came to be known.

When the evening's proceedings were opened, Professor Rivail took the floor and said, his voice quiet:

---

[1] Hence the name "White Table" given to Spiritism. However, this reference should have a different connotation to the one it has been given. In reality, it meant "table set" and, by extension, "charity", the main attribute by which the true believers in Spiritism should be recognized, according to a statement by Allan Kardec himself.

"Among the subjects on the agenda for this evening, first of all, we pass on to our Spiritual Guides the case brought to us by His Excellency, General du Servey, our permanent member, who submitted a written question about the health of the young Marquis de Montpelier, who has been suffering from mental insanity for a long time. Present at the session, in addition to the aforementioned consultant, were his worthy wife, Madame Constance–Yvonne du Servey, and the Marquise Amandine–Hélène Rounet, the august mother of the young Marquis de Montpelier, François–Armand."

The group of mediums actually working at the *Société Parisienne des Études Spirites* at that time was made up of the Baudin sisters, Julie and Caroline, who both possessed psychographic mediumship; Ermance Dufaux, also a psychographic medium; and *Madame* Plainemaison, an auditory and inspired medium; Ruth–Céline Japhet, psychographer; Aline Carlotti, psychographer and psychophonist; *Monsieur* Roustan, intuitive medium; *Madame* Canu, unconscious sleepwalker; *Madame* Leclere, psychographer; *Madame* Clement, talking medium and clairvoyant and *Madame* Roger, clairvoyant.

These people formed the mediumistic body of the *Société*; some of them had participated in the psychography of the first edition of *The Spirits' Book*, such as the Baudin sisters, Caroline and Julie. The others came closer over time, during and after the foundation of the Entity, when the sessions were still taking place in Professor Rivail's apartment.

Immediately after the verbal request made by the illustrious Codifier of Spiritism, Mrs. Plainemaison went into a trance.

"*J'écoute une voix!*"[2] – murmurs the woman, the owner of a spectacular and extremely capable mediumship, working in the early days of Spiritism.

"*Une jeune voix que pleure...*"[3]

"*Qui est là?*"[4] – asks the remarkable Allan Kardec.

"*Dissiez le votre nom s'il vous pla!*"[5]

"Sylvie..." – murmurs Madam Palinemaison.

"She says her name is Sylvie..." – on hearing that name, General du Servey exchanged a meaningful glance with his wife.

"What did the woman say?" – whispers Amandine to Constance.

"I could not hear what she said!"

"Sylvie!" – repeats the other, very excited.

"Did I not tell you? Things will clear up soon. Wait, my dear!"

"*N'est–ce pas possible!*"[6] – whispers Amandine into the other woman's ear.

"You said Sylvie! Could she be Edith–Aurore's daughter?"

"Yes! Who else? Now, shut up and pay more attention so you can hear what they are saying!"

---

[2] "I hear a voice...! (...) – A young voice crying...", in French.
[3] "A young voice that cries...", in French.
[4] "Who's there?", in French.
[5] "Please tell us your name!", in French.
[6] "It is not possible!", in French.

"Amandine! Amandine!" – exclaims Mrs. Plainemaison, in a mediumistic trance.

"*Moi?!*" – exclaims Amandine, tremendously frightened. And, turning to Constance, she tells her, highly astonished:

"That woman said my name!"

"Yes!" – replied the other.

"Sylvie's spirit wants to speak with you! Come on, raise your hand! Make yourself known, come on!"

"*Moi je!*"[7] – claims Amandine, hesitantly raising her hand.

"*Oui, lá!*"[8] – says Professor Rivail. And he continues:

"Madam Marquise de Montpelier, please confirm for us: was the person with that name related to you?"

"Yes, *Monsieur* Kardec!" – replied Amandine.

"She was my son's fiancée!"

"Amandine! Amandine!" – Mrs. Plainemaison continued in trance.

"*Je souffre pour François! J'écris...*"[9]

"*Parfaitement!*" – Rivail replied to the spirit, faced with enormous expectation that was building up in the audience present at the session.

Then Mademoiselle Ruth–Céline Japhet clearly showed signs of being in a trance. Her right hand began to tremble insistently, a sign that the spirit was ostensibly

---

[7] "Me", in French.
[8] "Yes, there...!", in French.
[9] "I suffer for François...! I write...", in French.

controlling the movement of her arm and hand. *Monsieur* Allan Kardec offered her a pencil and placed a small bundle of papers at her disposal. The medium then took hold of the pencil and, with incredible speed, began to write, uninterruptedly and in firm, precise strokes, the large letters, which quickly filled the pages, which were replaced with agility by the distinguished Codifier of Spiritism. The minutes passed in total silence, maintained by the assembly, which was at all times highly expectant of what the spirit was writing in Miss Japhet's hand.

There was no noise in the room except for the almost imperceptible rubbing of the graphite on the roughness of the paper. The young Japhet, taken by the spirit who had lent her hand, kept her eyes completely closed. Her head was thrown back, her neck slightly tilted to the left. Her features took an intense pallor, it would seem ghostly even to those observing her from a relative distance in the dim light of the room. Her face often took on expressive grimaces, as if the medium was suffering some kind of spasm while, while at the same time, almost imperceptible moans escaped from her loose and completely inexpressive lips. A few minutes later, the medium throws the pencil on the table and then stretches her limbs for a long time, as if disentangling them from an uncomfortable numbness, while at the same time showing slight tremors that literally sweep her body from top to bottom. Then, always assisted by Professor Rivail, the young Ruth–Céline Japhet opened her eyes and squeezed them tightly shut in order to adjust them to the light. At first glance, you would think she was waking up from a long period of sleep.

"*Merci beaucoup, Mademoiselle Japhet!*" – says Allan Kardec, smiling kindly at the young woman.

"*Vous avez été formidable!*"

Then, Mr. Kardec gathers up the psychographed pages and first examines them meticulously. Then he stood up, walked to the rostrum and, looking first and longingly at the expectant assembly, he said:

"Ladies and gentlemen! We have in our hands a message from someone called Sylvie. And, as we have already seen from Madame Plainemaison's perception, it may be a person who was related to the Marquise de Montpelier... Please pay attention to the following reading of Sylvie's words..."

"Dear Amandine, General du Servey, and Constance...

Friends... I cannot tell you how thrilled I am to be able to give you news of me after my death... Death... Oh, surely you cannot imagine how much of a decoy that now seems to me! There is no death, my dear friends!

When the disease struck me in Champagne, you cannot imagine how much I feared to die, to leave the world, so soon, so young! I thought about my mother, of her infinite pain would be when she lost me, and about my father, so far away in Algeria, when he received that merciless blow. But above all, I thought about my love, also far away in Africa, lost in the immensity of the sands of the Algerian desert...

I was suffering terribly from the throes of the inclement fever that was cooking me alive, but I was suffering even more, thinking of the immense pain that would come to the hearts that were so dear to me, after my premature departure... Oh, my dear, you do not know how my despair grew worse and worse as I sensed my life was rapidly being consumed by the fires of smallpox! I could see Maman's desperation, trying to do everything possible and even the impossible, with no resources at hand, in the far reaches of the countryside, to hold on to my rapidly dying body... Then the end, in the midst of unspeakable, slow agony...

I thought Maman would die with me, but she was strong and overcame the pain that has no name: the pain of the mother who loses a child, hugging him and clutching him so tightly and madly to her breast, overcome by despair, as if she wanted to fight for him by force, using only her trembling and powerless hands to try, even in this very uncompensated way, to snatch him from the hands of God who also wants him for Himself... Do you understand? Mothers even fight against God so that He does not take their children back! But what an unequal struggle it is! Death invariably wins... But they, the mothers, survive. They go on living, half mutilated, half stumbling, because it hey have had a large chunk of their heart ripped out...

Amandine, I know you are suffering the pain of seeing your son lost in the shadows of madness! I understand your pain, because it is my pain too! It is our pain! Do you think my heart does not despair when I see my love, my adored love, adrift, wandering aimlessly, lost in the dark meanders of dementia? You do not know how hard I have been fighting for François to be free of this horrible disease that afflicts him!

Our beloved François temporarily lost from us, and I advise you not to disturb his heart with your implications! The young nurse seems to be nothing more than the only and final support to restore him to a minimum of lucidity! Jealousy? No, Amandine, the love I feel for him masks this terrible deficiency in my soul! And if you want to know if it hurts me to see him turn to the other woman with eyes full of tenderness and passion, I will tell you yes! But I also know that this is the pure illusion of a mind gone mad! In that young woman, he sought me out, and perhaps in some trace, in the slightest remnant of my being that she might possess, he found me! And that is enough for me! It is enough for me to know that his love for me is still so great that, when he lost me, he searched for me endlessly until he found me again, even if it was in the eyes of another woman...

I kiss you, my friend, and also the others who are so dear to me: Maman and Papa (my dear Papa who is waiting for a sign from me!) But I especially ask you, Amandine, to kiss François for me! He will know that I am the one kissing him through your mouth...

Sylvie.

Mr. Allan Kardec finished reading the message and looked around the room. There was general emotion. Amandine cried softly, and Constance held her hands tenderly between hers.

"There is the proof, Amandine!" – says the General.

"It is clear that the people sitting at that table, and even Mr. Allan Kardec, were unaware of the wealth of details contained in the message! It is clear that this is Sylvie writing from beyond!"

"Absolutely, my dear!" – adds Constance.

"No one would have had prior access to so much precise information about your son and Sylvie! I have proof that we did not tell anyone about the case!"

"You are both right!" – says Amandine, letting her tears well up even more.

"But how can I make such things known to my son?"

"How to do that, I still do not know!" – exclaims the General.

"But surely *Monsieur* Allan Kardec will know!"

Sylvie's letter from beyond had brought hope and encouragement to Amandine. At last, François–Armand had the prospect of a cure through the sessions held every Tuesday at the Paris Spiritist Society. The disembodied young woman's parents, Edith–Aurore and Captain Hippolyte–Antoine Rousselet, were visited by Amandine the following afternoon, along with Constance and General du Servey, to tell them the news. At first, he Rousselet couple were a little skeptical about the news their friends had brought, however, when faced with the irrefutable proof they had at hand, and curious fact! Sylvie's handwriting and even her signature were very similar to the young lady's, as her mother was perfectly able to see.

"I always believed that Sylvie was alive somewhere!" – says Edith–Aurore, her eyes welling with tears.

"I still do not know exactly where, but I have a feeling that my daughter lives.."

"You can be sure of that, my dear!" – exclaims Constance.

"There you have, in your hands, incontrovertible proof that what you have always felt is true! Your little girl lives in the afterlife!"

"I always thought that people could not just go out like a flame in the wind..." – said Captain Rousselet.

"And for a long time now, ever since my dear Sylvie left, I have been yearning in my heart for some proof, no matter how small, that she really did not just vanish into thin air! And note that I told no one of this desire. Only I knew, not even Edith–Aurore!" – and with his hands trembling and his eyes filling with tears, the Captain continued:

"I know this is real! Did you see? She knew about my secret desire!" – and reread the passage:

"My dear Papa who is waiting for a sign from me!"

"That fact alone would prove everything, Captain!" – replies the General.

"It is impossible that those people gathered at the Spiritist Society could have been aware of something that was going on in your head! Not even your wife knew! Reason would refute any kind of fraud in that case, do you not agree? Notably, your daughter's spirit will have read your mind. I believe there is no other explanation for such a phenomenon! However, we need to bring this further proof to the attention of Mr. Allan Kardec. Such confirmations will help him to prove to the skeptics of the world that what Spiritism proclaims is based on logical and scientific foundations! And, despite what is read in the newspapers, which are highly uninformed about the true character of Spiritism, this Doctrine is not the fruit of 'numb and schizophrenic minds', as a writer recently wrote, in the *Journal des Débats*!"[10]

---

[10] The "Journal des Débats" was a French periodical, published between 1789 and 1944, and which changed its title a few times. Created immediately after the first meeting of the "States General" in 1789, it was, after the outbreak of the French Revolution, the faithful record of the debates of the National Assembly; it was then published under the title of Journal des Débats et des Décrets" (Journal of Debates and Decrees). It endured even during the occupation of France by the Nazis during the Second World War, but ceased to circulate in 1944.

"In fact, General! – continued the Captain.

"The press is definitely not giving up on Spiritism and, consequently, on Mr. Kardec. They are even calling him a hoaxer and a charlatan..."

"I recently read a defamatory article in the Gazzete, in which the journalist called Spiritism a false doctrine, created to deceive the foolish and the naive..." – observes Constance.

"Worse than all that!" – adds Amandine.

"It was what I read in *Le Constitutionnel* just yesterday! They wrote that Mr. Kardec is getting rich quick, amassing an incalculable fortune with Spiritism..."

"Oh, poor thing!" – exclaims the General. And shaking his head sadly, he continued:

"I am the one who knows how extensive Professor Rivail's fortune is! Did you know that he financed the first edition of *The Spirits' Book* at his own expense, using the savings from years and years of hard work, together with Madame Allan Kardec?!"

"Yes!" – says Constance.

"I have known Professor Amélie Boudet since she taught girls at the Lycée des Arts! She is a lovely creature! Lovely! I am not at all surprised that she has given her full support to the cause espoused by her husband! They are both undoubtedly very worthy people! And I do not think they are making money out of Spiritism! On what grounds? From selling books? I know that little profit is made from that! What is more, if he does not charge anything for the consultations that take place at the *Société*! As far as I am concerned, I do not see any basis for such unreasonable claims!"

"I take it all for slander, my friends!" – observes the General.

"There must be a lot of hidden interests embedded in the slanderous campaign that the newspapers are already launching against Spiritism! There are a lot of people who do not like what the spirits have revealed at all! You know how it is; such things have been hurting their business, do you not agree?"

"Yes, General..." – agreed Captain Rousselet.

"Especially those of the modern peddlers of the temple! Do you not think that Spiritism could embarrass them?"

"Oh, you are absolutely right about that, my dear!" – agrees General du Servey.

"Christianity has been shredding and selling the body of Christ, at retail and at a premium, for long time! In fact, that is what their biggest income is... Simony!"[11]

"Exactly!" – said the Captain.

"And Mr. Kardec must beware of this simoniac villainy, or he will soon be asked for his head! In fact, I still do not know how the persecutions have not started! They are masters at it! Persecuting, arresting and keeping quiet are their specialties!"

"They have to take care of the rents!" – exclaims Constance laughing.

---

[11] Deliberate purchase or sale of spiritual things, such as sacraments and sacramentals, or temporal things inseparably attached to spiritual things, such as ecclesiastical prebends and benefits.

"Without the pasture, how will they keep feeding their oxen? And how will they stay fat and shiny, sleeping like pigs in their rich palaces?"

"I think it will always be foolhardy to poke them with a short stick..." – said General du Servey.

"But if no one ever does that, how will the truths about spiritual things reach us, as the spirits themselves have done so magnificently through someone as competent and moral as Professor Rivail? It is certain that he will pay the price, in fact, the high price that has always been paid by those who have sought to bring a little more of light into the darkness of our world! Christ himself is proof of that! What have we done to Him? There has not been anyone purer and more perfect than Him to dwell among us in all of humanity's history, but..."

"I do not know how they have not released *The Spirits' Book*[12] on the *Index*[13] yet!" –exclaims Constance.

---

[12] On May 1, 1864, just a few years before the events described above, "The Spirits' Book" was published on the dreaded *Index Librorum Prohibitorum*, an index of books censored and banned by the Catholic Church, created in 1559 by the Sacred Congregation of the Inquisition to "prevent the corruption of the faithful".

[13] The *Index Librorum Prohibitorum* is a list of forbidden publications that were considered heretical by the Roman Catholic Church in 1559 at the Council of Trent (it was the longest in the history of the Church: it is called the Council of the Counter-Reformation, 1545-1563); Pope Paul IV (1555-1559), in his last year of pontificate, officially instituted the censorship of publications in the "Sacred Congregation of the Inquisition". The 32nd edition of the Index, published in 1948, included four thousand censored titles, and there is no surprise at all about the censorship, since the Church has always persecuted any line of thought that diverges from its own, ever since the institutionalization of Catholicism; what is really surprising is the list of names of expressive personalities, such as Galileo, Voltaire, Victor Hugo, Pascal, Spinoza,

"Are they asleep at the switch or are the winds of change finally starting to blow?"

"If we were still in the Republic, my dear, I would still believe that if they did not forbid it…" – replies the General.

"And if the Republicans were still in power and eventually defended the free circulation of books, it would only be in order to punish the Church's leader! I can assure you that it was for no other reason than that! Just petty! I do not think that the politicians of today, when the monarchy is being restored, have any interest in persecuting or shutting up the institutionalized religious!"

"The revolutionaries tried!" – Amandine adds.

"But you can easily see that they have not succeeded, *ma chérie*!" – observes Edith–Aurore.

"At the time of the Revolution[13], the clergy had a hard time of it; however, with the return of the monarchy, the Church was once again hugging and kissing temporal power…" – and he adds, after a brief chuckle of irony:

"Spiritual and material monarchies have always gotten on wonderfully! They are made of the same stuff!"

"And Mr. Kardec beware!" – exclaims the Captain.

"Sooner than you think, the counter–attack will come! It will only be a matter of time!"

"I totally agree with what you are saying, Captain!" – says the General.

Shakespeare, among others, cited throughout history, in this index of Forbidden Books. The Index was abolished by Pope Paul VI in 1966.

"Very soon, I believe, the ostentatious and intensive attacks on the Doctrine of the Spirits will begin, with the intention of suffocating it in the bud.! But I think this is a war in which the enemies of Spiritism will have already been defeated! They think they are fighting against the Christ Consoler and they do not even know it! The things that come from God, dear friends, no man can stop or extinguish!"

"Yes..." – Constance adds.

"Man only allow himself to destroy what he himself creates; what is divine; however, not even if all human strength is mustered, will it be possible to stop even a millimeter of the power of Creation!"

"It is true!" – agrees the General.

"And he continued, always emphatic.

"Man himself is responsible for changing or destroying only what he himself creates! The things of God, however, cannot be overturned or changed, since they already appear perfect and eternal! We have systematically received guidance from the spirit of Saint Louis, telling us about the mission that Spiritism will have on Earth! And anyone who takes a stand against the march of these revolutionary new ideas about faith is simply fighting against God! The advance of truth will inexorably take place, whether its detractors like it or not! You will see!"

"Yes, but to return to the letter Sylvie sent us, how do you think we should proceed from now on, sir?" – Edith-Aurore asked General du Servey.

"As I am sure you can imagine, Constance and I have become regulars at the *Société*'s sessions..." – replied the General.

"And I will tell you something else: we have become followers of this new Doctrine because we consider it to be the Second Coming of Christ! It contains in itself unusual teachings that come with the purpose of enlightening, not confusing or arousing even more doubt or disbelief, as institutionalized religions do, which have always presented a series of absurd dogmas that enslave rather than liberate consciences! We believe that the main function of a religion should be precisely to liberate man, not to enslave him more and more, imprisoning his reason and making him lose himself in a labyrinth of dogmas, of inexpressive and empty rituals which are only aimed at external conduct! And, in order to justify any questions that may be asked, for man is an inquisitor by nature! They have created a succession of countless and unfathomable mysteries, casting an enigmatic and hermetic veil over the most serious and profound questions involving faith! Where reason fails, superstition steps in, my friends! Spiritism postulates that unshakeable faith is only that can face reason face to face at all times! No other! How can one deny the value of science and not have it as a companion to our faith? Is God not the greatest of all scientists? Man, in fact, creates nothing; He only rediscovers what already existed..."

"You are absolutely right, General..." – says Amandine thoughtfully.

General du Servey remained silent for a moment, deeply moved, after his economistic words about Spiritism and, looking at the small group of friends gathered there, he continued:

"The main mission of Spiritism will be to console!" –he continues with a firm voice.

"Wherever there is pain and despair, there Jesus will manifest Himself there, through the hands of Spiritist workers! And if you will notice, that is what we are already doing, those of us who actually take part in the *Société*:

"*Our main motto is: without Charity, there is no salvation!*"

"We already share tasks among ourselves: there are those who work directly with the spirits and those who are willing to mitigate and alleviate the pains of the world... In this way, a series of tasks are carried out to help and assist those in need of material bread, but above all with regard to spiritual issues. Cases of madness and disturbance, as well as incurable diseases, have often been solved with the help of the spirits who systematically appear there to provide assistance, either through the guidance they give us in writing, or through the phenomenon of incorporation, when the spirit speaks to us directly through a medium, borrowing their body, or through direct or indirect magnetization of the patient, from a distance. There is also, as instructed by spirituality, the magnetization of water, a fact that has led to extraordinary cures![14] As for François–Armand's, I am sure

---

[14] It is worth remembering here that, in the early days of Spiritist practice, much of the vocabulary or even the techniques currently used in Spiritist Centers were not yet effectively known, such as "fluidized water", "medium" or even "obsession", "disobsession", "pass"... The techniques and the relevant vocabulary gradually emerged as Spiritist practice became institutionalized.

that, under the wise supervision of *Monsieur* Kardec, his treatment will take place. That is how it has been. Whenever the Société has been approached with similar cases, there has been the greatest willingness on everyone's part to attend to them, and the cures have actually happened in almost every case! I have faith that François–Armand will also be freed from the illness that afflicts him!"

"Oh, God willing!" – exclaims Amandine, filled with excitement. And then she asks:

"And when will we look for Mr. Allan Kardec again?"

"Next Tuesday, we will go to the *Société!*" – replied the General.

"And I extend the invitation to you, Captain, and your wife!"

"Oh, of course we will be there, *n'est–ce pas, mon chéri?*" – Edith–Aurore hurried to say, looking at her husband.

"Yes, General…" – replied the Captain.

"You can be sure we will be there!"

After the visitors had left the house, very late in the afternoon, the Rousselet couple were filled with new perspectives. That revelation had been quite unexpected! Sylvie had written them a letter from beyond… To know that she was alive, or rather, to now be absolutely certain that their little girl, who had left them so quickly and so unexpectedly, was remembering them and writing to them from somewhere else, was truly heart–warming! Still sitting in the drawing room, they both remained silent, locked in deep thoughts. After a while, Captain Hippolyte–Antoine Rousselet took his wife's hand and squeezed it tightly. His eyes were filled with tears and, as he looked at his wife's face, he noticed that she was crying too. Then they look into each other's eyes for a long time and continue to shake hands and smile. Who knows, maybe from then on, life would stop being so empty for them, so full of such great sadness that there would be no end to it?

Chapter 16

A Case of Healing...

The fact that Sylvie had written the letter came to Captain Berg's attention through General du Servey.

"You say Sylvie wrote a letter after she died?" – Céleste–Marie was startled by the news, which her husband extremely excited, bringing her as soon as he set foot in the house.

"The General told me as much just now, while we were having coffee at *Le Procope!*"[1] – replies Berg, highly excited by the news.

"And there is already talk of spiritual treatment for François–Armand at the *Société Spirite*, under the responsibility of *Monsieur* Allan Kardec! Do you not think you could also ask for such a treatment?"

"Oh, Wilfred!" – she said, with a sigh that reflected the constant discouragement in her soul.

"We have tried so many things! We have traveled to different places in search of treatment, but as you know, nothing has worked! I remain the same!"

---

[1] Founded in 1686 by the Sicilian Francesco Procópio dei Coltelli, Le Procope is the oldest café-restaurant in Paris and also one of the most famous today, located at 13 Rue de l'Ancienne Comédie.

"Oh, darling!" – he says, taking her in his arms and tenderly stroking her hair.

"It does not hurt to try once more; do you not agree? Surely it must be something new, something completely unusual that is being done in Spiritism!"

"No, I do not know, my dear!" – she replied, overcome with sadness.

"I know that I suffer and make you suffer! And I also know how unhappy you are by my side! In fact, I still do not know how you put up with me! Sometimes I wonder how you can put up with my constant bitterness, my frequent mood swings! I am a failure! I could not even give you the heir you dreamed of! Sometimes I wonder how you can put up with me!"

"Oh, if I can stand it, it is because I love you, *ma chérie*!" – he says, with strong emotion in his voice.

"If I did not love you, I would have certainly left by now... And the son, we still have plenty of time to order him, do you not agree?"

"You are indeed a very good man, Berg... The best man in the world!"

"Oh, you exaggerate, *ma belle*!" – he says, with a slight smile. Then, holding her head with his hands, he looks her straight in the eye and continues:

"I beg you, do it for me! Once again! Let's look for *Monsieur* Allan Kardec... Please, I beg you! I love you so much and I want to see you happy by my side..."

"Oh, what I would not do for you, Berg!" – she says, opening a sad smile.

"You know how much I love you! However, I have made it clear that I will only do it for you! As far as I am concerned, I already consider myself crazy, with no hope of a cure! But I will ask you something else: I know you are enthusiastic about Spiritism, perhaps because of the influence of General du Servey, whom you admire so much. However, do not be so thirsty! What if I disappoint you again?"

"Oh, silly!" – he exclaims, hugging her tightly.

"How can you think that you will eventually disappoint me if you do not get any better?" – and shaking his head, he continued:

"And if that happens, *ma belle*, you will definitely not be to blame! Why should you blame yourself?"

"I do not know, Berg!" – she says sadly.

"I tend to blame myself for everything bad that happens to me! Then an infinity of accusations come to mind! You cannot imagine the hell my life is! If something bad happens to you, I blame myself; if Maman suffers because of me, I blame myself! This situation is terrifying! I am constantly tormented! Torment and affliction come to me out of nowhere, and I am terrified just thinking that such a thing or such a situation could happen to you or Maman... Then I panic and despair! *Oh, mon amour*, I am so tired! I have no peace! I do not know what joy is... I think I have always been crazy... I think I was born that way, Berg!" – and poignant sobs shook her insistently.

"Try to calm down, my darling!" – he says, stroking her wavy black hair.

"Have confidence! We will find a cure for your ills yet!"

"Oh, I am so unbelieving!" – she continues, between sobs.

"I cannot even pray! My ideas get confused when I try to connect with God! I simply cannot pray, Berg! You do not know how difficult it is for me! Maman has been going to church every day. I know she prays fervently for me and she has been doing so for a long time! You know, darling, Maman is tireless! I envy her persistence! I know she is making so many promises to the saints, poor thing! But look! We have had nothing so far! I am getting tired of it all. But, Maman keeps going, she never lets up!"

"Marie–Louise does these things because she has so much faith, *ma chérie!*" – says Berg, tenderly stroking his wife's hair.

"And also, because she loves you! Your mother loves you too much, Céleste–Marie, and that is why she never tires of begging God for you..."

"And with that, you make me suffer even more!" – she continues tearfully.

"I really am a wretch! God does not hear her because I am cursed, Berg!" – and bursts into highly convulsive weeping.

"Calm down, darling!" – said Berg, drawing her more tightly into his arms.

"I understand your anger, but you must never lose faith! If God has not given you grace yet, it is because the time has not come yet!" – and trying to get her out of that deep crisis of anguish, he continued:

"Look, maybe He is listening to you right now? They say that the *Société Spirite* is promoting miraculous cures!"

"I am afraid of such things, Berg!" – she explodes in despair.

"They say they deal with ghosts and hauntings there!"

"Oh, surely all that is just a fantasy in people's heads!" – he observes with a smile.

"What I do know is that they do serious research on the dead there!" – and trying to convince her otherwise, he continues:

"Did you see what Sylvie said? A series of things exactly confirming that she was the real author of the letter! There's no reason not to accept it! It is all very obvious..."

Céleste–Marie answered nothing. With her face hidden in her husband's chest, she continues her deep, painful crying. And Berg, hugging her tightly, continues to stroke her wavy black hair. Then he kissed the top of her head repeatedly and squeezed his eyes tightly to stifle the tears that were still in their eyes, then a deep knot rose in his throat. A solution had to be found urgently. Céleste–Marie was exhausted. How long could she endure such an ordeal?

Céleste–Marie cried for a long time, holding him close. Then, unburdened, she lifted her tear–washed face and, facing him, said:

"Berg, if *Monsieur* Allan Kardec and Spiritism manage to cure me, will you give me a baby?"

"Oh, of course, *mon amour*..." – he replies without hesitation.

"Of course!"

There was so much emotion in Céleste-Marie's voice that Berg did not even think to answer. He would do anything to get her back to health. Anything, really! Unusually happy, she hugged him and kissed him repeatedly.

"You are a good man, Berg..." – she says, beaming.

"You are a good man..."

On a Tuesday in November 1858, at the ordinary session of the *Société Parisienne des Études Spirites*, under the chairmanship of the distinguished Professor Hippolyte-Léon Denizard Rivail, the spiritual treatment of François-Armand began. Present at the session were General du Servey, Constance, Amandine as well as Captain Berg, Céleste-Marie, Marie-Louise and Sylvie's parents, Colonel Rousselet and Edith-Aurore. As always on that Tuesday, the simple hall of the Paris Spiritist Society was packed with people. It was not uncommon for those present to include high-ranking foreign personalities who had come to see the famous meetings of Monsieur Allan Kardec, which, with incredible and unusual speed as had never happened before, were becoming known in all parts of the world, even the most remote.[2]

As usual, patients were not taken to the Spiritist Society; the treatment consisted of applying spiritual

---

[2] It's worth remembering here that, in less than twenty years after its launch, The Spirits' Book which, at the time, represented a milestone in the speed with which an idea could be disseminated, given the difficulties that still existed in the means of communication in the mid-19th century, when only the telegraph was used, and even then, covering relatively short distances. It wasn't until 1866 that the first regular transatlantic telegraph transmissions were made via a submarine cable linking North America to Europe.

resources from a distance. The patient's name and address were given to the spirits, who gave their opinion, whether through psychography, psychophony or any other mediumistic modality.

After Professor Rivail opened the session, the list of requests for assistance and clarification of doubts and questions was read out, as usual, since it was common for number uncertainties to arise regarding the communications received from the spirits, which was of people to be uncertain about the communications received from spirits, a fact that was understandable given that spiritist practice was still in its early times and still unknown at the time. Then, under the silent expectation of the audience, the spirits began to manifest themselves through the mediums present in the session.

Time went by while the mediums wrote page after page of paper, receiving news from beyond. *Monsieur* Kardec followed everything with great attention. Nothing escaped his attention. And he had the collaboration at of two other effective members of the Société to help him systematically: *Madam* Plainemaison and *Monsieur* Baudin who, as well as being bearers of unique mediumship, also helped him with the difficult and complex task of assisting and supporting the mediums trance. After more than an hour, the communications gradually ceased.

Now all those messages had to be put together and read carefully and rigorously! We had to be very careful about what the spirits said. Do not just accept everything they wrote. It was essential to analyze every word, every idea expressed, before making it public!

Monsieur Kardec knew very well what ground he was treading on. There were so many risks surrounding mediumship, so many pitfalls! One false step and the enemies of light would be there, always on the lookout for the slightest opportunity to throw all kinds of obstacles and confusion. As time went by, Rivail began to realize just how misleading one of those messages could be! He remembers the wise advice of the Apostle John[3] and smiles slightly. He should not give credence to any spirit; first, he had to test their origin[3]. When it came to what he was doing, there was always too little care...

"Ladies and gentlemen, today we have a series of communications..." – says the Codifier of Spiritism, after having carefully read one or half a dozen psychographed messages.

"We will begin with the one addressed to *Madame* de Longchamp... It is about her august husband..."

"Oh, Pierre! Pierre!" – exclaims a distinguished lady who, standing up, highly excited and tearful, cuts *Monsieur* Kardec's words.

"*C'est mon bon Pierre!*" – she continues, bursting into tears.

"I knew it! I felt it!"

"Come closer, Madam, *s'il vous plaît*!" – says Professor Rivail, inviting her to approach the table.

"Here is what your husband is telling you! Please, read it and then, if you wish, you can confirm to those present the veracity of the facts!"

---

[3] I John, 3:4.

"Yes! Yes!" – exclaims the woman, holding with trembling hands, the bundle of handwritten papers that Monsieur Allan Kardec had given her.

"*Monsieur* Alphonse–Auguste de Pérault–Devron..." – continues Allan Kardec.

"We have something from Marguerite... Can you confirm that?"

"Oh, yes! Yes!" – exclaims an old man, approaching somewhat unsteadily and leaning on a cane.

"*C'est ma fille!*[4]"

And then, a series of messages were sent to people who consulted the spirits about the most varied subjects: news of deceased relatives, searching for missing persons, curing serious illnesses...

"*Madame et Monsieur Rousselet!*" – calls Allan Kardec.

"News from Sylvie..."

"*Oh, mon Dieu!*" – exclaims Edith–Aurore bursting into tears.

"She has written to us again!"

An hour and a half later, all seated around a table at Le Procope, having a snack, they were excitedly commenting to each other on the extraordinary fact that had been repeated.

"Did I not tell you that what *Monsieur* Allan Kardec is proposing to do is extremely serious?" – remarks General du Servey, overjoyed.

---

[4] "She's my daughter...!", in French.

"Today we have all had even more irrefutable proof of the authenticity of the message received!"

"Yes!" – agreed Captain Rousselet.

"My daughter refers to details of her existence that only her mother and I know!"

"All the more so as he promised us François' cure!" – adds Amandine, full of spirit.

"And we will have even more proof if my cousin actually heals!" – says Berg.

"Yes!" – exclaimed Edith–Aurore, who was holding her daughter's writings in her hand, insistently re–reading them.

"Look at what she says here:"

"Our dear François is already under the care of the eminent team of doctors here, and his full cure will only take a little more time... Let's be patient, pray with faith and wait..."

Strong hope then strengthens the spirits of the group of friends. Amandine takes Edith–Aurore's hand and gives it a firm squeeze.

"I know your daughter is looking after François!" – she exclaims, her eyes brimming with tears.

"They loved each other so much that such intense love could never be broken by death..."

"Yes, *ma chérie*!" – says the other, her eyes also welling up with tears.

"Their love transcends death itself..."

The friends look at each other. Things were changing. Now there was a new hope on the horizon. There was a chance to be happy again and they laughed. And his laughter mingled with the discreet alacrity of Le Procope, literally overwhelmed by the beauty and brilliance of the what was most elegant and luxurious in Paris. Times were changing; things were finally taking on a firmer and more plausible meaning...

That same night, when Amandine arrived home, François-Armand was snoring peacefully, leaning back on a divan in the living room. At the slight rustle of his mother's dress, the boy woke up and looked at her, surprise and frightened.

"Where have you gone, Maman?" – he asked, highly strung. His eyes were swollen from the long and deep sleep.

"Oh, I went out with some friends..." – she says. And she lies to him, deliberately.

"We went to the Comédie..."[5]

"Ah, and what are they staging at the Comédie?" – he asks, showing great interest.

"They're carrying *Rotrou's*:[6] *Cleagénor et Doristée*!" – Amandine replied, sitting down in front of her son on a chaise

---

[5] *Comédie – Française*, or *Théâtre – Français*, is the only state-owned theatre in France and one of the few to have a permanent troupe of actors. It is located in the 1st *arrondissement* of Paris. The *Comédie – Française* was founded by a decree of Louis XIV on 24 August 1680 to merge the two major Parisian companies, the *Hôtel Guénégaud* and the *Hôtel de Bourgogne*, into one. Today, the *Comédie – Française* has a repertoire of some 3,000 plays and three theatres: the Richelieu Hall, the *Théâtre du Vieux* – Colombier and the Studio – Théâtre.

[6] Jean de Rotrou (1609 – 1650) was a French poet and playwright. Rotrou's first play, *L'hypocondriaque* (first produced in 1631), dedicated to Louis de Bourbon, Count of Soissons, was placed on the stage when the author was barely eighteen. Still in the same year, a collection *OEuvres poétiques*, which include praise, epistles and religious verses. He also

longue. And looking him straight in the eye, she observes his facial features. François was serene, unusually calm.

"When were you sleeping?"

"I do not know!" – he replies, laughing breezily.

"I think I have slept for a hundred years!"

"And your nurse?" – Amandine asks, looking around.

"Where has she gone?"

"You mean that idiot you set me up with who wants to shove medicine down my throat all the time?" – he says, mocking.

"I left her grounded in her room! I told her I did not want to see her hanging around here, trying to get on my nerves!" – and, getting up, he stretches his arm exaggeratedly, stretching them above his head.

"Gosh! I am getting rusty! I need to go for a walk!" – and, approaching the window, he looks out and sys:

"Too bad it is already dark..."

Amandine stares at him, dumbfounded. She could not believe her eyes! It was her son back after so long! Had he suddenly healed? She thought it would take some time. I could not believe my eyes! François was still peering out of the window, and she decided to make sure.

"And Sylvie... Do you still want to see her?"

The boy stares out the window for a moment. Then he turns around slowly and looks his mother in the eyes.

---

wrote: *Diane, La Bague de l'Oubli, Cleagénor et Doristée, Les Occasions Perdues, L'Heureuse Constance,* among many others.

"Sylvie is dead, Maman..." – his gaze full of sadness.

"Do you not know she has died?"

Amandine lowers her eyes. A strong emotion overwhelms her chest. It was true! He reacted normally! He no longer called her a liar, nor did he get angry when she stated that sad fact! But we had to go further:

"And Marie–Victoire?"

"Do with her what you will!" – he said, returning to his seat in front of his mother. His eyes were sad, but there was no trace of insanity on his face or rebellion in his voice.

"Did you know that Sylvie wrote to us from the other side?" – said Amandine, taking a risk. She needed to make sure of her son's reactions. Anxiety gnawed at her.

"She has already written two letters! And she is asking for you!"

"If you say so..." – murmurs the boy, now lowering his eyes even more sadly.

"I thought you would be happier..." – says Amandine, getting up and approaching him, taking his head and bringing it close to her own. And, while stroking his unruly hair, she continues:

"Sylvie is still worried about your health... She promised to help you and I see that she has kept her promise, even sooner than I thought... You have come to your senses again!" – and kissing the top of his head repeatedly, she continued:

"I can see that you are all right! Oh, *mon chéri,* you do not know how much you are easing my heart by accepting this fact and choosing to face it head on! I know how painful it can be for you, but that is life! We have to accept the pain as God sends it with resignation!" – and insistently stroking his son's hair, she adds:

"I believe that now, finally, you will be able to give your life a direction..."

The boy does not respond immediately. Only slight soft sobs shake him insistently. After a few moments, he raises his head and, his eyes blurred by tears, stares at his mother.

"If what you are trying to tell me is to forget Sylvie, Maman, you are wasting your time!" – and, getting up, he continued to look at his mother and continued, tears wetting his words.

"I will never forget Sylvie, Maman... Never, do you understand? And until the day comes for me to join her again, I will go on living, yes! And I will no longer hide behind the mask of madness, if that is what you are afraid of! Do not worry! From now on, I will be me again! Or almost... If it were possible for a dead man to come back to life... But I will go on! Even though I am dead inside, Maman, I will go on!" – and walked out with firm steps.

Amandine looked at him as he left resolutely. She had no more doubts: it was her son coming back! Or almost him... Then she sighs deeply. The first great battle had already been won... All that remained was to persist in the fight. Alone in the large living room, the Marquise de Montpelier thought. She closed her eyes and, very satisfied, began to recall the last events of that day. Good heavens!

It was incredible! When she had left for the session at the *Société Spirite*, she had left the boy totally hopped up by the narcotics given to him by that stupid little nurse! However, when she came back, he was completely different! Good heavens! How was that possible? Would the spirits that attended *Monsieur* Allan Kardec's séances act so quickly? Amandine found it hard to believe. Everything seemed so impressive to her! So fast? That was incredible! Her friends were sure to be pleased with the result of the clear improvements she was seeing in her son immediately after the treatment she had received. Gradually, Amandine felt herself relax; the days of tension and extreme worry were over... And deep down, she was rejoicing for yet another reason: she was looking forward to the unbridled pleasure she would get from getting rid of that overbearing little bitch once and for all, as soon as the day dawned! Oh, she would love to see the disappointment creep into that slut's face! And then a smile of complete satisfaction came to her lips and, even with her eyes closed, the Marquise de Montpelier sensed that she was no longer alone in the room. She opened her eyes slowly and, on the threshold of the door, the little girl was looking at her, already a little disheveled.

"What do you want?" – Amandine asks, making herself rude. She did not want to hide the fact that she did not like that stuck-up little girl one bit.

"Pardon me, *Madame la Marquise*, for interrupting your rest..." – said Marie–Victoire.

"But I must tell you that François–Armand is refusing to take his medication! In fact, since the beginning of the night, he has been behaving strangely!" – she continues, approaching Amandine.

"He peremptorily refused to take his medication and treated mw harshly..." – and she adds, almost tearfully:

"I would say that he was downright rude to me today, Madam! Your son had never treated me like this before!"

"And what about that?" – remarks Amandine, looking at the girl with contempt.

"My son can and must do whatever he wants in this house!"

"But it is extremely important that he takes the medicine, Madam!" – exclaims the nurse, her eyes welling with tears.

"If he does not, he will go into crisis and have to be admitted to the clinic!"

"Is that so?" – says Amandine, looking at her with disdain. She continues staring at her acutely:

"As a matter of fact, I was going to tell you this tomorrow, but since you have gone ahead, I will tell you now: when the day dawns, get out of here! The only reason I am not kicking you out right now is because it is getting dark; otherwise, you would not be here a moment longer! François does not need you anymore! If you have not realized it yet, fool that you are! Now I am telling you in no uncertain terms: my son does not need you anymore! Get out of my house!"

"But, Madam, what about Dr. de la Roche? What will he say?"

"I will deal with Dr. de la Roche!" – Amandine replied.

"Now, pack your belongings, because as soon as dawn breaks, I want you out of my house!" – and storms out of the room.

Marie–Victoire suddenly felt the ground disappear from under her feet. So that was the pay she was getting? For years, she had devoted herself to the sick boy. She had become attached to him body and soul and had become so used to his soft, tender voice, calling her Sylvie...

Sylvie! Suddenly, a deafening hatred seized the nurse's heart. Tears flooded down her cheeks in a rush of pain, deep pain, blunt pain, pain of disappointment...

"I hate you, Sylvie!" – she murmured, her words soaked in tears.

"Even if you are dead, I hate you, damn you!"

Back in the small room she had inhabited for so long in that mansion, Marie–Victoire therw herself on the bed and cried. Her sobs shook her violently and she punched the pillow in a rage.

"Oh, how unhappy I am!" – she says between sobs.

"How will I live without you, my love?"

Marie–Victoire was overcome with despair. She had gotten too involved with François–Armand. They had gone too deep in that relationship. She had given herself to him, body and soul. There had been so many years of intimate relationship... Amandine was suspicions... And she was right, the damned woman! Yes, they had both given in to intense passion, yes, and she now felt like throwing it all up in the face of that insensitive snob, who had always treated her like an abject and vile being! Just because she was poor? So what? Did the poor also not have feelings? They could not fall in love, could they? You wretch! If it had not been for her unbridled intransigence and intolerance, she could have been married to François a long time ago. In the meantime, she would had to lie, she would had to pretend that she had no feelings for the boy! Oh, how difficult and cruel it had been for her to hide that feeling, which was so great that it barely fit in her heart! There were times when her love for the boy grew so strong that it seemed to want to burst her heart into a thousand pieces! Meanwhile, that insensitive wretch was always humiliating her and watching every step she took in that house! And yet, she and François always found a way to circumvent her surveillance and how they loved each other! They loved each other, madly, wildly, even though he always called her Sylvie in the midst of his outbursts pf passion and infatuation! Oh, and that other wretch had to be between them all the time! But, until then, she had not attached so much importance to that fact, had she?

All she cared about were François' tender touches and sweet kisses, always exchanged slyly, far from Amandine's eyes, who suspected all this, but knew nothing for sure... Amandine! Oh, damn you, you wretched! She would be gone, all right! Like a hydrophobic bitch, but if she would go! She would suffer the penalty of hell, far from her love, but she would go!

"But I will not wait until morning, no, you wretched!" – says the young nurse, getting up from the bed. Resolutely wiping her eyes with the back of her hands, she hurriedly gathered up her few belongings and clumsily threw them into a small cardboard suitcase.

"I am out of here today, you bastard!"

Once the small suitcase was packed, Marie–Victoire left the small room she had occupied for a long time. Without turning around once, and walked silently to the door of the vestibule and went out into the darkness of the city night.

Once on the street, she takes one last look at the gray granite house and mutters through his teeth:

"I will get even with you, you wretched aristocrats! I will get even!"

Resolute, Marie–Victoire threw herself into the darkness of the night and was literally swallowed up by it. She walked with a firm and determined steps. She had a long way to go that night. A lot, in fact, until she reached the poor suburb where she had once lived. It was not going to be easy for her to resume her life in that tiny, cold house! She had become accustomed to the spaciousness, the cleanliness, the good food and, above all, the warmth of her love... But, what would life hold for her from now on?

"*Froid...*" – murmured Marie–Victoire, as she walked with difficulty through the dark and bumpy streets. The icy early morning wind was cruelly blowing in her face. Desolate, she put thet collar of her coat around her neck and continued in a harsh whisper, as if spitting out the words, soaked in hatred:

"*Froid et solitude... Rien plus...*"[7]

---

[7] Cold... (...) Cold and loneliness... Nothing more... - in French.

Chapter 17

A Chance Encounter

Leaving the Marquise de Montpelier's house, Marie-Victoire walked, stumbling and without much haste, carrying her suitcase, through the bumpy and dark streets of the city. It was high in the morning and the biting cold hurt her exposed face, causing her great discomfort. However, she felt more uncomfortable, deep down in her soul, terribly wounded by François-Armand's mother's harshness. François! He himself had hurt her terrible by rejecting her like that! How had he suddenly acted like that out of the blue? Come to think of it, it was not very surprising, was it? Marie-Victoire had extensive experience of the clinic! She then remembered that sometimes some of the mentally ill patients there spontaneous recovered! It was inexplicable, but it happened... How many did not come out of crisis of deep hysteria without the aid of any medical action or medication? They were the mysteries of the soul! They would spend years immersed in complete alienation and then, in a second, they would come to their senses! They were totally cured! François had certainly been one of those cases. Worse for her! But accepting her current situation was not at all comfortable for her! For a long time, she had cherished the idea of becoming François-Armand's wife, of leaving her misery behind once and for all! Deep down, she had always hoped that the boy would never come to his senses, that he would remain alienated for the rest of his days, and that she, there, would always be asked by him and supposedly replace his dead beloved! But, oh, no lucky!

"*Oh, malheurs! Disgrâce!*"[1] – mutters the young nurse, walking with difficulty through the darkness.

At this point, she feels tired. She stops for a moment to catch her breath and also to locate herself. Towards the center of town, the streets began to be lit by gas lamps[2], casting their bright white light on the uneven paving stones. She had been walking for more than two hours uninterrupted and was able to see things a little more accurately. She raised her head and could see the towers of Notre–Dame: two dark shadows looming in the distance against the faint light of the moonless sky. She was arriving at the Cité. At that moment, she was walking along the Rue de Rivoli, under the trees of the Jardin des Tuileries. Through the trunks of the trees in the grove, she saw the glint of the Seine; she was now very close to the bridge. Her intention was to reach Boulevard Saint–Germain, which was much wider and brighter than the dark alleys that bordered the river, and walk down it to the Île de la Cité. There was hardly anyone on the street at that time. one or two carriages drove past, almost running over some drunks who were stumbling down the middle of the street in their characteristic zigzags. After crossing the bridge, the young woman hesitated for a moment: what if she walked along the

---

[1] "Oh, misfortune...! Disgrace...!" in French.
[2] Public gas lighting in the center of Paris began in 1819.

river to the Île? It was much closer than walking to the Boulevard Saint–Germain, further on.

All she had to do was walk along the Quai Voltaire and Quai de Conti and she would find herself at the Île de la Cité, where she intended to stay until dawn, in front of the cathedral.[3] There, it would certainly be brighter and there would be more people. For a moment, Marie–Victoire stood at the end of the bridge, resting from her intense walk. She places her small bag on the parapet of the bridge and, stretching her neck, looks down at the dark waters of the river flowing silently and enigmatically below

"*Êtes–vous perdue, mademoiselle?*"[4] – she was startled by the powerful voice coming from behind her.

"*Moi–je?! Más non, Monsieur!*"[5] – she replied, turning around in an flash, her heart beating wildly. Then, instinctively holding her hands to her chest to show how frightened she was, she continued, still breathing hard:

"I was just resting..."

"Oh, excuse me then, please, miss!" – he exclaims, giving her a long bow.

"Honestly, I thought you were lost..."

"No, I was not, sir..." – she replies. And, looking more closely at the boy's face, even in the dim light of the gas lamps,

---

[3] A reference to Notre-Dame Cathedral, which is located on the Île de la Cité – an island in the River Seine in the center of Paris. Seine, in the center of Paris.
[4] "Are you lost, miss?" in French.
[5] "Me?! No, Sir!", in French.

she could see that he was still young and handsome. So, she decided to correct herself:

"I mean, in a way, I thought I was lost, yes. I was wondering which way to go: along the river or towards Boulevard Saint-Germain..."

"Oh, but without a shadow of a doubt, if you take the *Quai Voltaire*..." – and pointing to the alley that started right there, at the end of the bridge:

"The one that is there, you will get to the Cité more quickly..."

"I know that, sir..." – she said, picking up her suitcase from the bridge parapet.

"But that was not exactly the point. It is just that, as you may well noticed, Quai Voltaire is rather dark! I think Boulevard Saint-Germain is a bit brighter, even though it is much further away from here..."

"I understand..." – says the boy, now observing her better in the faint light of the lamp. He continues:

"If you will allow me, I can keep you company, because I was just on my way to Île...."

"Oh, really?" – she observes, carefully studying his features. The boy did not have a bad face and he seemed very kind and polite. She made up her life and, standing next to him, continued:

"Well then, let's go..."

They walked a few steps in silence, side by side, studying each other closely out of the corner of their eyes.

"Where do you come from, miss?" – he asks, now deliberately changing his treatment.

"From Clichy..." – she replies laconic.

"Wow!" – he is amazed.

"You have come all this way?"

"I did not have much choice!" – she says.

"It was urgent that I got out of there!"

"Did you have any trouble?" – he asks. And then apologizing:

"Oh, how rude of me! We have been walking for a while and I have not even introduced myself: Pierre Durand..."

"*Enchanté!*"[6] – she replies, laughing, and giving him a slight nod, she says:

"Marie–Victoire Bernardi..."

"*Enchanté*, Marie–Victoire!" – he says in turn.

"You have a beautiful name! And what were you doing in Clichy?"

"I was a nurse..." – she replies.

"*Une infirmière!*"[7] – exclaims the boy, amused.

"You really do have the makings of a nurse!" – he jokes.

" Even if you are not wearing the white coat, you have got it..."

"Why do you say that?" – she asks, puzzled.

"You are a bit serious?"

---

[6] "Nice to meet you!", in French.
[7] "A nurse!", in French.

"Just for that reason?"

"No, but it is characteristic of nurses, don't you think? They tend to be serious and quite uncompromising when they try to shove those horrible potions down our throats!"

"If we play soft, it is the big boys like you who usually give us the biggest headaches when they have to take their medicine..." – she observes, amused.

"We are just doing our duty, my dear!"

"Really?" – he continues, looking playful. He did not know why, but that little girl he had found lost in the darkness of Paris had the gift of making him happy. How long had it been since he had had such a carefree chat with someone? It had been a long time. In fact , he had not laughed like this since another young lady, as jovial as this one, had left...

"Tell me, Marie–Victoire..." – he continued, squinting at her as they walked.

"It must have been something very serious that happened to you where you were to risk going out alone in the dark streets of the city..."

"If it was..." – she replies.

"They literally threw me out!"

"Oh, you must have been up to something!" – he says, laughing.

"Not so much!" – she exclaims, reddening slightly.

Then she quickly pulls herself together and, turning her face away, faces him and continues, her voice full of disdain.

"Those aristocrats are ungrateful! They suck us dry and then, when you no longer meet their needs, they throw you away without the slightest ceremony..."

"Ah, you served the aristocrats then, huh?" – he says, looking at her.

"But you are right to be indignant! These people are not good! When they get the chance, they trample all over us... So, did they mistreat you?"

"Yes, they did!" – she replies, highly indignant.

"They humiliated me until they could not! The old Marquise was the worst... She was dying of jealous of her son, afraid that I would insinuate myself into his life! What a wretch! She drained me like a mangy dog! These people seem to be disgust with the poor, Pierre!"

"Apparently?" – he replies, full of disdain.

"I think they have a real dislike for anyone who is not one of their own kind! The revolutionaries tried to erase this stain from the world by guillotining them by the thousands, but they did not succeed! Here they are springing up again, like worms in the wild..."

"Are you a Liberal or a Republican?" – she asks.

"What is the point of being a Liberal or a Republican? Or socialist or monarchist?" – he continues, with bitterness in his voice.

"Regimes change, but men remain the same. Misery keeps growing, corruption tends to increase..."

"You are right..." – she agrees.

"It seems that the Republic is not catching on..."

"Yes, and there we have the abject monarchy restored!" – he says.

"It seems that the people missed the stench of the aristocracy..."

"The political unpreparedness of Republicans and Liberals, my dear!" – she says, now laughing.

"So much so that the king is back! I do not think there is any way out of this. The solution is to conform..."

"Conform?!" – he replies.

"Never! All it takes is for another Republican Army to appear and I will join it without hesitation... I hate aristocrats!"

"Maybe one day we will learn to manage ourselves, won't we?" – she says with a deep sigh.

"For now, we are swallowing the misery and abandonment heaped on us by the powerful. We will learn yet!"

"I am not as conformist as you, my dear!" – he says, getting angry.

"I question this ignoble right of a few to have so much and many to get by with so little. Especially with the crumbs that fall from the tables of these indecent pigs!"

"But that is the way it has been since the beginning of the world, my dear!" – she says.

"Did the Revolution[8] not try to change these things? And what was achieved? A river of blood flowed through these streets that we now tread and what happened? The same as before! Here they are again, and what is worse, by the very

---

[8] Reference to the French Revolution of 1789.

will of the people!⁹ Do you think that, if the people really did not want him back, the king would be there?"

"I don't know, my dear!" – he says thoughtfully.

"This time the army was not on the side of the people! On the contrary, it defended the coup d' état, putting the tyrant on the throne! How many did not lose their lives trying to prevent misfortune from returning?"[11]

"Louis Bonaparte carried out the coup, taking advantage of the chaos!" – she says.

"The parties could not get along..."

"In fact, they were always fighting among themselves, forgetting the main thing: promoting real changes that would actually benefit the great persecuted: the people!" – and, finally realizing that she understood politics very well, he asked, highly intrigued:

"I see you are up to date with everything that is going on in the country! That is a rare thing for women... Especially young women like you!"

"Oh, have you forgotten that I live surrounded by people?" – she replies.

"I am poor and uneducated, but I have spent a few years of my life around people from the most varied

---

[9] In December 1848, Louis Bonaparte, nephew of Napoleon Bonaparte, was elected President of France and, in December 1851, he carried out a coup d'état, closing the Assembly and having absolute power. This coup became known as "Louis Bonaparte's 18th Brumaire". From then on, the New Empire was established, which would last until 1870.

backgrounds. In Charenton, the clinic where I started as a nurse, as you know, receives mainly wealthy people..."

"Yes... You're right..." – he agrees, thoughtful.

"Even the rich go crazy, *n'est–ce pas*?"

"If they stay! There are madmen from all walks of life..." – she replies.

"However, only those who can afford it go there! For the poor, there are only a few spaces in the basement!"

"Oh, so that is how it works over there, is it?"

"Only there?" – she observes, ironically.

"Does discrimination against the poor not exist everywhere?"

"You are right.!" – he agreed, trying to swallow the anger that was clogging up his throat. He was even shaking with hatred at the memory of the situation the country was in, mired in the darkest abandonment and relegated to total neglect by the highly corrupt rulers. The rise in cost of living; almost general unemployment; factories closing their doors, one after the other, producing waves and waves of unemployed swarming like flies through the streets. The rise in crime, caused by the lack of opportunities in the job market.

"Where do you live, Pierre?" – she asks.

"I rent a small room in an attic on the Quai de Bercy..." – he replies.

"Oh, so we are close to your house!" – she observes.

"Yes, just below, but we will have to cross the bridge. But were you not going to the Cité?"

"Yes!" – said Marie–Victoire, pausing for a moment to catch her breath. Then the young nurse put the small suitcase on the floor and rubbed one hand against the other to relieve them of the cold. She then straightens a lock of hair which, when she bent down, had come loose from the clip holding her clumsy hairstyle, certainly done in a hurry. As she fixed her hair, he looked at her, longingly, studying her features, every gesture she made... A silence fell between them. The night went on slowly, coldly. The sky was now covered in a light mist, making everything darker and colder. In the distance, the whistle of a locomotive pierced the air, poignant, mournful, like the cry of an animal being slaughtered.

"Let me carry your suitcase..." – he offers.

"*Oh, merci beaucoup!*" – she says, handing him the small suitcase and feeling relieved.

"I am getting tired... I have been walking for hours!"

"Where do you work, Pierre? – she asks.

"You have a *raffiné* manner... I do not think you are a lowly ship's worker or stevedore!"

"You are right, Marie–Victoire!" – he replies.

"For a long time, all my life in fact, I have lived with big people! In fact, I was brought up by a rich family and worked there as a butler until very recently!"

"And why did you leave?" – she wonders.

"Did you leave a good thing, a light service like that, in such a crisis?"

"Yes... You're right..." – he says, lowering his head.

"But I was not happy there..."

"And you exchange that post for another one, I presume..."

"Not yet..." – he replies, with extreme bitterness in his voice.

"Did the rich humiliate you?" – she asks, halting her steps and looking at him steadily.

"They are quite capable of that!"

"No, they did not humiliate me!" – the boy hurried to reply.

"It is just that I did not fit in that house anymore!"

"So, it must have been very strong reasons indeed to make you exchange your daily bread and a clean-smelling bed for a cold, damp room!" – she observes.

"Yes," he replies laconically.

"Very strong reasons!"

Marie-Victoire cracked a small, mischievous smile. She understood the very strong reasons! And, for a moment, she said nothing. They continue walking, side by side, along the alleyway bordering the Seine, which, unalterable and insensitive to the hardships of the people who lived in that great, inhuman city, flowed meekly, cutting through it and receiving tons and tons of sewage from it, tainting its waters gradually, making them black and heavy, as it winded its way, like an immense dark serpent, through several of the districts of the great French capital.

"These very good reasons you mentioned are actually things of the heart, *n'est ce pas?*" – she observes, looking at him with an almost mischievous expression in her eyes.

"They are…" – he replies tersely. And, after walking for a long while in silence, he continues without much enthusiasm:

"We have arrived: there is *Place Parvis*."[10]

"Whew!" – exclaimed the girl.

"Now, I can finally sit on a bench and wait for dawn!"

"Are you really going to stay right here, Marie-Victoire?!" – asked the young man, placing her suitcase next to her on the bench where she had sat.

"Among the drunks and prostitutes?"

"Yes!" – she replied, finding his question strange.

"Why not? I think it is quite safe here, it is well lit and, besides, did you know that I still have nowhere to go? I will have to wait until daylight and walk to Puteaux, where I used to live, in *Madame* Démieux's house. Hopefully, I will get back the room I was renting there!"

"Puteaux! Where is it?"

"Beyond the Bois de Boulogne…" – she explained.

"Too far! I still have to cross the river after the big bend. And then I will have to talk to the staff at the Clinic where I used to work. I do not know if they will want me back!"

"Can I sit down?" – he asks, after staring at Marie-Victoire's face for a moment.

"Oh, of course!" – she exclaims, pulling the suitcase closer to her and making room for it on the bench.

"I thought you were going home…"

---

[10] The square where Notre-Dame Cathedral is located in Paris.

"I was going to..." –he replied in a sad voice.

"I was going to try to sleep..." – and, as if to get something off his chest, he says, without looking at her:

"Actually, when I found you near the bridge, I was wandering around, with no certain branch..."

"I see..." – she says, looking at him sideways.

"Do you not want to open up? I can see that you are carrying a huge avalanche in your chest..." – and, with a gentle smile, she continues:

"I do not think you will be able to contain it in for long and it will certainly explode! And when it does, it might tear your heart even more!"

Pierre just tried to swallow the thick lump in his throat. She was right. Marie–Victoire was very perceptive. The cataclysm that he had been keeping contained in his chest at great cost was suffocating him and hurting him intensely. He really had to let it out, let it flow...

"You know, Marie–Victoire..." – he said, his voice low and not looking at her:

"You are right... The pain in my chest is killing me little by little, slowly, mercilessly..."

"Pain of passion, isn't it?" she asks, looking at him in the face.

"Why do you not fight for your love?"

"She is dead..." – he says with a breath.

Marie–Victoire said nothing. Slowly, she stopped looking at him and, thoughtfully, stared at the toes of her shoes, soiled by the mud of the street. A crowd of drunks and prostitutes pass by them, crossing the square, making fun of each other in a big racket. The young nurse remains silent. The boy next to her was also silent, his gaze lost in emptiness; a sad, dull look. In fact, Marie–Victoire had noticed that Pierre's eyes were extremely sad. And even when he laughed, his eyes remained sad... The girl lifted her face and looked at him longingly. He was still mute, cold and distant. The group of drunks and prostitutes was now almost at the end of the square, on the other side, and in the distance they could be heard singing in a disharmonious chorus of laughter:

"*Cadet Rousselle! Cadet Rousselle! Cadet Roussette c'est un bon garçon!*"

"I'm sorry..." – murmured Marie–Victoire at last.

Pierre turned to looked at her. His eyes were welling up with tears. Then he wiped them away slowly withf his fingertips.

"Things have not been easy for me lately..." – he said, staring into nothingness again. "I am alone in the world! Everyone has gone!"

"Consulate yourself with me, *mon chéri!*" – she exclaims.

"I do not have anyone else around here either! Except for an old aunt I left in the South!" – and, making a silly gesture with her hand, she continued:

"She may not even be alive anymore..."

"Yes, I think we are two lonely people in this horrible city!"

Marie–Victoire simply nodded, looking him in the face.

"It is all over!" – he murmured; his voice extremely sad.

"Everything has gone... Empty..."

Then Pierre stood up and looked longingly at the sky, which was now dark and heavy with mist. Marie–Victoire followed his movements with her eyes.

"Come!" – she invites.

"Sit down!"

"Are you not hungry?" – he asks, looking at her.

"By then, on the Quai de Voltaire, there should be a joint open where we can have a hot coffee and a something to eat."

"If you want, I will keep you company..." – she replies.

Café Le Loup, on *Quai Voltaire* was open. A few drunks and vagabonds occupied some of the grimy tables, sipping beer or ordinary wine from small glasses opaque by the constant drool. Pierre and Marie–Victoire sit down at one of the little tables with a grimy white marble top. A waiter with a pale face and black hair, straight and shine from the excess of oil, wearing a dirty apron, approaches them, with an unlit cigarette wet with saliva hanging from the corner of his mouth.

"*Qu'est–ce que voulez–vous?*"[11] – he asks, not very cheerfully.

"Coffee, bread and dumplings, *s'il vous plaît!*" – Pierre replies. The waiter walks away, ostentatiously scratching his greasy hair.

---

[11] "What would you like?", in French.

"Has she been dead long?" – Marie–Victoire asks.

"It's been... I think almost seven years..." – he replied, after a moment of silence. His voice had come out with a bitter taste, a taste of infinite sadness.

"So, she was very young when she passed away..."

"Yes... She was quite young when she died of smallpox."

"Smallpox?" – she exclaims.

"What a pity! That is a terrible disease! And, poor thing, if she had not left, she would certainly have been even worse off, with her whole body marked by spots... Death was preferable, then! There is nothing worse for a woman than catching this disease!"

"I would love her just the same!" – Pierre exclaims, bitterly. "I loved her soul, you know? Do not appeal...!"

The waiter returns, carrying a tray.

"The coffee is good!" – says Marie–Victoire, after taking a long sip of the comforting liquid.

"Drink it before it gets cold..."

Pierre just looked at her briefly. Then he lowered his eyes and stared at the dark liquid steaming in the white cup. He felt so desolate that he did not even want to drink the coffee.

"Have you ever fallen in love, Marie–Victoire?" – he asks, without looking at her, and, after bringing the cup to his lips and taking a long sip of coffee, he continues:

"I mean real, deep passion, which hurts more than it brings pleasure and joy..."

"Yes..." – she replies, laconic.

"And where is your love?"

"I left him a little while ago in Clichy..." – she says.

"So that is why you left, isn't it?"

"Yes. His mother was against it..."

"Because were you poor?"

"I think so..." – she replies.

"In fact, she never liked me! François was admitted to the clinic; that is where I met him..."

"Have something to eat..." – he remarked, passing her the brass plate on which half a dozen dumplings were swimming in an appetizing *sauce grise.*

"Smear the bread with the sauce!" – and gives a slight smile. Then, becoming serious, he continued:

"So, your beloved was mad?"

"Oh, Pierre!" – she reproaches him.

"Are those ways of referring to my love?"

"I'm sorry... I did not mean to offend you..."

"François was sick, Pierre!" – she exclaimed, after a few moments of silence.

"Terribly sick in the soul! A passion had driven him mad..."

"Really?" – says Pierre, showing deep interest in the case.

"Poor boy! Today I know that it is perfectly possible for someone to go mad with love!" – and, after reflecting for a moment, he continued:

"But if he went mad with passion, it certainly was not for you! And where do you come into this? I do not quite understand: how did you get into his life?"

Marie–Victoire then went on to tell hin in detail about François–Armand's case, Sylvie's death, his hospitalization in Charenton. As he learned the facts, Pierre began to pale and his hands began to shake uncontrollably.

"What is the matter, Pierre!" – Marie–Victoire asked, realizing that the boy was shaking enormously as she told him her story.

"You are as white as a ghost! What has gotten into you?"

"You cannot even imagine, *ma chérie*!" – he says, running his hand over his cold forehead. Then, taking her hands between his, he continues, looking into her eyes.

"How small this world is, my God!"

"Why do you say that?" – she asks, still not understanding.

"The girl who died of smallpox, Sylvie, as you said, was my love, Marie–Victoire!" – he says, his eyes welling up with tears. "– and François–Armand, the boy you are in love with, was her fiancé!"

Marie–Victoire looks at him in amazement.

"What are you saying?! Are you sure of what you are saying?!"

"All the certainty in the world, *ma belle*..." – he says.

He went on to narrate facts that fitted in precisely the other part that Marie–Victoire had reported.

"You are absolutely right, Pierre!" – she exclaims, still stunned.

"This world is too small!"

"All in all, it was a good to meet you, Marie–Victoire!" – he exclaims, squeezing her hand.

"It was for me too!" – she said, her eyes welling up with tears.

"I was beginning to feel so lonely in this world!"

Outside, the day was beginning to brighten. The city, like a giant that had spent hours in deep sleep, was waking up. The locomotives and steam engines of the factories blew their shrill whistles into the air, as if signaling the start of terrible daily struggle that began in yet another stage that emerged in the middle of a cloudy, cold and sad day.

Chapter 18

A Friendship is Born

It was already light when Pierre and Marie–Victoire left Café Le Loup on Quai Voltaire.

"Are you really going back to Puteaux?" – asked the boy, as they walked side by side down the alleyway that bordered the Quay. He was now starting to fear the loneliness that would surely invade his soul once again.

"Yes!" – she replies.

"I have nowhere else to go. And I must thank heaven if *Madame* Démieux can rent me one of her small rooms..."

"Look, why do you not try something right here in the center?" – he suggested, trying to hold her close. Suddenly, he was afraid of losing sight of her.

"There are so many mansards, in Bercy, or on the Quai de Conti or the Quai de Voltaire..."

"Oh, but the rent would be too high for me!" – she exclaims, with a chuckle of disappointed.

"Did you know that I have very little savings and, even if I get my job back in Charenton, my salary will be a pittance? I appreciate your goodwill, but it would be unfeasible for me to live in the city center!" – and then, suddenly becoming melancholy, she continued, looking down at the floor:

"I wish I could..."

"And why do you not try at least?" – he continued, insisting. He could not understand why, but there was something that attracted him to that woman. He seemed to have known her for a long, long time...

"Oh, I do not think it would be worth it! Then again, I hardly know anything about this side of town!"

"But I know everything around here like the back of my hand!" – he exclaims.

"I could go with you! Why do we not try the place where I live? Maybe we will find a room that has been vacated! So many people are moving out of the city because of unemployment! Do you not want to look for my landlord?"

"I don't know..." – she hesitates.

"What I have will barely survive me for a few days! If I have to spend all I have, how will I afford food?"

"I do not have much, since the money given to me by the Rousselet couple, as a gratuity for the time I served them, is barely enough to keep me going ever since... In the meantime, I have been getting a few odd jobs to do and so I have managed to get a few francs for food, even though I have been restricting my diet since I left my former employers' house..." – and, heaving a deep sight, he continues:

"I do not know how long I will be able to stand it, because this galloping inflation coming down on us like a cloud of locusts devouring everything and everyone, without exception!"

"Oh, there are exceptions, my dear!" – she corrects him.

"For those who speculate on the famine, everything is going extremely well! And let's not forget the rich! They are never really hit by anything!"

"You are right, *ma belle!*" – he says, smiling slightly.

"In this sort of thing, the weaker part is the one who always falls apart, *n'est ce pas?*"

"And in this case, you and I and the vast majority of our compatriots!" – she says, spreading her arms wide.

"The vast majority of French people go hungry!"

"Yes..." – he agrees.

"But I was saying that I can help you out in the early days until you get on your feet, if you decide to stay permanently in these parts."

"Really?" – she asked, sending him a look full of tenderness. That strong boy, although tremendously sad and crushed, surprised her at every time.

"Will I not be a burden to you? It will not be easy for me to get my job back in Charenton..."

"You did not even try!" – he says, giving her a look of almost reproach.

"Everything is very difficult for everyone these days, my dear. If we do not join hands, most of us will inevitably perish, because those in charge of our nation's destiny care little or nothing about us!"

And in a spontaneous gesture, made without thinking, driven more by her heart, Marie–Victoire took the boy's hand and held it, squeezing it tightly. He smiled, moved, and returned the touching gesture of affection, and then intense emotion overtook them both. They look at each other, locking firmly into each other's eyes.

"*Merci beaucoup, Marie–Victoire!*" – he murmured, his eyes welling with tears.

"*Merci Beaucoup*, Pierre..."

Céleste–Marie had decided to start treatment at the Paris Spiritist Society. At first, she had been a little reluctant, but when she heard that François–Armand had recovered almost immediately, and in addition to the constant pleas for her husband and mother, she decided to accompany them to another of *Monsieur* Allan Kardec's sessions, only this time as a patient.

On that Tuesday evening in December 1858, the *Société Parisienne d'Etudes Spirites* was, as always, packed with faithful visitors. Céleste–Marie, Wilfred Berg and Marie–Louise were looking for one of the front rows. General du Servey and Constance were already seated at the front. They greeted each other lightly and settled down next to their friendly couple. The was a respectful and general silence in the meeting room. The table, set up at the back of the room, on a slightly raised platform, standing out from the level of the floor, a dozen people sat, highly serious and in absolute silence. At the head of the table stood the illustrious Codifier of Spiritism, who, with great concentration, was examining a series of papers with exceptional attention, adding notes in the margins as he read them. Before long, *Monsieur* Allan Kardec took his watch out of his coat pocket and examined it carefully. Then, standing upt, he walked over to the small pulpit and, looking at the distinguished audience, said:

"*Mesdames et Messieurs!* Thank you sincerely for coming to our session. On the agenda, we have a series of questions for the consideration of our spirit guides, whom we ask in advance for their helpful collaboration..." – and he read out the minutes of the sitting that had taken place the previous week. He then listed the topics that would be discussed that evening.[1]

Céleste–Marie, since she had decided to go to the Spiritist Society, had experienced an exacerbation of the strange sensations that had always plagued her throughout her life. She had even told her husband that she was thinking of giving up going because she was so ill. Then, Berg, with extreme affection and skill, convinced her not to give up, to go ahead. There at the *Société*, however, she felt herself getting even worse; in fact, from the moment she had set foot in the hall, she felt suffocated and had the urge to break free from her husband's hold and run out of there. However, with

---

[1] At this time, the end of 1858, it is worth noting that Spiritist practices were still being established and until then had not had the character we now know them to have; it should also be added that Spiritism effectively developed as a religion in Brazil in a crescendo, and it was only towards the end of the 19th century that it was truly established as such. On November 1, 1868, Allan Kardec gave the famous opening speech at the Paris Society's commemorative session for the Day of the Dead. This speech is important for understanding what the Codifier of Spiritism meant by "religion", how he viewed the role played by religions, his vision of the Spiritist Doctrine within this context and why he preferred not to present Spiritism as a religion. The speech was published in the Spiritist Review of December 1868. The first Spiritist Center in Brazil was the "Family Group of Spiritism", set up on September 17, 1865, by Luís Olímpio Teles de Menezes, in the city of Salvador, Bahia. On January 2, 1884, the Brazilian Spiritist Federation was established at Rua da Carioca, 120 – sobrado – Rio de Janeiro, with Major Ewerton Quadros as its first President.

unusual strength, she managed to control herself, even though her breathing was difficult and her chest was oppressed by strange sensations and the fear that that place and those people imposed on her. Berg held her hand, firmly to give her courage and often looked at her stealthily. When he felt her hand shaking uncontrollably, he whispered in her ear:

"*Courage, mon amour! Coruage!*"[2]

Then the séance began, when the mediums went into trance and began to communicate with the spirits present at the séance. Allan Kardec supervised everything with full attention and dedication; nothing escaped his observation and insight. The pencils ran fast in the mediums' hands, filling pages after pages of paper. It was spirituality that was ostentatiously projecting itself, opening the doors to the afterlife with such clarity and seriousness as to systematically shake up the old secular concepts, eaten away by time and covered by the accumulated dust of absurd dogmas, miracles and superstitions, which muzzled and masked the face of the truth! For the first time, the world was receiving, in such a grand and spectacular way, the incalculable proof that life is not limited to the tiny space between the cradle and the grave. There is something beyond this existence we know! A new life, as real and perhaps more complex than the one we know in this world, was manifesting itself! And with each session that took place at the *Société Parisienne d'Etudes Spirites,* and as the spirits brought news of the "dead" through the mediumship door, proving irrefutably that they were as alive as ever, one could see that no longer the astonishment of the

---

[2] "Courage, my love...! Courage...!", in French.

beginning, but the incontestable certainty that life was continuing! And, invigorated by the faith that was based, above all, on reason and common sense, Spiritist ideas spread like wildfire, filling the periodicals of the time, surpassing the borders of Paris, gaining the whole France, Europe and the world...

"*Madame Berg!*" – calls Allan Kardec at the end of the session.

"*C'est toi, mon amour?*[3] – Berg asked sweetly.

" *Monsieur* Allan Kardec is calling you!"

"*Moi!*" – exclaims Céleste–Marie, raising her hand.

The Codifier of Spiritism made a sign with his hand, urging her to come closer. Berg also got up and accompanied his wife, as he was very anxious about the outcome. *Monsieur* Kardec was holding a series of sheets of paper written by one of the mediums.

"Here you are, gentlemen, the result of the consultation!" – said Professor Rivail, holding out the bundle of paper to Celeste–Marie's trembling hands.

"Read it carefully and, if you have the slightest doubt, do not hesitate to contact us here at the *Société*... I have read it all beforehand and I can assure you that what you find there is the purest expression of the truth! You can check every page for my seal of approval!" – and, shaking both hands firmly, he bade them farewell and continues to attend the other queries.

Berg, Céleste–Marie, Marie–Louise, General du Servey and Constance, all highly anxious about what those

---

[3] "He's my daddy...! (...), in French.

psychographed pages contained, set out to find a suitable place where they could read them carefully and discuss their contents. After a short and discreet discussion, they decided on a quiet café in the Galerie des Valois.

Shortly afterwards, they were all sitting around a table at Café Le Rouget. The place was not very busy at that hour, and the waiter had arranged the steaming cups of coffee in front of each of them.

"Read it, Berg!" – urged General du Servey, hardly suffering the anxiety that was eating away at him.

"Yes! Yes!" – Marie–Louise exclaims.

"Read it, our hearts are pouring out of our mouths with so much distress!" – and burst into nervous laughter.

Captain Berg then began to read in a slow, clear voice:

"Ma petite,

I know that you remember little about me, because when I left this world, you were still a delicate little girl of five! Your were brought up by your mother, my beloved Marie–Louise, the lioness, who was your mother and father, defending you and protecting you from the hardships of this cruel world! And she did it so well! You are a hero, Loulou! You filled in for me in front of our 'petite poupée' and you did magnificently!

You know, ma 'petite poupée', the cruelty of war has take me away from you and your mother, but you can be sure that I never abandoned you! The so–called dead live on, my loves! Now you have incontrovertible proof of this fact! And I have always remained by your side, offering you my protection–discreet but constant–and whispered words of consolation and encouragement in your ears, Céleste–Marie, so that you could continue in your inner struggle against the suffering that is plaguing your being! I know how much you suffer! And there is a reason for it, ma 'petite poupée'! A reason so bizarre and unusual for you to understand that, until recently, it would have been impossible for you to know about it! All this ailment that is afflicting you has its roots in your past life! I want you to know, 'ma petite', that we have not lived only in the world once! There are so many journeys along the path of flesh that we even lose count of them! Your sufferings, my dear, have their origin in the revenge that an enemy of yours, a man whom you hurt very much in the past and who now, living in the world of spirits and still holding a deep grudge against you in his heart, continues to persecute you! He loves and hates you at the same time! He was in love with you and lost his life in a duel because of you. He thinks you are to blame for that misfortune and is persecuting you today. All this may seem absurd to you, but it is! Did they not take you to a multitude of doctors and did you not ingest so many medicines? Has anyone really found out what is wrong with you? And tell me honestly: have any of the medicines you have been prescribed worked? I know you do not! So, believe what your father tells you! This is the right way! You will find a cure here! I have added my prayers to those that your mother has always said for you, and today I know that they have been heard! God, in His infinite mercy, has determined it, and enlightened spirits are here taking care of your case! Trust in Divine Providence and pray too!

I kiss you and your mother, Guillaume–Philippe"

Berg finishes reading the message, highly emotional. Céleste–Marie was crying quietly. Marie–Louise's had tears in her eyes. General du Servey and Constance were highly moved.

"*C'est mon papa!*" – murmured Céleste–Marie, her words wet with tears.

"*C'est, vraiment, mon papa!*"[4]

"Extraordinary!" – comments the General.

"Truly fantastic! If I had not met Colonel Guillaume–Philippe Coty, I might have doubted it! But I know it is him! What do you say, Marie–Louise?"

"I know it is him, Genera!" – exclaims Marie–Louise, through tears.

"From the beginning of the reading, I knew it was him! No one else in this world would call me Loulou!" – and a deep, painful tears overtook her.

"There is the evidence!" – observes Berg, very moved.

"Colonel Coty quotes very intimate things about the family! Those people at the *Société* could never have known about them!"

"What Guillaume–Philippe says is incredible!" – says Constance.

"An evil spirit is tormenting Céleste–Marie... What a terrible thing!"[5]

"Yes, my dear..." – said the General.

---

[4] He really is my daddy...!", in French.
[5] Very little was actually known about obsession – the ability of the disincarnate to persecute and torment the incarnate – since more specific studies on this subject only took place with the release of the 2nd edition of "*The Spirits' Book*", extensively revised and expanded by Allan Kardec, on March 16, 1860, and the appearance of "*The Mediums' Book*", in 1861, and "*Heaven and Hell*", in 1865.

"I am absolutely certain that Spiritism will yet reveal very important things to us about how those who preceded us on the 'great journey' lived and acted..."

"I confess to being very impressed!" – exclaims Captain Berg.

"Even the affectionate way Colonel Coty used to call Céleste–Marie when she was still a little girl!"

"*Poupée!*" – says Céleste–Marie through tears.

"My father used to call me doll! *Ma petite poupée!* – and cries, deeply moved.

Since that session at the *Société Parisienne d'Études Spirites*, Céleste–Marie had gradually shown evident improvements in her behavior. At the moment, she could often be seen smiling and even laughing, things that had rarely been seen in her before.

"How are you feeling, *mon amour*?" – asked Berg one morning, hugging her lovingly.

"Oh, very well!" – she replies.

"I have never felt this before... You know, Wilfred, after I received that letter from Papa, things started to change for me... The fears, the unfounded fears and anguish that clogged my heart disappeared, almost completely! Not to mention the constant nightmares, the feeling that they were chasing me, that they were watching every step I took, and the incessant fear! I was really scared! Today, however, I no longer feel this constant dread of everything! Afraid of people, afraid to go out in the street, afraid that you would die! Oh, you do not know how horrible everything was for me! How can you explain such a change, just by receiving those words from Papa?"

"I assume that it is not just your father's words behind all this, *ma belle!*" – he observes seriously.

"I think deeper things are happening to you, things we do not even know! Your transformation is clearly noticeable!"

"Do you really think someone dead was after me, Berg?" – she asks.

"I do not doubt anything anymore, my dear!" – he says, gently stroking her hair.

"Maybe something we do not know yet all about was going on with you! But what really matters is that you are improving your behavior!"

"Oh, and do you not feel happy about that?" – she asks, hugging him, full of tenderness.

"It feels like I can finally be a little bit happy by your side!" – and whispering in his ear:

"Do you not think we will be able to order our baby now?"

"You never give up, do you?" – he says, looking her in the eye. And with a smile, he continues:

"Let's wait a bit longer. If you continue showing such obvious improvements, we will certainly have our little boy!"

"Oh, Wilfred!" – she exclaims, hugging him tightly.

"I am so happy!"

"If you are so happy, why do we not go to the Opera today?"[6] – he asked.

"It is been so long since the two of us went out! What do you think? Then we can have dinner at *Le Procope*!"

"Yes!" – she says, without hesitation.

"I would love to go out with you!"

Berg looked at her, full of satisfaction. Céleste–Marie was changing, and that filled him with great joy. He stares deep into her eyes. Things would certainly work out.

"Not before time!" – he thought.

"Not before long!" – and let out a deep sigh.

Marie–Victoire and Pierre, that morning when they met after leaving the café, walked together to Quai de Bercy, where the boy lived, and managed to rent a modest room for her, coincidentally in the same house and next to the tiny room the boy occupied.

"You will do much better here than in that horrible suburb where you lived in before, *ma belle*..." – exclaims the boy, as they both inspected the poor room she will now occupy.

"But I do not know if I will be able to pay the rent!" – she exclaims, full of fear.

"It is almost double what I would pay there!"

"Do not worry about that!" – he says, comforting her.

---

[6] Reference to the Paris National Opera (in French, *Opéra National de Paris*), a musical institution, successor to the one founded in Paris by Louis XIV in 1669 under the name of "Royal Academy of Music" (*Académie Royale de Musique*). It is one of the oldest "institutions of its kind" in the world.

"I will help you in the beginning. And if you want, I will come with you to Charenton today to see if you can get your old job as a nurse back..."

"Oh, will you do that?" – exclaimed Marie–Victoire, filled with joy. It was the first time in a long time that she had someone to be her friend, to care about her, to keep her company all the time.

"I would not be able to do anything else today!" – he says, making an inane gesture with his hands.

"It is very late, and freelancers have to get up early if they want to earn a few pennies as wagon loaders at the railway terminal..."

"So, that is how you can earn a few pennies..." – she observed.

"I would starve to death if I had to carry so many heavy loads on my back, like those poor bastards do, for so many hours at a time!" – and looking at him with pity, she asked:

"How can you do that, Pierre? You certainly were not used to such heavy and tiring tasks when you worked as a butler!"

"Oh, you get used to everything in this world, *ma chérie!*" – he exclaims.

"In order not to starve, you will do anything!"

"What a life we have!" – she says, sitting down on the old iron bed that creaks under her weight. And, looking at him, who was standing at the doorframe, she invites him:

"Come, sit here!"

"Poverty is degrading, Marie–Victoire!" – he says, looking around the girl's meager little room. His eyes wander over the grimy, mildew–stained walls, then up to the ceiling blackened by the soot of the years, and finally to the rough, grimy floorboards, and his face twitches in disgust.

"All this misery disgusts me!" – he exclaims. And he continues, his voice full of revolt.

"I have never lived in a shack like this before! I was poor, but I always lived in the mansion of my former employers. In fact, my parents had served the Rousselet couple since long before I came into the world, and they both died there..."

"Unlike me, who has always lived in places like this..." – she says in a sadly.

"I only got a taste for luxury and refinement after I took care of François–Armand..."

"And you got used to the good stuff, *n'est ce pas*?" – he observes, with a slight tone of irony in his voice.

"*Oui...*"

"And who does not?" – he continued, getting up and going to the tiny window to look out for a few moments. Then he turns around and, looking at her, continues:

"I do not blame you, *ma chérie*! Everyone would act like that! It is very easy to get used to what is good! It is hard to go to the other way, as we both did: back to the mud.!" – and, after letting out a deep sigh of discouragement, he continued:

"And if you really want to go to Charenton, we should leave now, because the hours are advancing...."

Three hours later, Pierre was waiting for Marie-Victoire in front of the high gates of the venerable secular institution. It had been almost an hour since the young nurse had entered the gates; she had disappeared down the long avenue that led to the hospital main entrance and was slow to return. Pierre was impatient. He walked back and forth, like a caged animal, often bringing his face close to the thick iron bars of the gate and peering longingly down the little path that merged into the grove at the end. Finally, after some more waiting, he saw a silhouette walking along the yellow gravel road. Pierre held his gaze and, at last, it seemed to be her. But not at all excited. On the contrary, her hands were down by her sides and her head was lowered. The boy guessed, even from a distance, that she had achieved nothing.

"How did it go?" – he asks anxiously as she approaches the gate.

"Nothing, Pierre!" – she says, very discouraged.

"They have already hired someone else to take my place! And there is no prospect of them taking me back. I think my old boss has already warned them. In fact, they did not care about me! A hospital of this size always needs experienced people"

"Let them go!" – he exclaims and, looking at her tenderly, tries to comfort her:

"We will manage! Do not despair! There are other hospitals in Paris! We will rum to all of them and, if we are lucky, one of them will need nurses!"

"Oh, how optimistic you are, Pierre!" – she exclaims, taking his hand and squeezing it tightly.

"I am glad I have gotten you by my side, cheering me up!"

"I do not let myself down that easily at the first disappointment, my dear!" – he exclaims.

"I tend to be quite persistent in my endeavors... However, there is no time for that today. It's is late afternoon and we have a long way to go back..."

Pierre and Marie-Victoire, in order to save the little money, they had, decided not to take the bus back; they preferred to walk the little more than ten kilometers to the center of Paris.

"Are you hungry?" – he asks, as they walked side by side along the road to the city.

"A little..." – she replies.

"However, from now on, I will have to get used to the martyrdom of an empty stomach, just like before..."

"I have never felt hungry before..." – he says, holding her hand as they walk.

"Now, however, I know how much it can hurt someone..."

"It really hurts..." – she agrees.

"You cannot rest, you cannot sleep; your thoughts do not flow. You stagnate on one and only goal: to satisfy the demon of hunger that mercilessly devours our insides!"

"If you want to punish someone with cruelty, simply deny them his daily food!" – observes Pierre.

"I agree! And they still inventing the most hideous instruments to torture men!" – she says, her voice full of irony.

"None of that would be necessary: all they would have to do is cut off their food, that is all!"

"Anyone who has never kept the monster of hunger inside does not really know what it is capable of, *ma belle*!" – continues the young man.

"Before, I could not imagine what it was, because until then I had always had good food, all the time! Today, however, thrown on my own luck, I know what it is like have to limit things to the maximum!"

"But you threw yourself at your own fate voluntarily!" – she exclaims.

"As far as I can tell from what you have told me, your former employers did not throw you out!"

"Yes..." – he says.

"But what was the point of having a stable life if I was not happy, if I suffered all the time, immersed in the memories of my love, that tormented night and day, without giving me the slightest respite?"

"But something intrigues me, Pierre, about this whole affair: Sylvie was not in love with François–Armand!" – she asks.

"And if smallpox had not taken her so young, surely they would not have been married by now? And how would you have solved it if things had turned out differently?"

"I was thinking about killing François–Armand if that actually happened!" – he replied, keeping his head down and not looking at her. His voice came out almost in a whisper, charged with uncontainable rage. Marie–Victoire just stared at him, full of amazement. She had sensed, from the tone in which the boy had answered her, that he was not joking with her. A heavy silence then fell between the two of them; you could tell that they were in deep thought.

"Would you really have had the guts to murder François–Armand?" – she risks asking after a while.

"Let him dare to take her away from me and he will see what I am capable of!" – replies Pierre, without looking at her.

"But the wretch was lucky: God took her for himself first, and I spared him.! That is the only reason, understand? Otherwise, that asshole would not have taken her from me, ever! I would kill him! I swear to you, I would have killed him first!"

Suddenly, Marie–Victoire felt afraid. Who was Pierre in fact? Who was she really getting involved with? Then she looked at him sideways as they walked lightly, still holding hands. Pierre was a handsome, dark–haired boy with slightly wavy, full black hair, cut short at the nape of the neck, as was the custom at the time. His velvety black sideburns framed the soft complexion of people who had always lived in the shade, away from the scorching sun. His slightly hooked nose adorned his face more than making it ugly; his prognathous chin gave him an almost arrogant air, and his thick, shapely neck completed the ensemble, adding to his truculent shoulders, muscular arms and broad, large chest.

"Are you scared or cold?" – he asked, looking at her and now giving her a slightly cute smile.

"Your hands are suddenly cold..."

"Oh, it is cold!" – she exclaims with a nervous giggle.

"Be calm, *ma belle*!" – he said, looking at her tenderly and squeezing her hand tightly. "In this world, I would kill nothing but cockroaches and that bastard! No one else!"

Marie–Victoire returned his gaze, followed by a deep sigh of relief. In the distance, the first houses of the Paris suburbs could already be seen…

Chapter 19

A fatal accident

On the next few days, Marie–Victoire and Pierre visit all the main hospitals in Paris in search of a place for the young nurse. However, given the calamitous situation in France at the time, it was difficult to find a job for anyone who was unemployed. The Industrial Revolution that had taken place since 1850 had at first promoted a real rural exodus: cities were swelling, factories were multiplying, but in less than a decade, political destabilization had thrown the economy into chaos. Corruption was rife in the upper echelons of government, and spending on the wars of imperialist colonialism drained the public coffers, throwing the country out of the control and into unbearable rates of inflation, especially for workers who depended on the smooth running of the manufacturing export business. Paris was swarming with unemployed and underemployed people! Many were leaving the city for the countryside, where life was deceptively more pleasant. Meanwhile, as an eminently agricultural country, France was lost in the midst of a modernization policy designed to benefit only the "new rich", entrepreneurs and wealthy merchants, to the detriment of the proletariat, always relegated to the hardship of lacking everything.

"Oh, I feel so discouraged!" – Marie-Victoire exclaims, as she and Pierre return from yet another unsuccessful attempt to find a job, now in a hospital further away from the city center. Sitting on the bed in her very poor room, she continued, while taking off her feet, which were tremendously sore from the strenuous walk:

"There is nowhere else to look! Day after day, I can only see the failed attempts adding up! Expectations are running out! There is no way out for me!"

"Why be discouraged before your time, *ma belle*!" – remarks the boy, sitting next to her on the bed and trying to cheer her up.

"If you cannot work as a nurse, there will be other jobs... Why do you not try your hand at weaving?"

"Oh, how naive you are, Pierre!" – she exclaims, highly dejected.

"When it comes to weaving, I can barely get a thread to the bottom of a needle to mend my old clothe! What is more, the weavers who have practice on the looms are also out of work, because the weaving mills are closing down one after the other! I would not stand a chance! I am already starting to despair. My savings, which were not much to begin with, are running out quickly! Soon, I will be on the steps of some church, begging!"

"Oh, you exaggerate!" – says the boy, barely cracking a smile.

"To go that far, only if I die first!"

"*Mon bon, Pierre!*" – she exclaims, throwing herself around the boy's neck and hugging him gratefully.

"You are quite a man! If I was not in love with someone else, and you with someone else..."

"You know, Marie–Victoire..." – he said, returning her the hug.

"We are two lonely people in this world, aren't we? I have been thinking... Why do you and I get married and emigrate?"

"Emigrate?" – she is urprised by the idea.

"Gosh, I had never thought of it."

"Yes!" – he says, getting up and standing in front of her. And, highly motivated, he continues:

"If France does not offer us any conditions, if we are on the verge of starving to death here, then why do we not go to a new land where there will certainly be plenty of opportunities? Look, the country has so many colonies overseas: in America, Africa and Oceania! There is no shortage of places: there is plenty to choose from!"[1]

---

[1] It was in Senegal, Africa, that the French first settled, founding warehouses in 1624; however, they did not create real colonies there until the 19th century, limiting themselves to trafficking slaves to their possessions in the Caribbean. In the Indian Ocean, the French colonized *Ile Bourbon* (now Réunion) in 1664; Ile de France (now Mauritius) in 1718 and the Seychelles in 1756. During Napoleon's reign, Egypt was also conquered for a brief period, but French domination never extended beyond the area immediately around the Nile. France's real interest in Africa manifested itself in 1830, with the invasion of Algeria and the establishment of a protectorate in Tunisia in 1881. From then on, they expanded inland and to the South, forming the colony of French Sudan (now Mali) in 1880 and, in the years that followed, occupied a large part of North Africa and Western and central Africa. In 1912, the French forced the Sultan of Morocco to sign the Treaty of Fez, turning that country into a protectorate.

"Oh, would you really have the courage, Pierre?" – she asks, suddenly becoming very interested.

"If you accept..." – he replies, with a smile.

"We will be able to forget our personal frustrations by dedicating ourselves to each other... Or would you rather remain in black misery and regret what was not yours?"

"You are right..." – she says thoughtfully.

"But do you think it will work? Deep down, I know that you do not love me and that I do not love you either..."

"So, we are two rejects!" – he jokes, taking her by the hand and holding her close in his strong arms and trying to kiss her lips.

"Not yet, Pierre!" – she says, turning her face away.

"I beg you, please, not yet! The wounds are still bleeding..."

"I understand..." – he murmured, loosening his arms.

"Are you not hurt?" – she asks, after letting go of his arms. She slowly sat back down on the simple bed and noticed that he had suddenly become quiet.

"Look... I..." – she stammered.

"No!" – says Pierre, gesturing with his hand.

"I do not need to say anything or try to explain yourself! I Have already told you that I understand! It is just that we men are just like that. It is difficult for us to hold a woman in our arms and remain unchanged! Sometimes it becomes irresistible, uncontrollable! Do you understand? It must be the smell..."

– Yes..." – she says thoughtfully.

"That must be it..."

A silence then fell between them. The afternoon was falling fast and the night was fast approaching. Pierre remained standing, leaning against the musty wall and, with his face raised, he could spy on the roofs of the houses on the other side of the river through the tiny window of the mansard.

"It is getting dark..." – says Marie–Victoire, getting up and insistently forcing open the drawer of the small bedside table, the only piece of furniture in the room apart from the bed, and taking out a stub of a candle. Scratching a matchstick on the floorboard, she lights the candle, which flickers for a moment and then steadies its weak yellowish light.

"Are you not hungry?" – Marie–Victoire asks. In the candlelight, Pierre's face had turned into a ghostly blur.

"Sit here!" – she asked, gently.

Without saying a word, he sat down next to her. The young woman takes his hand and squeezes it tightly. Pierre looks into her eyes.

"Kiss me, Pierre..." – says Marie–Victoire in a low voice. It was a slight whisper, an almost imperceptible murmur...

When dawn broke, Pierre opened his eyes and squeezed them tightly shut to adjust to the dim light. Then he looked around and realized that this was not his room. He felt squeezed, cramped even, in that bed. He found himself cuddled up to Marie– Victoire, who was also snoring very tightly in his arms.

"Good heavens!" – he thinks.

"And is not it..." – he laughed, looking at the face of the young woman who was sleeping soundly in his arms. Pierre tried to get up without waking her, but soon found out that this was an impossible task, since they were both lying down and squeezed tightly together in the girl's small bed. The slight movement he made woke her up involuntarily.

"*Oh, bonjour, Pierre!*" – exclaims Marie–Victoire, opening her sleepy eyes.

"Are you there?" – and laughs.

"I am..." – he says, a little awkwardly. He gets up and gets dressed.

"It is dawn, and I need to go to the station. Maybe I will find some work!" and he smiles.

"Or we will have to fast today too..."

"Oh, what a shame!" – she exclaims, sitting on the bed and running her fingertips over and over again through her still very sleepy eyes.

"I wish I could go out and earn a few bucks too! But where to?"

"Do not worry..." – he says, finishing putting on his boots.

"If I am a bit lucky, I will defend our lunch today!" – and bending down, he kisses her on the cheek.

"Go back to sleep! I have already looked outside, and the weather is awful!"

"Pierre!"

"What is it?" – he says, turning around, about to open the door to leave.

"*Merci!*" – and smiles.

"It was my best night yet!"

Pierre simply returned her smile and blew her a kiss. And, opening the door, he hurried out.

Marie–Victoire lies back on the simple bed and covers herself with the thin wool blanket. She closed her eyes, and the image of Pierre kissing her remained in her mind, and a wave of tenderness for the boy washed over her. Suddenly, however, the images of Pierre and François are superimposed on each other, blurring together in her mind. She felt confused. She loved François–Armand without a shadow of doubt. She had devoted so much of her life to him, night and day, and what had she gotten out of it? Humiliation and more humiliation. Pierre, however... Pierre... Pierre had been tender and friendly to her from the beginning; he had protected her, even to the point of supporting her at the moment.

"Oh, Pierre..." – she murmured softly.

"How I wish I could love you like I love that other man who despised me!"

When Pierre returned, it was almost nine o'clock at night. He was dirty and very tired.

"Oh, you are a mess, *mon chéri!*" – says Marie–Victoire, making him sit on the bed and loosens the laces of his boots.

"I worked like a camel!" – he exclaims, letting himself lie loosely on the bed, which creaks under his weight. "

We unloaded countless bales of cotton from the wagons!"

"Oh, it must be a horrible job!" – she said trying to cheer him up, while sitting next to him and giving him light massages to the muscles in his very tired arms.

"And I do not even have a cup of comforting tea to offer you!"

"I have you to comfort me!" – he exclaims, laughing and, drawing her to him, kisses her long on the lips.

"I see you have not eaten today!" – she says.

"You are shaking with weakness!"

"You have not eaten anything either, *ma belle*!" – he says, looking her in the eyes.

Marie–Victoire answered nothing and looked away to keep from crying. She could not cry at that moment, sinse she did not want to melt him. Despite his tiredness, he seemed cheerful.

"Wait a little while, until I have regained my strength, and we will go out for dinner!" – he exclaims, gently pulling her chin with his fingertips, forcing her to look at him.

"Hey! Do not be like that!" – he continues:

"All of this is temporary! Do not let it get you down? Have you forgotten our plans? Come on! Clear your head! It is just a storm and it will pass!"

"Oh, Pierre!" – she exclaims, hugging him on the bed.

"You are stronger than I am! You do not let yourself down easily!"

"No!" – he says, straightening up in bed.

"I will never let myself overwhelmed! I will always fight to the end of my strength! I will always go down fighting!"

"I wish I had half your audacity!"

"If you follow me wherever I go, that will be enough for me!" – he says, getting up from his bed, more refreshed, at least in his spirit.

"Come on! I will go to my room and wash up, while you get ready too, and then we will go out to eat…"

The night fell cold with a fine, persistent rain. The sky remained dark, weighed down by the clouds which, tangled by the wind, passed but lightly, almost brushing the roofs of the houses and the tops of the tallest trees in the woods and boulevards.

"Have another cookie!" – says Pierre, offering Marie-Victoire the polished brass tray on which some meat dumplings are dancing in the middle of a thick, oily sauce.

"Help it with the bread. You're getting pale! If you do not feed yourself, you will certainly get sick.!"

"You eat!" – she says kindly, and she lies:

"I have not had much of an appetite lately! It must be the heartbreak of disappointments! But you eat well, or you will not last the day at the station!"

"You know, Marie-Victoire…" – he says, purposely lowering his voice.

"I have been thinking seriously all day today about the possibility of leaving France for America! We could emigrate to one of our American colonies! So many of our compatriots have already done so! And, if you look closely, hardly anyone has returned from there, a sign that things might be going better than they are here, do you not think?"

"I have also been thinking about it all day too, Pierre..." – she says.

"In the meantime, I have realized that you and I have nothing, nothing at all!"

"To take the first step! How do you think we will manage there in the beginning?"

"Yes, you are right!" – he says, after thinking for a moment.

"We do not really have anything we could sell to raise a little money for the trip and the start! We would run the risk of starving to death along the way, since we could not even imagine what we would find there…"

"I have heard reports in Charenton of people who had relatives who emigrated and who wrote back to tell of their incredible experiences in America! There are the dangers of the journey, there are the savages, with whom you have to dispute possessions of the land. There are also the unknown diseases, you know, there are an infinite number of risks inherent in undertakings of this magnitude!"

"You are right, *ma belle!*" – he agrees thoughtfully.

"However, are we not running similar risks if we stay here? Who cares about us? Are our rulers promoting our well-being or are they only concerned with filling the pockets of those who already have plenty?"

"Those who are down on their luck, like you and me, Pierre, are at risk everywhere!" – she says with sad eyes.

"For us, living is always dangerous..."

A short silence falls between them. Outside, the wind had risen, becoming ululating, and it was hurting the trees that lined the Quai de Bercy, forcing them to contort in a frenetic dance.

"So, what are we going to do?" – he asked, preparing to bite into a piece of bread that he had dipped into the thick sauce on the tray.

"We will find a way..." – she said, staring him in the eye.

Pierre was staring at the ceiling of the Café Saint-Louis as he chewed the piece of bread in his mouth. His eyes wandered randomly across the varnished wooden ceiling, and he thought. Quietly, Marie-Victoire just stared at him as he chewed his piece of bread slowly.

"I think I have gotten an idea!" – he suddenly exclaims, staring at her.

"But I will not tell you anything here! Let's go home!" – and reaching into his coat pocket for a crumble note, he smoothed it out in his palm and then signaled for the waiter who was standing sleepily by the counter.

"What did you think?" – asks Marie-Victoire, as she hangs her worn-out wool coat on the makeshift clothesline that stretches along the musty wall.

"Sit here!" – he says. Then he takes her hand between his and, holding it firmly in her eyes, continues:

"You were quite right when you said we had nothing for the journey, and I agree with you that it would be extremely dangerous for us to embark on such an endeavor without a penny in hand." – and, as if he was having a hard time saying what he wanted to say, he fell silent for a moment and got up. He walks over to the narrow window and looks out. Then he turns and faces her. Then, summoning up his courage, he continues:

"Pay close attention to what I am about to explain to you: I do not know how long I will be able to put up with the work at the station... I confess that the work there is exhausting, and if I do not eat properly I will not be able to stand lit for long! And apart from that job, there will not be another one for the moment! There is no choice, Marie-Victoire! Either I submit to it, or we will both starve!"

Marie-Victoire followed his words in silence. She had not realized what he wanted to say to her, but she was already feeling sorry for him. She suspected that he would not be able to stand it for long.

"So, with that said, there is only one solution to propose: someone will have to finance our trip!" – he adds.

"Finance?!" – she is amazed.

"But who would do that for us? We are so poor that we would not have any credit!"

"There is only one person in all of Paris who can do this for us, *ma belle*!" – he exclaims.

"And I know he will do it for you! François-Arman! Is he not rich enough?"

"François?" – she is surprised.

"Do you think he will do this for us?"

"Not for us!" – he corrects her.

"For you!" – he says, giving her a slightly disdainful smile.

"I know he will never do it for me! He hates me as much as I hate him! The hatred between us is mutual and true!"

"I do not know..." – she hesitates.

"Have you forgotten that his mother hates me? What if she finds out? Besides, has he regained control of his life? Before, it was his mother who took care of everything! How do you think François will lend us some money without his mother knowing? I really think that is impossible!"

"If we do not try, we will never know!" – he says, trying to encourage her.

"And we will make sure his mother does not know!"

"If I were to accept what you are proposing, how would you act?" – she asks.

"I thought you should write to him and arrange a meeting first!" – Pierre continues.

"And once you are alone with François, you will ask him! I do not think he will deny you such favor! Besides, it will only be a loan! And let's be clear: we will pay him back!"

"Well, under those terms, I could try!" – exclaims the young woman.

"Oh, I knew you would!" – says Pierre taking her in his arms and hugging her tightly. And, taking her by the hand, they sit down on the edge of the bed.

"So, we need to make plans..."

In high spirits, the young couple began to talk while the night fell, greatly disturbed by the wind that continued to howl furiously outside, like a pack of wolves lured by the bright moonlight.

Two days later, François–Armand received an unexpected letter at his home. Strangely Marie–Victoire invited him to meet her alone, but she did not say anything else and asked for complete secrecy. At first, the boy found it strange and even thought of telling his mother about it. However, as he was starting to make little trips into town on his own, and knowing that his mother could not stand the nurse, he preferred to say nothing to herti and decided to comply with the request contained in the letter. François re-read those words written on paper and thought: he no long felt anything for this woman. He was aware that, strangely enough, he had taken an interest in Marie–Victoire when he was sick. Now he felt nothing more for the girl, apart from tinges of gratitude and friendship. He had regretted having been rude to her and now had the opportunity to make amends for the bad impression he had made on his companion of so many years. He even felt happy to be able to meet her again. Yes, he was going to see Marie–Victoire again and try to make up on her when she left.

On the afternoon of the following day, Marie–Victoire waited for François–Armand in front of the house where she lived on the Quai de Bercy. Fine rain was falling, wetting and chilling everything to the bone.

"Do you live here?!" – François–Armand asked, staring in amazement the decrepit house. Then he kissed her gently on the cheek.

"Thank you for coming!" – Marie–Victoire exclaimed, smiling slightly. Then she takes François's hand and gives it a firm squeeze. Then she looked at him carefully. He had recovered a lot since the last time she saw him. He had put on a bit of weight and his face was flushed, al though his eyes remained sad.

"Do you want to go somewhere, or you would rather come up to my room?" – she asked.

"I think I prefer your room..." – he replies.

Deep down, the boy did not want to be seen with Marie–Victoire. The city was full of snoopers, and there was always the risk that he meet one of them and his mother would find out. What François–Armand did not want at this moment was to get in trouble with his mother.

The musty smell of Marie–Victoire's room immediately made François–Armand feels sick. He immediately took his handkerchief and undisguisedly wiped his nose.

"Good heavens!" – he thought!

"How can anyone live in such a place?"

"Sit down!" – invites Marie–Victoire, a little crestfallen, indicating to the sordid bed to the boy.

"There are no chairs..."

"*Non, merci!*" – replies the boy, deliberately approaching the small window of the mansard. The air in that cubicle was simply unbreathable. And pointing to the latch of the small pane:

"May I?"

"How are you?" – she asked, after agrreing to his request. A breath of cold air invades the small space.

"Well..." – he replied, feeling a little more comfortable with the fresh air. The smell of extreme poverty made him feel sick. Running his eyes over the moldy walls, he continued:

"And you?"

"You see..." – she says, making a broad gesture with her hand!

"I do not lack anything..." –and flashes a smile full of irony.

François felt embarrassed by her attitude. He still did not know why she called him to this meeting. He just stared at her, full of anguish. This place was really doing him a disservice, a lot of disservice.

"Well, Marie–Victoire..." he says at last, bluntly and high aggravated.

"What do you want from me?"

"I'll tell you bluntly, because I know that this is not a healthy environment for your health..." – bluntly.

"I need you to get me some money!"

"Money?" – he was startled by the unexpected request. He had imagined a thousand things that Marie–Victoire might possibly ask for the coach ride from his house to her. However, not once it occurred to him once that she would make such a request. Feeling caught off guard, he nervously wiped his face and the corner of his lips with his handkerchief, and after the initial shock that had caused him such a sudden request. "Why do you need money for?" he asks, still surprised by the abruptness of the request.

"I am going to emigrate..." – she replies, without stopping look him in the face for a moment.

"I want to leave France. There is nothing to do here! If I stay, I will succumb to hunger!"

François did not answer at first. He just looked at her, saddened. He knew that poverty was rampant among the poorest sections of the population, and that droves and droves of emigrants were seeking colonies overseas.

"How much do you need?" – he asks.

"Fifty thousand..."

"All that?" – he is amazed. And, pulling himself together, he continues:

"But you will not have to pay for the ticket; the government will provide it for you. Where do you want to go?"

"Maybe to America..."

"But I insist again that it is a lot of money!" – he says.

"You do not need that kind of money to travel alone!"

"I am not just going..."

"Oh, no? And who will go with you?"

"My future husband..." – she answers, now not looking at him.

"So, you intend to get married and emigrate to America with him? But I do not have that much money to give you!"

"Oh, I correct myself: we do not want your money!" – she says, frowning, full of pride.

"I should have said from the beginning! It is a loan! We will pay you back as soon as possible!"

"Even so, it is a big sum!" – says François.

"Maman would probably find out! There is no way to raise that kind of money without having to go to her!"

"I thought you had your father's inheritance!" – she says, ironically.

"Do you not even have access to that part?"

"Oh no!" – he replies.

"What Papa left me ended up being managed by my mother. I had to go to war, remember? Besides, you know I got sick afterwards..."

"If you do not have access to that amount, how much can you lend me?"

"I do not know right away!" – he replies. "I will have to check the safe and even sell some jewelry!" – and after thinking about it for a moment, he asks curiously:

"But tell me, who is the man you want to marry? If I am going to lend you my money, I will have to get to know him first! What is more, you will need to sign a bill of exchange! I need guarantees, Marie–Victoire!"

"I thought you would trust my word!" – she says, offended. And she moves on to emotional blackmail.

"I never thought you would make such a demand, especially of me, who has lived by your side for so long! I think you know me enough, don't you?" – and finishes, irony leaking from every pore:

"And when I gave you those medicines that Dr. La Roche did not prescribe for you, which, by the way, did you a lot of good! I did not t ask for any guarantees, remember?"

"It's not a question of trust, my dear..." – he continues, now standing firm.

"In business matters, sentimentally does not come into it! If I really am going to lend you some money, it is going to have to be like this. Besides, why do you not want to introduce me to your fiancé? Does he have something to hide?"

"No!" – the young woman hurries to reply. However, if François knew who the man she wanted to marry really was, he might not like it, and everything would be irretrievable lost.

"My fiancé is a distinguished, hardworking young man! It is a pity he is not here; otherwise, you could have met him right away!"

"It's a pity, Marie–Victoire..." – says François, getting ready to leave.

"But if I do not meet your fiancé, there is nothing to do..."

"Oh, do not leave yet!" – she said, getting up from the bed on which she had been sitting the whole time and, taking him by the arm, tried to hold him back. She knew that if she let him go, he would not come back. So, she insisted:

"Wait a little longer, he will be here soon. He does not delay, I swear..."

"Look, Marie–Victoire..." – exclaimed the young man, highly aggravated by the girl's insistence.

"I have a series of appointments and I do not intend to miss them!"

"Oh, you will not lose any of them, I guarantee it!" – she insists, holding onto the arm of the boy who was feeling very uncomfortable about the situation.

"Stay there and I will watch the stairs. He should be on his way up right now. He will not be long, I guarantee it..." – and went out the door, very distressed.

Marie–Victoire had deliberately lied. Pierre was next door, in the same corridor, in his little room, waiting for the events to unfold. By mutual agreement, they both concluded beforehand that François, who had hated Pierre for a long time, would certainly not tolerate him proposing such a deal. So they decided that Pierre would stay in his room while Marie–Victoire was convincing the other. However, things did not go according to plan.

"He insists on meeting you!" – Marie–Victoire whispers to Pierre. She only had to walk a few steps to reach the fiancé's room.

"And he is adamant!"

"What are we going to do?" – asks Pierre, taken aback by the unexpected.

"If he leaves, he will never come back!" – she explains.

"I know him very well. We would better take our chances. Come on!"

"All right!" – Pierre decided to follow her, after briefly examining the situation. "If I do not go, we will end up losing everything!"

"You?!," – exclaims François–Armand, astonished, as he realizes who the boy was who had come in following Marie– Victoire.

"François!" – said Pierre, holding out his hand to the other man, who was looking at him, high scandalized.

"Get out!" – shouts the young Marquis de Montpelier, ignoring the hand Pierre was offering him to shake.

"Get out of here!" – he shouts, possessed, trying to force his way through the narrow door.

"I do not want any contact with vulgar people!"

"François!" – shouts Marie–Victoire, trying to hold the boy by the brim of his coat.

"No! S'il vous plaît, halte!"[2]

"Get off me, you filthy whore!" – shouts François–Armand, possessed. And, realizing that he was being forced to go against his will, he turned around and punched the girl violently in the face, and she staggered and felll onto the bed.

"Ah, you bastard!" – Pierre shouts, enraged by the other man's violent attitude of the other man.

"You bastard!"

Pierre throws himself on François, grabs him by the neck and drags him out into the narrow corridor. A fierce fight broke out between the two boys. Had it not always been like this? François and Pierre could not stand each other,

---

[2] "François...! (...) No...! Please stop...!", in French

animosity was inherent between them. And the exchange of punches and blows was inevitable.

Marie–Victoire, recovering from the dizziness caused by the punch she had received, ran to the door and, shouting for help, tried futilely to break up the two quarrels that were now clinging tightly to each other and approaching the banister of the spiral staircase that went down four floors. And, taking turns, they threw themselves against the precarious wooden railing, which wobbled dangerously in the face of the strong bumps on the boy's backs, engulfing them in a fierce struggle. And sometimes one, sometimes the other their backs against the railing, then suddenly, there was a pop! A terrible snap and astonishment! Pierre reached out, trying to grab the other man, who plummeted into the void, his scream of terror ending in a deafening thud at the bottom of the stairwell...

Chapter 20

Reality and Dreams

François–Armand's death hit Parisian high society like a bombshell. The newspapers reported the tragedy, taking it a priori as the disastrous consequence of an unsuccessful attempt at kidnapping. However, as the police investigated the facts, listening to witnesses and analyzing the scene, it turned out that it had all been accidental, but the fatal outcome of a fight between the two adversaries, a fact that somewhat mitigated the sentence handed down to those involved in the case: Pierre and Marie–Victoire.

What incriminated the young nurse enormously was that the police investigators found the letter she had sent him in one of the pockets of François's jacket, arranging their meeting at the scene of the accident and, and from being condemned to death at the guillotine, their sentences were reduced to the banishment to one of the overseas island colonies in the Caribbean, a French possession in Central America. For both of them, there was perpetual exile, with a sentence of forced labor in the vast sugar cane plantations. The punishment, however, was still terrible, since the intention of both of them was not to murder François! None of those involved actually intended unexpected outcome! Reality for the two young people was now infinitely worse than what had previously seemed difficult and unbearable! Pierre and Marie–Victoire's dream of rebuilding their lives in America was thus extinguished for good!

Time had passed; it was six months since the inauspicious event that had victimized François–Armand. In Captain Berg's house, there was a new air, beginning with the jovial countenance of Céleste–Marie's who, reclining on the comfortable divan in the living room, knitting a small, delicate piece of wool.

"You look beautiful with your big belly!" – exclaims Wilfred Berg, sitting down next to her and sweetly caressing her bulging belly, which is showing an advanced state of pregnancy.

"What do you think?" – she says, proudly showing off the wool cardigan she had been patiently knitting until then.

"Oh, so tiny like that?" – he observes.

"You did not get the recipe wrong, did you? Maman says I came into this world quite big. What if he takes after me?"

"And who is to say it is him and not her?" – jokes Céleste–Marie.

"You could be wrong, *mon chéri*! We never know!"

"You are right!" – agrees Berg.

"We will not know until the time is right!" – and, looking at her with mischievous eyes, he continues:

"But why are you knitting all those little jackets in blue wool?"

"Oh, pure mother's intuition!" – she says, laughing.

"Something tells me it is going to be a boy…" – and she strokes her belly longingly with her hand, in wide circular gestures.

"And you, I think you would prefer it to be a boy, *n'est-ce pas?*"

"No, you are wrong about that!" – he replies.

"I want you to know, *mon amour*, that boy or girl, anyone is welcome among us! I really do not have any preferences!"

"You know, my dear…" – says Céleste–Marie.

"It is amazing how, from the moment we took part in that memorable session at *Monsieur* Allan Kardec, things began to change for me! Today I am sure, without a shadow of a doubt, that it was the spirits who gave me a hand![1]

I cannot tell you how grateful I am that you insisted that I accompany you there that day. I confess that, at first, I thought I was skeptical about what they were saying about Spiritism! Today, however, I know I was saved through my father's intercession. The spirit that was persecuting me probably understood the harm it was causing me and left me!" – and letting a deep sigh, she continued:

---

[1] The above events occurred at the end of 1858, a year and a few months after the publication of the 1st edition of *The Spirits' Book*, which took place on April 18, 1857, and it is known that Allan Kardec would only complete the bases from the Codification, during the following almost 12 years, until his disincarnation, which took place on March 31, 1869, and that the knowledge on which Spiritism is based was gradually gathered through the revelations that the spirits made to him, in addition to carrying out a series of serious and systematic experiments and observations, made during all these years.

"For the first time in my life, I am at peace!"

"That is good!" – he says, squeezing her hand tightly.

"I'm happy to see that you are happy too!"

Berg then hugs Céleste–Marie and kisses her tenderly on the top of the head. The words of *Monsieur* Allan Kardec came to Berg's mind when Berg, a few days after taking her to the *Société*, had sought out the illustrious Codifier of Spiritism and had had a conversation with him alone, without his wife knowing anything about it:

"Your wife, Captain, suffers from an illness that is still totally unknown to me, but which I have been researching for some time now!"

Monsieur Kardec told him, looking him seriously in the eye, as was his wont. He went on to clarify:

"However, beforehand, I am almost certain that in such situations, the same ones your wife is going through, a spirit persecutes its incarnate victim, becoming their tormentor and judging them relentlessly, and causing them suffering and often even causing them to fall morally, thus throwing their enemy into situations that denigrate them in society, and all with the sole purpose of taking revenge!"

"Really?" – he replied to the venerable Professor Rivail.

"But as far as I know about Céleste–Marie, she has never harmed anyone." – he said with conviction.

"And how can that be?"

"However, as I told you beforehand, Captain…" – continued *Monsieur* Kardec:

"Your wife may not have done anyone any harm in this life; however, I have been seriously researching the possibility of palingenesis actually occurring, a fact that, in itself, would justify a series of questions which, until now, had been considered inexplicable by current logic."

"So, the ideas put forward by Mr. Schopenhauer are ill-founded!" – Berg observed.

"In terms, yes, Captain. But this subject still lacks effective study and systematic observations. Personally, I think that the root of the vast majority of the ills that affect humanity lies precisely there: in the multiplicity of human existence! There is no more rational explanation than that! I confess to you that I still know very little about this subject. However, reason urges us to think seriously about it. Furthermore, your wife's cure, if it actually takes place, will be more than irrefutable proof to us that the cause we presuppose really is!"

The memory of such a dialog with the eminent Codifier of Spiritism fills Berg with emotion.

"You know, Céleste Marie..." – he said, looking seriously at his wife's face.

"I did not tell you before, but a few days after we went to *Monsieur* Kardec's session, I secretly went to see him and had a private conversation with him about your case. He told me at that time that if you were cured, it would be full proof that you were in fact under the influence of a spirit that was harming you. You had the intercession of your father, who obtained for you the help of benevolent spirits to help you heal from your illness."

"Do you really think so, Berg?" – she asks.

"If not, it would have been a tremendous coincidence, would you not agree?"

"I would..."

"Now, then, we need to go back to Mr. Kardec and tell him of the result. I know that this will be of utmost importance to him. He told me that he was doing serious research into this disease, that affects many people and for which, until now, there had been no known effective treatment..."

"Only I know how terrible such a thing is!" – exclaims Céleste Marie, snuggling into her husband's arms.

"I almost went mad and had to be admitted to Charenton. If it had not been for your constant help, plus Maman's persistence, who never gave up on finding me a cure, I do not know what would have become of me! Possibly, it would have had a tragic end, as I know has already happened to many people! Today I think I know the possible cause of so many unexplained cases of suicide out there!"

"Perhaps *Monsieur* Allan Kardec is right when he says that the cause could lie in the pernicious influence that disaffected spirits would exert on us!" – remarks Berg, thoughtfully.

"You know, *ma cherie*..." – he continues:

"By observing your case carefully, we know that you have improved, without having ingested a single drop of anything! You only received your father's words promising you help, nothing more than that!"

"Yes!" – she agrees.

"And I can assure you that from that moment on, I feltl better! And look, when I got there, I was having such a bad time that I almost embarrassed myself. I had to restrain myself a great deal; I had to use extraordinary self–control, which I do not even think I was capable of employing, in order not to run out of that hall like a possessed person!"

"Without a shadow of a doubt, your father helped you from beyond, my dear!" – says Berg.

"And it is our duty now to tell Mr. Kardec what happened! I know he will be pleased!"

Berg and Céleste Marie's son was born at the beginning of 1859. He was a robust boy who was named after his maternal grandfather, Guillaume–Philippe.

"Is he not beautiful?" – said Céleste Marie to her husband, who was gazing at her while she breastfeeds the baby.

"Yes!" – replied Berg, his voice laced with emotion.

He sat down next to his wife and kissed her tenderly on the cheek. Then he gently strokes the sparse blond hair of his son with his fingertips, who, still oblivious to the world around him, was busy sucking voraciously on his mother's breast. Captain Berg's thought then flew back to three months ago, when, highly satisfied, he had sought out *Monsieur* Allan Kardec at the end of another of the very popular sessions at the *Société Parisienne d'Études Spirites*.

"Do you have a moment for me, *Monsieur* Kardec?" – he asked him, as he prepared to leave the hall. The Codifier of Spiritism was visibly tired after the exhausting task of conducting the session and having attended more than twenty people who wanted to speak with him in private.

"*Oh, sûrement, Monsieur le Capitaine...*" – the distinguished Professor Rivail answered courteously, opening a kind smile, despite being on the verge of exhaustion.

"*Je me suis à votre service!*"[2]

"I do not want to cause you any more trouble, sir, but it was essential that I tell you about my wife. She is completely cured of her disease that afflicted her!"

"Really?" – replied the eminent Allan Kardec. And, with a broad smile of satisfaction, he continued:

"So, we were right?"

"Yes, you were absolutely right! Since then, Céleste Marie has been behaving as affably and calmly as ever, and what is more, she got pregnant!"

"Really? My congratulations, Captain!" – said Mr. Kardec, shaking his hand effusively. And, saying goodbye, he stated categorically:

"If your wife is expecting a baby, Captain, then you can consider her cured once and for all..." – and left hurrying towards the exit of the hall. Berg stood for a moment, absorbed in *Monsieur* Kardec's final words, which sounded somewhat enigmatic to him. What had he meant by that?[3]

---

[2] "I am at your service...!", in French.

[3] Possibly, Allan Kardec had alluded to the fact that the obsessive spirit of Céleste-Marie is reincarnated and takes him as a mother, as an appropriate instrument, in this way, the obsessive relationship between them ends, as usually happens in these cases.

"To whom do you intend to give the baby to be baptized?" – asks Céleste–Marie.

"I have been thinking of General du Servey and Constance..." – he replies.

"What do you think?"

"That is perfect for me!" – she agrees. And, cradling her son in her arms, she squeezed him and kissed him effusively, and over and over again on his tiny cheeks.

"I love you so much, *mon petit*!"

And the baby, as if touched by the maternal tenderness so effusively shown to him, opens his little mouth and, for the first time, smiles slightly.

"He laughed! He laughed!" – exclaims Céleste–Marie happily.

"*Mon petit garçon m'a souri!*"[4]

Berg looks at both of them with tenderness. Mr. Kardec was right: Céleste Marie was completely cured. We would not recognize her hugging and kissing her son now, in a clear display of affection. He, Berg, then felt a well-disguised twinge of jealousy in his chest: and was not it that that little guy was now stealing all of Céleste–Marie's attention?

"Hey, there is not a scrap left for me, is there?" – he says, protesting.

"Oh, you are a fool, Berg!" – she exclaims, pulling him by the hem of his coat.

---

[4] "My little boy smiled at me!", in French.

"Come on! Sit down here!" – and looking at him, full of malice, she continues:

"You want to suck too, don't you?" – and pulling up the neckline of her blouse, she shows off her voluminous breast leaking from milk from the nipple.

"Look, there is one left for you!"

"Ha! Ha! Ha! Ha!" – he bursts out laughing.

"Only you, Céleste–Marie, could say such a thing!" – and becoming serious, he looks at her tenderly and says:

"You had an unsurpassed sense of humor inside you, you know?" – and, in a wide and fearful embrace, he wraps his wife and little son in his arms.

"You are a good man, Berg!" – murmured Céleste–Marie, caressing her husband's face.

"You are a good man..."

Outside, the winter day was cold and gray, but the little family, in the warmth of their home, seemed happy. Berg would now feel like a fulfilled man, were it not for the chaotic situation his country was in.

"Wilfred..."

"Ahn?"

"Are you still going to war?"

"I hope you understand that I have not yet done my patriotic duty, *ma chérie*!" – he replies, after thinking for a few moments.

"I know it bothers you enormously, but you know it must be done!"

"If that is what you want..." – she says, lowering her head. Deep down she knew that she would end up alone... That, just as it had happened to her father, it would possibly happen to her husband. She would end up having to raise her son alone. Suddenly, a wave of revolt swept over her. Why did all men have to be like that.? Why did they always have to be involved in wars, killing each other?

"Come on, do not be like that..." – says Berg, noticing that she has gone silent and that her countenance become somber. He then lifts the tip of her chin with his fingertips and, focing her to face him, continues:

"Nothing will happen to me, I assure you!"

"You cannot guarantee me anything, my dear!" – she exclaims firmly.

"In this particular case, you cannot predict anything! Do we not lose a lot of our patricians every day, stupidly dying on the battlefields? They died honorably defending their sacred patriotic duty, say the stupid ones who see nothing but cold, insensitive immediacy... But, what about life, Berg? And love? Where is love in this sordid mess? Struck down by human greed, carelessness and foolishness! How long will men fuel stupid wars, making misery and more misery, increasing the already large number of widows, orphan, and the miserable around the world? No, Berg, do not try to convince me that war is good or useful, that my head cannot understand it!" She got up and become to nurse the baby, who had started to whimper insistently. Then, realizing that it would be better for her to put her son to sleep in his crib, she offered to leave her husband's company in the living room, and concludes:

"And if you really want to know what my true opinion is about these patriotic rants that are going on in your mind, know that I think you still do not love us enough to make your final choice!" – and she stormed out of the room, leaving him dumbfounded.

Berg remains alone in the room, mulling over Céleste-Marie's words. His wife could never understand what was going on in his soul. He was going to war for them! It was out of the excess of love he had for them, if need be, he would give his life! There were so many things still to be established in the world! So many were the shackles that stubbornly remained tied to people's wrists and ankles, restricting their freedom and keeping them firmly tied to ignorance and misery! If he did not fight now for future generations to have a better world, things would never have adjusted! A new order was needed, and at first there was no other choice: only force! Berg was not under illusions: fine words alone could not bring about revolutions! The sword was still needed! France had given the world a delicious taste of freedom, and the process was not over yet. It had only just begun! We had to move forward, we had to continue.! Why stop now? The pain of his wife's incomprehension had wounded his soul deeply. He had tried so many times to convince her that he had an ideal, that he was not going to war just for the sake of adventure... He knew that there were adventurers, those who loved danger, who hated the boredom of domestic life, but that was not the case with him. He was fighting for a purpose, fighting for an ideal!

Tremendously embittered, Wilfred Berg got up and looked outside. It was still raining and very cold. He was not going to give up! No, even if Céleste–Marie did not understand, he would not give up! For her and for his son, he would die, if need be, so that a new, fairer and more equitable world could take the place of the one that, until then, had always been so inhuman and so cruel!

Amandine Rounet stopped in front of the exuberant life–size oil portrait of her son and ran her eyes over the majestic figure of François–Armand, decked out in his aspiring military uniform. The boy displayed his usual, almost mocking smile, even there, wearing the severe uniform of the French army.

"*Ah, mon petit! Mon petit!*" – murmured the Marquise de Montpelier, her eyes streaming with tears, as she ran her fingertips along the features of her son's face, faithfully painted on the portrait.

Then, turning around, she sat down on the red velvet divan and continued to stare at the portrait hanging on the border wall, next to the exuberant figure of her husband, also masterfully portrayed in his brilliant blue uniform. Then her eyes move from the figure of her husband to the figure of her son.

"You both left me alone!" – murmured Amandine, her eyes tinged with tears.

"Did you see what you did to me? You have consigned me to the darkest loneliness! – and sobs shook her violently.

Then the Marquise de Montpelier's eyes locked onto her son's face. His features were still so youthful! How old was he when he allowed himself to be portrayed? Seventeen? Eighteen? She could not quite remember.

"You are gone so fast, *mon François!*" – she says between tears, talking to her son's portrait.

"And it is all that unqualified woman's fault! Oh, how I hate her! From the moment I laid eyes on her, I knew she was no good, the wretched! And you would not listen to me! Did you have to go after her? Did you not realize that all she wanted from you was your money? So much so that she set you up, along with her lover, to entangle you!" – and, sobbing deeply, she continues:

"You had to go there, didn't you? Why did you not tell me? You knew I would forbid you to go, didn't you? But you have always been so stubborn! You have always done what you wanted!"

Amandine took a handkerchief from the pocket of her pink silk peignoir and noisily blew into it. Then, she stares again at the portrait, her eyes swollen and reddened from crying too much. Her thoughts then flew back to a few months ago, when, unexpectedly, on that rainy late–autumn morning, she had received a visit from the police inspector.

"To what do I owe the honor of your visit, Inspector?" – she asked, highly apprehensive.

"I bring you bad news, Madam!" – the policeman had been direct.

"Your son has had an accident!"

"Accident?" – she sought.

"My son rarely leaves the house and whenever he does, he is accompanied by his coachman! He never goes out alone!"

"This time he was, Madam..." – replied the man, as cold as ever.

"And he fell from the top of a ladder!" – and, for the first time, he swallowed dry before delivering the final blow.

"It was fatal!"

The word 'fatal' had not entered Amandine's ears, but had struck her directly in the heart, like the blade of a very sharp dagger piercing her flesh.

"Wha... What did you say?" – she had stammered, her eyes darkening at the starkness of the news.

"Your son is dead, *Madam!*" – repeated the policeman.

"He fell down the four–story stairwell!"

At the terrible confirmation, Amandine had fallen to the ground. She could not bear the weight of the tragedy! Her little boy was dead!

Terrified, the servants rushed to her aid and gave her salts to smell, and she regained consciousness. When she returned to reality, the pain that had seized her chest was stabbing, unbearable. No, something must be wrong. It could not be real. François, dead?!

Amandine gazed at her son's smiling figure, masterfully depicted in the portrait: his eyes sparkling, his radiant face, his lips sporting that mocking smile that charmed her so much... "Oh, how she missed him!" – her chest tightened and tears flooded her eyes.

"*Oh, mon petit! Mon petit!*" – she exclaims, full of despair.

"What will become of me now that I find myself so alone?"

Despair overtakes the Marquise de Montpelier. Where could she find the strength to go on, living with this pain that was relentlessly eating away at her chest, night and day, without truce? She wanted not to think about it, not to ask herself why it had had to happen! Had François not gotten better, had he not come out of the insanity that had afflicted him for years? She had rejoiced so much at her son's recovery, and then, all of a sudden, that misfortune happened! Why was God taking such a toll on her? First, her husband, at such an early age! Now, her little boy was going like this, too, in the prime of his life!

She recalls the shock at seeing him dead at the scene of the accident. Berg, who had been notified in a hurry, had accompanied her to the scene of François's death. They did not understand, *a priori*, what he had come to do there, in that decrepit place, on the Quai de Bercy, an disreputable place inhabited almost exclusively by vagrants and prostitutes! Amandine feels a shiver run through her as she remembers, for the thousandth time, how terribly hopeless it was for her to see him slumped on the dirty floor of that gloomy foyer, the ghastly entrance door to that sordid old building!

"*Oh, mon Dieu! Mon Dieu! Quelle disgrâce!*"[5] – she cried out, overcome extreme despair, as she threw herself on her son's corpse. If it had not been for her nephew's kind but firm presence to support her, she would not have been able to resist.

"We cannot touch the body yet, *Madam*!" – the police inspector had warned her.

---

[5] "Oh, my God...! Oh, my God! What a disgrace...!", in French.

"The police draughtsman needs a little more time to finish his work!"

It was only then she saw the man with the pad of paper and the crayon minutely recording the lugubrious scene of the crime. Amandine had the urge to throw herself at the man and tear from his hands the paper on which he had been so meticulously tracing his drawing, and to tear it into a thousand pieces! Why does perpetuate such an appalling thing?

"The police need to record everything, so that it is on the records, *ma tante!*" – Berg said to her, taking her in his arms and pulling her away.

"It is presumed that my cousin was murdered!"

"What?!," – she shouted, appalled."

"And who was the wretch who took my boy's life?"

"Marie–Victoire, in cahoots with her lover..." – Berg had said.

"Surely, they were trying to extort money from François–Armand! That is what Inspector Villeneuve told me!"

"That wretch!" – Amandine roared, foaming with hatred.

"That wretch had the audacity to lure my little boy into a trap and then kill him?! Oh, damn her! A thousand times damned! Oh, I knew it! She was no good! I suspected as much!" – and, filled with fury, she continued shouting:

"Where is that wretched?! I want to kill her with my own hands! Come on, tell me, Wilfred, where is that damned thing?! Because before I send her to hell, I want to pierce both her eyes with my nails!"

"The police have already arrested both of them, *ma tante!*" – said Berg, trying tremendously hard to control Amandine.

"Restrain yourself, the guillotine awaits them!"

"Oh, and I will be there!" – roared the Marquise de Montpelier.

"I will be there watching their heads roll! I will have these last joys before I die! By God, I will have them!"

At the memory of such sad things, Amandine sobs harder and, getting up, approaches the portrait. Once again, she runs her fingertips over her son's face, carefully outlining every feature of his physiognomy. Those memories hurt her so much! How much she struggled to forget, not to throw himself back into that sad, revolting past! But, she could not; a mixture of pain and hatred alternated in her chest. How she longed to remember no more, to forget everything! However, as much as she reluctantly tried, the memories came back to her more vividly: François' wake in the drawing room; the consolation of friends and the few relatives he had left; the mass at the Church of Saint Sulpice... Amandine sobbed and stared at her son's portrait, while those sad memories ran through her head. That was how her life had been ever since. It was all about crying and mourning the premature loss of her son.

Although her sister and nephew were often there to visit her, Amandine never left the house. General du Servey and Constance had already insistently urged her to go and see

Monsieur Allan Kardec at the *Société Spirite*; however, she refused to go. The revolt still held her back; she was not content to see her son's murderers simply condemned to banishment! She wanted them dead, beheaded at the guillotine! She wanted to be there, in front of their terrified eyes, to mock and deride them and throw all her hatred and resentment in their faces! But justice had taken a different view and, after a long and agonizing trial, the magistrates ended up sentencing the defendants to perpetual banishment!

"Damned!" – murmured Amandine, gritting her teeth with hatred.

"Wherever you go, my hatred will follow your footsteps as if it were your own shadow! Oh, how I hate you!"

Then, overcome with deep sorrow, the Marquise de Montpelier let herself back on the *chaise longue*.

"Hatred will help me swallow the rest of the absinthe that God still has in store for me!" – she murmured, overcome with deep unease.

"From now on, only hatred will suffice!" – and sobs softly.

Suddenly, however, she felt as if highly subtle hands were affectionately stroking her gray hair. Inexplicable relief floods her chest and she resolutely wipes her eyes with her fingertips and looks around, intently scrutinizing her surroundings.

"François?" – she murmured, filled with joy.

"*C'est toi, mon chéri?*"[6]

---

[6] "Is it you, my dear?", in French.

"*Oui, Maman!*" – whispers the spirit in his mother's ear.
"*C'est moi, ton François!*"[7]

Amandine then cries. She cries, copiously, but no longer of pain or longing or revolt. Her chest was filled with unexpected joy. Yes, it was him, her little boy! There was no mistaking it! Suddenly, hope returned! No, she had not made a mistake! Yes, she had heard his unforgettable voice in the depths of his soul and felt the soft touch of his hands on her hair! She could not be wrong; he was there! She was absolutely certain of it! Resolute, Amandine got up and went to the window.

With a wide gesture, she opened the heavy curtains and daylight flooded into the room. In and unusual mood, she looked outside and smiled: spring was back...

---

[7] "It is me, Uncle François!"

Epilogue

François–Armand opened his eyes and gradually adjusted them to the soft ambient light. At first, he did not immediately realize where he was. He was lying on a bed and, highly intrigued, he scrutinized the place in detail: it resembled a hospital room in every way.

"Oh, will I be back in Charenton?" – he thought, highly dismayed.

"But it is different from what was there! Have they carried out such a structural and significant renovation of the building in such a short space of time?"

As he forced his mind to remember something, François felt dizzy. Waves of intense drowsiness alternated strangely with expressive spaces of lucidity, a very clear lucidity in which, in an unusual way, his senses seemed sharper, clearer; the colors of his surroundings seemed more vivid, and even the air entered his nostrils more lightly. A strange silence enveloped the place. The door was locked and the large window was guarded by a light white lace curtain, gently swaying in the comforting breeze coming in from outside. Through the thin lace of the curtain, François could see a glimpse of a well–tended garden and, beyond that, bordering the extensive lawn, the edge of a lush park, and that it was dusk, since the cobalt–blue sky was flooded with a brilliant golden light!

Making extreme efforts, the boy tried to get up, but felt faint; inexplicably, his strength disappeared and, the sleepiness envelope him again. He struggled desperately to keep awake, he tried harder and harder, and eventually his lucidity returned. How strange those sensations were to him!

Time passed slowly and he tried hard to remember. However, all he could think of was an emptiness, a huge lapse of forgetfulness! He could remember older things; but, of recent events, not a trace came to mind! Outside, he noticed, through the window, that night was slowly falling. He tried to get up once more, but the strange weakness returned accompanied by tinges of intense drowsiness. Good heavens! How strange those sensations were for him!

Tired of fighting, François eventually fell asleep. In the morning, he woke up to the first rays of the rising sun. He was amazed again, until he rediscovered where he was. Little by little, the memory of the previous evening came back to him. What was that place? There was no noise, except for the joyful trill of the birds that sang in the bushes full of bright flowers permeating the green lawn of the garden outside his window. The boy had once again forced him to think. A loud ringing sound came to his ears, and he remembered! Good heavens! An intense shiver ran through his body. Marie–Victoire! Pierre's bandit! The fall down the stairs! And the terrible images came to his mind: his back hitting the rail at the top of the banister; the terrible crack of the wood splintering; the terrible sensation of emptiness behind him; the amazemnt; Pierre's futile attempt to reach out to him in desperation, his face fading like a ghost's as he realized that he was fatally lost, plummeting into the void! Good heavens! François recalled, stunned. The scream of terror that escaped from his throat, during the terrifying, light flight, culminating in the deafening, soft thud of the dirty stone floor of that gloomy lobby! What had he felt in those terrible moments of falling? Extreme despair; the certainty he was going to die! Only a few seconds! But did they not last an eternity? Did he not look up as he fell? Did he not see the face of the wretch with whom he had been sparring until then, looking at him with horrible eyes? He did see his face moving away at dizzying speed, but even at that moment, he realized that something strange was happening: the landscape was different, and Pierre was different. The odious Pierre had long hair tied back at the nape of his neck; he was dressed exquisitely and wore a three-cornered hat, and he was riding! And insistently, he chased after him, François, who was riding a few meters ahead of him... Suddenly, a deep precipice appeared in front of both of them, and he, François, in the last few moments, had skillfully maneuvered his horse away from the imminent danger. Pierre, however, overwhelmed by surprise, had involuntarily thrown himself and his horse into the depths of the colossal abyss![1]

François felt confused! What were those strange memories? Things just blending together in his mind! Suddenly he saw himself in a different time. Pierre was different too! Then he tried to understand the facts that were mysteriously adding up in his mind, but he could not come

---

[1] This scene can be found in the book *"The Stone Smile"*, also written by Monsignor Eusébio Sintra.

up with any plausible explanation. Finally, tired by the effort, he closed his eyes. A slight drowsiness insisted on taking over his consciousness, and he began to doze off. A sweet, tender slumber then took hold of him and he closed his eyes. Sometime later, he felt his forehead lightly touched with lips in a gentle kiss, and he opened his eyes.

"Sylvie!" – he shouted in a jubilant cry.

"Is it you, my love?!"

What followed were not words, since words could never describe that scene of love! What had happened was a wild succession of tight hugs hoarse cries and kisses as crazy as any the world had ever seen before...

Zibia Gasparetto's Greatest success stories

With more than 20 million titles sold, the author has contributed to the strengthening of spiritualist literature in the publishing market and to the popularization of spirituality. Learn more of the author's successes.

Romances Dictated by the Spirit Lucius

The Life Force

The Truth of each one

Life knows what it does

She trusted in life

Between Love and War

Esmeralda

Thorns of Time

Eternal Bonds

Nothing is by Chance

Nobody is Nobody's

God's Advocate

Tomorrow Belongs to God

Love Won

Unexpected Encounter

On the Edge of Destiny

The Sly One

The Morro of Illusions

Where is Teresa?

Through the Doors of the Heart

When Life chooses

When the Hour Comes
When it is necessary to return
Opening for Life
Not afraid to live
Only love can do it
We Are All Innocent
Everything has its price
It was all worth it
A real love
Overcoming the past

Other success stories by André Luiz Ruiz and Lucius
The Love Never Forgets You Trilogy
The Strength of Kindness
Under the Hands of Mercy
Saying Goodbye to Earth
At the End of the Last Hour
Sculpting Your Destiny
There are Flowers on the Stones
The Crags are made of Sand

Books of Eliana Machado Coelho and Schellida

Hearts without Destiny

The Shine of Truth

The Right to be Happy

The Return

In the Silence of Passions

Strength to Begin Again

The Certainty of Victory

The Conquest of Peace

Lessons Life Offers

Stronger than Ever

No Rules for Loving

A Diary in Time

A Reason to Live

Eliana Machado Coelho and Schellida, Romances that captivate, teach, move and

can change your life!

Romances of Arandi Gomes Texeira and The Count J.W. Rochester

Lancaster County

The Power of Love

The Trial

Cleopatra's Bracelet

The Reincarnation of a Queen

You Are Gods

Books of Marcelo Cezar and Marco Aurelio

Love is for the Strong

The Last Chance

Nothing is as it Seems

Forever With Me

Only God Knows

You Make Tomorrow

A Breath of Tenderness

Books of Vera Kryzhanovskaia and JW Rochester

The Revenge of the Jew

The Nun of the Marriages

The Sorcerer's Daughter

The Flower of the Swamp

The Divine Wrath

The Legend of the Castle of Montignoso

The Death of the Planet

The Night of Saint Bartholomew

The Revenge of the Jew

Blessed are the poor in spirit

Cobra Capella

Dolores

Trilogy of the Kingdom of Shadows

From Heaven to Earth

Episodes from the Life of Tiberius

Infernal Spell

Herculanum

On the Frontier

Naema, the Witch

In the Castle of Scotland (Trilogy 2)

New Era

The Elixir of Long Life

The Pharaoh Mernephtah
The Lawgivers
The Magicians
The Terrible Phantom
Paradise without Adam
Romance of a Queen
Czech Luminaries
Hidden Narratives
The Nun of the Marriages

Books of Elisa Masselli

There is always a reason
Nothing goes unanswered
Life is made of decisions
The Mission of each one
Something more is needed
The Past does not matter
Destiny in his hands
God was with him
When the past does not pass
Just beginning

**Books of Vera Lúcia Marinzeck de Carvalhoç
and Patricia**

Violets in the Window
Living in the Spirit World
The Writer's House
Flight of the Seagull

**Vera Lúcia Marinzeck de Carvalho
and Antônio Carlos**

Love your Enemies
Slave Bernardino
the Rock of Lovers
Rosa, the third fatality
Captives and Freed

Books of Mónica de Castro y Leonel

In spite of everything

Love is not to be trifled with

Face to Face with the Truth

Of My Whole Being

I wish

The Price of Being Different

Twins

Giselle, The Inquisitor's Mistress

Greta

Till Life Do You Part

Impulses of the Heart

Jurema of the Jungle

The Actress

The Force of Destiny

Memories that the Wind Brings

Secrets of the Soul

Feeling in One's Own Skin

World Spiritist Institute

www.ingramcontent.com/pod-product-compliance
Lightning Source LLC
LaVergne TN
LVHW041737060526
838201LV00046B/842